MOSES AND POLITICAL PHILOSOPHY

Representations of the figure of Moses are both central and pervasive in the history of Western political thought. The story of Moses, as depicted in the Books of Exodus, Numbers, and Deuteronomy in the Hebrew Bible, has generated an immensely powerful set of images that have left a lasting mark on both Western and global culture.

Moses and Political Philosophy explores the enduring tropes drawn from this narrative, which continue to shape political discourse up to the present. The book examines why these interpretations retain such a lasting relevance in contemporary debates and explores how an appreciation of them can enrich our engagement with the centuries-long dialogue that has shaped the tradition of Western political theory. Offering a comprehensive analysis of the Moses story, the book investigates various appropriations of the tale, the characterization of the Mosaic regime, the politically charged implications of Moses's authority, and the most intriguing puzzles and paradoxes within the narrative. In doing so, *Moses and Political Philosophy* sheds new light on the profound and lasting influence of the Moses story on the evolution of political thought.

RONALD BEINER is a professor emeritus of political science at the University of Toronto.

HARRISON FLUSS is an assistant professor of philosophy at St. John's University.

RONALD BEINER AND HARRISON FLUSS

Moses and Political Philosophy

UNIVERSITY OF TORONTO PRESS
Toronto Buffalo London

Toronto Buffalo London
utppublishing.com

Printed in Canada

ISBN 978-1-4875-4115-6 (cloth)
ISBN 978-1-4875-4116-3 (paper)
ISBN 978-1-4875-4118-7 (EPUB)
ISBN 978-1-4875-4117-0 (PDF)

Library and Archives Canada Cataloguing in Publication

Title: Moses and political philosophy / Ronald Beiner and Harrison Fluss.
Names: Beiner, Ronald, 1953- author | Fluss, Harrison, author
Description: Includes bibliographical references and index.
Identifiers: Canadiana (print) 20250142171 | Canadiana (ebook) 20250142198 | ISBN 9781487541156 (cloth) | ISBN 9781487541163 (paper) | ISBN 9781487541170 (PDF) | ISBN 9781487541187 (EPUB)
Subjects: LCSH: Moses (Biblical leader)—Influence. | LCSH: Political science—Philosophy.
Classification: LCC BL65.P7 B45 2025 | DDC 320.55—dc23

Cover design: Jennifer Stimson
Cover image: *Moses receiving the Tablets of Law* by Marc Chagall. Oil painting.
Source: WikiArt

We wish to acknowledge the land on which the University of Toronto Press operates. This land is the traditional territory of the Wendat, the Anishnaabeg, the Haudenosaunee, the Métis, and the Mississaugas of the Credit First Nation.

University of Toronto Press acknowledges the financial support of the Government of Canada, the Canada Council for the Arts, and the Ontario Arts Council, an agency of the Government of Ontario, for its publishing activities.

Canada Council for the Arts
Conseil des Arts du Canada

Funded by the Government of Canada
Financé par le gouvernement du Canada
Canada

For Gabriel
RB
For Samantha
HF

Contents

Preface

This book has been written by a political theorist and a philosopher. It should not be assumed by the reader that the two authors agree on everything, nor that we have been able to harmonize our two minds into one mind. We agree on many things; we disagree on many things. In that respect, it will likely be helpful to the reader to know that Beiner is responsible for the introduction and chapters 1, 2, and 4; Fluss is responsible for chapter 3.

Beiner and Fluss happen to be Jewish, but we write in our identity as theorists, not in our Jewish identity. Jewish philosophers ought to follow the example of Spinoza in not letting Jewish piety get in the way of submitting the Hebrew scriptures to fearless theoretical interrogation. We have no wish to slight the long tradition of Jewish interpretation of the Hebrew Bible; but it is a matter of simple honesty to say that our competence lies elsewhere. Neither of us would claim to have spent his whole life studying the Hebrew Bible and the traditions of commentary on it, whereas many other scholars obviously have. However, all of us, whether specifically schooled in biblical scholarship or coming from other disciplines, should bring our own particular competence to bear on a dialogue concerning a text of universal import, which is what we believe the Hebrew Bible to be. Jewish tradition obviously embodies a special relationship to the text at stake in this study, and commentaries from within the world of Jewish piety have a legitimate, but surely not privileged, voice in the dialogue about its human significance. Intra-Judaic interpretation and debate is important, but so is extra-Judaic reflection on and engagement with the text. The text, then, doesn't belong exclusively to Jews as Jews. The Hebrew Bible is a towering work of Western culture – or, it might be better to say, of human culture full stop. All thinking human beings should be able to contribute to the dialogue about its meaning and normative implications.

Our purpose in this book is not to impugn the centuries of biblical interpretation that have shaped contemporary Judaism. We have made the Five Books of Moses the focus of our hermeneutic exertions because, even considered as a work of wholly profane literature, it is a fascinating text, and leading thinkers within the theory tradition have rightly expended enormous effort in trying to draw upon it as a signal intellectual and narrative resource. Moreover, because normative judgment is intrinsic to the business of political philosophy, we have not hesitated to apply critical normative judgment to the Hebrew Bible's presentation of the Moses story where such judgment seems called for. To be sure, it would be interesting to engage in full dialogue with the long tradition of intra-Judaic interpretations if we felt competent to do so. What we have here are two rich traditions of interpretation engaged in a perennial tug of war over the same text, and each must be true to its own integrity. Nor should we discount intellectual attempts to reconcile these two traditions. And of course even *within* each of these traditions, there is a tremendous diversity of interpretations, characterized by intense intramural contestation. But allowing for the quite different purposes of these traditions of interpretation, we certainly can't decide between opposing interpretations with a coin toss. In the end, interpretations within each tradition assert truth claims, and a true interpretation, properly vindicated, would be true for all readers of the text, not just those inhabiting a particular tradition, whether secular or religious. That, at least, must be what one aspires to, however far one falls short in practice.

It's probably stating the obvious to say the following, though there's certainly no harm in stating the obvious: There is much that's highly problematic in the Hebrew Bible, just as there's much that's highly problematic in the Koran; yet it would be a big mistake to assume that Judaism is "essentially" defined by what's in the Hebrew Bible or that Islam is "essentially" defined by what's in the Koran without considering how these two religions have evolved and revised their self-understandings over the course of a very lengthy history. The latter is not something we attempt to do in this book. The central purpose of the book is to map out a space of dialogue constituted by theoretical encounters across the centuries with one of the founding texts of Western thought and culture. It cannot be hoped that it surveys all relevant voices in that dialogue, since that would engage a much larger ambition than this small book can realize. Still, it can be hoped that the book offers an interesting selection of such voices, and hence, precisely in its manageable scale and limited ambitions, succeeds in sketching the rewards of opening that space for others who may seek to pursue further this open-ended dialogue.

RB
HF

MOSES AND POLITICAL PHILOSOPHY

The Moses Story in Exodus, Numbers, and Deuteronomy

Political thinkers throughout much of the Western intellectual tradition have their own versions of the Moses saga and its theoretical relevance. But what is the Hebrew Bible's version of the story? For anyone unfamiliar with the life of Moses as the Hebrew Bible presents it, the fairly sparse or minimalist character of its narrative content is quite striking and more than a little surprising. What follows is a compressed summary of the biblical story, to make it easier to compare the multitude of theoretical appropriations of the story to the original version from which those appropriations are drawn.[1]

The Israelites in Egypt are a subject people: the pharaoh of Egypt imposes forced labour on them. They are in need of a liberator.[2] Feeling threatened by the growth of the Hebrew population, Pharaoh issues an order that all male Hebrew infants shall be murdered at birth. Yet the Hebrew midwives defy this order. A son is born to two parents of the tribe of Levi, namely Amram and Jochebed. A papyrus ark containing the child is set upon the waters of the Nile, and with some help from the baby's sister, the pharaoh's daughter rescues the child and names him Moses. Again with some help from the sister, the baby's real Hebrew mother is engaged as the child's wet nurse. Moses is raised within the Egyptian royal court, though we are told nothing about his early life. "Some years later," Moses witnesses an Egyptian overseer beating a Hebrew labourer.[3] Recognizing the slave as a "brother," Moses kills the bully, thinking that his avenging deed was seen by no one.[4] But it turns out that it was seen, forcing Moses to flee Egypt in order to evade Pharaoh's justice. He settles in Midian. Moses (referred to in this context as "an Egyptian man")[5] provides assistance to some girls at a well, and comes to marry one of them, namely Zipporah. Moses and Zipporah produce a son: Gershom. At this stage of his life, Moses is a shepherd, tending the flock of Zipporah's father, Jethro (also called Reuel),[6] a Midianite priest.

It is in his capacity as humble shepherd that Moses undergoes the transformative experience at the famous burning bush. This is where YHWH recruits Moses to rescue the Israelites (whom God refers to as "my people")[7] from their oppression in Egypt. Moses is mightily reluctant to take on this mission. "No man of words am I, ... for heavy of mouth and heavy of tongue am I!"[8] God doesn't take no for an answer. To help seal the deal, he offers Moses's brother, Aaron, as a deputy (Exodus 7:1: "Aaron your brother will be your prophet.")[9] Given that Moses was raised by an Egyptian princess, it seems a little hard to fathom how he would have any acquaintance with his Hebrew siblings (Miriam and Aaron), but the two siblings go on to play a quite significant role in the subsequent narrative. Jethro gives permission for Moses to return to Egypt with Zipporah and "his sons" (Exodus 18:4 informs us that Moses had a second son by Zipporah named Eliezer).[10] So the adventure of national emancipation begins.

What follows is perhaps the most bizarre episode in the whole of the Mosaic narrative. Moses had somehow been negligent in circumcising his son (Gershom? Eliezer?)[11] – though one obviously wonders how the founder of Judaism could be negligent in performing a ritual so central to Judaism.[12] God is so infuriated that Moses's life is in danger: "YHWH encountered him and sought to make him die."[13] Zipporah rushes to resolve the crisis: she finds a flint with which to perform the circumcision, and God releases his death grip on Moses (Exodus 4:24–6). The next story is the reunion of Moses and Aaron, organized by God, and the two brothers proceed to their confrontation with Pharaoh. Rather than telling him that they demand the emancipation of the Israelites, they merely ask for a trip to the desert for a religious ceremony honouring God. Pharaoh responds by making the burdens of the Israelites even more severe. Exodus 7:7 tells us that at the time of the encounter with Pharaoh, Moses was eighty and Aaron, the elder brother, was eighty-three. What follows is a contest of magic tricks, such as turning staffs into serpents, but Pharaoh's sorcerers lose the competition. Still, Pharaoh is unmoved. The contest between God's magic and Pharaoh's magic undergoes dramatic escalation with a succession of plagues (reeking of the Nile with blood; swarming of frogs; a plague of gnats or lice; a second swarm of insects; a pestilence striking down livestock; boils; hail; a horde of locusts; darkness), culminating in the final and devastating tenth plague: death of all firstborn in Egypt. Several times along the way, Pharaoh's resolve seems to weaken a bit, but God suggests that he "hardened the heart of Pharaoh" (Exodus 9:12, KJV) in order to impress all the more powerfully upon the Egyptians the supreme power of the Hebrews' god.

Finally, the Israelites are allowed to depart Egypt. However, they don't leave empty-handed. "They despoiled Egypt," collecting "ornaments of silver and ornaments of gold and cloaks" (Exodus 12:35–6).[14] Not only do the Hebrews make off with a significant quantity of Egyptian property, but they also somehow constitute a properly equipped army: "The Children of Israel went up armed from the land of Egypt."[15] It appears that the Israelites are not the only people involved in this mass migration: "A mixed multitude went up with them."[16] As the people enter the wilderness, God leads them, "by day in a pillar of cloud … and by night in a pillar of fire" (Exodus 13:21–2, KJV). But having released the Israelites from their servitude, Pharaoh promptly has a change of heart, ordering that the fleeing exiles be pursued. Hence the famous episode of the dividing of the Red Sea (or Sea of Reeds). As before, Pharaoh's behaviour is shaped by God's notion of "hardening Pharaoh's heart" (Exodus 14:4) in order to display all the more compellingly God's amazing powers. Even as the chase goes on, the Israelites are wracked with doubts: "Is it because there are no graves in Egypt that you have taken us out to die in the wilderness?"[17] Moses tells the people to "stand fast," but there is a consistent pattern, throughout the wanderings in the wilderness, for the Hebrews to be ever-doubtful that God is committed to taking special care of them, despite Moses's constant assurances on that score.[18] God provides the protection that Moses has promised by drowning the pursuing Egyptian army. Still, the trials of the Israelites have barely begun.

The first crisis in the wilderness is a lack of water. "The people grumbled against Moses."[19] God makes the water drinkable. At the beginning of Exodus chapter 16, the people are again grumbling. This time the complaint is a lack of food. The children of Israel scold Moses and Aaron in the following words: "Would that we had died by the hand of YHWH in the land of Egypt, when we sat by the flesh pots, when we ate bread till (we were) satisfied! For you have brought us into this wilderness to bring death to this whole assembly by starvation!"[20] YHWH supplies food (Exodus 16:4: YHWH promises "to rain down … bread from the heavens"), since as Moses points out, "YHWH hearkens to your grumblings which you grumble against him."[21] But there is a "test" and an "instruction" attached to this food. All food provided must be duly collected, and since the Sabbath must be honoured, God gives the people two days' worth of food on the sixth day. But the people are not great at following these instructions or meeting God's test, eliciting Moses's "fury" (Exodus 16:20).[22] At the end of chapter 16, the standard fare for the people becomes the famous manna (Exodus 16:31: "like coriander seed, whitish," with a taste similar to "a wafer with honey"), which we're told was eaten by the children of Israel "for the forty years, until they came to settled land [at] the edge of the land of Canaan."[23]

At the start of Exodus chapter 17, the topic of the people's grumbling swings back to the issue of lack of water.[24] The complaints become so serious that Moses starts to worry that the people will stone him (Exodus 17:4).[25] YHWH resolves the crisis by allowing Moses to strike the rock at Horeb with his staff, miraculously producing water. However, in the version of the story narrated in Numbers 20:2–13, Moses errs in how he performs God's instructions, with eventually fatal consequences for himself and his hopes (and Aaron's hopes) of entering the Promised Land.[26] We next get a battle with Amalek, with the fortunes of the Israelites rising and falling in accordance with the raising or dropping of Moses's staff.[27] This is where Joshua, Moses's eventual successor, makes his first appearance (Exodus 17:9 and 17:13–14). The chapter ends with a declaration of eternal war between Israel and Amalek. With Exodus chapter 18, we get the reappearance of Jethro within the Mosaic narrative. It's a very happy reunion between father-in-law and son-in-law, and Jethro takes the opportunity to give Moses quite good advice about devolving a substantial portion of his judicial responsibilities to "men of calibre" appointed for this purpose.[28]

Chapter 19 begins to lay out what is arguably the core of the Mosaic narrative, namely YHWH's covenant with the Hebrews. They are to be, he tells Moses, "a kingdom of priests, a holy nation" (Exodus 19:6).[29] The elders of the people convened by Moses accept this covenant: "All that YHWH has spoken, we will do" (Exodus 19:8).[30] God promises to "come down before the eyes of all the people, upon Mount Sinai" (Exodus 19:11). And come down he does: as "a heavy cloud on the mountain," with lightning and thunder, in "fire" and "smoke," with the trembling of the mountain (Exodus 19:16 and 19:18). Moses is called to the top of the mountain and told to warn the people (including its priests) not to approach or attempt to see God. The next time he is to meet God on the mountain, he is supposed to bring only Aaron with him.[31] Moses then descends the mountain to deliver the Ten Commandments, laid out in chapter 20. What follows is a set of much more detailed divine regulations in chapters 21, 22, and 23.

Another divine audience is arranged in chapter 24. Aaron and two of Aaron's sons, as well as seventy elders of Israel, are allowed to "bow down from afar," but only Moses is permitted to approach YHWH (Exodus 24:1–2).[32] Twice more (in Exodus 24:3 and 24:7), the people commit themselves to abide by the words of YHWH – that is, to honour the covenant. At the conclusion of chapter 24, Moses is invited to ascend higher in order to receive God's stone tablets, accompanied up the mountain, at least a bit further, by Joshua (Exodus 24:13).[33] The others, however, are told to wait where they are. Thus commences a Mosaic visit with God lasting forty days and forty nights (Exodus 24:18).

Most of the next seven chapters (chapters 25–31) are devoted to an extremely detailed and precise specification of the requirements for what Everett Fox calls the "Dwelling," the "Tent of Appointment," or the "Tabernacle."[34] It's only in the very last verse of chapter 31 that we learn that God and Moses have completed the business of transmission of "the two tablets of Testimony … written by the finger of God."[35] So the narrative really resumes in chapter 32. Here we get the most memorable action in the book of Exodus – the part of the story that has most intensely engraved the Mosaic saga upon subsequent cultural consciousness. The people become impatient waiting for Moses to return from his conclave with YHWH. So they prevail upon Aaron to construct a gold idol, and he doesn't seem to have any problem going along with this sinful idea. This molten calf very quickly becomes Israel's substitute god, one that had supposedly "brought [them] up from the land of Egypt."[36] God rightly observes to Moses that notwithstanding the covenant, "they have been quick to turn aside from the way that I commanded them" (Exodus 32:8).[37] This occasions God's famous characterization of Israel as "a stiff-necked people."[38] He offers to destroy them and create a whole new people descending from Moses himself (Exodus 32:10). At this point, Moses does a good job of reasoning with God and pacifying his anger, actually managing to get God to express regret for, so to speak, overreacting (Exodus 32:14).[39]

Now it is Moses's turn to explode with anger. As he descends the mountain to see for himself how egregiously the people have violated YHWH's covenant, Moses flings the stone tablets written by God and smashes them. When he arrives at the camp, he grounds the calf into powder and forces the children of Israel to drink it (Exodus 32:20).[40] Aaron tries to talk his way out of guilt for his betrayal, and somehow gets himself off the hook. To cleanse Israel of its sin and to re-establish authority within the reign of YHWH, Moses initiates a wholesale bloodletting executed by the swords of the tribe of Levi. The Bible tells us that three thousand Israelites are massacred in order to purge the sinners, or at least their leaders (Exodus 32:28).[41] As John Geerken rightly underscores, Moses tells the Levites that *God* has ordered the slaughter of the apostates ("Thus saith the LORD God of Israel"[42]), whereas the narrative in Exodus makes clear that God orders no such thing.[43] Even if one accepts the biblical view that Mosaic policies generally originate with God rather Moses, here is at least one instance where, according to the Bible's own version of the story, Moses puts his own decision "in the mouth of the immortals," to borrow Rousseau's memorable formulation, or pretends that his precept was "the dictate of some God," to borrow Hobbes's.[44] In any case, when Moses returns to God, he offers to sacrifice himself as redress for the sin committed by Israel.[45] God refuses to let Moses bear responsibility for the people's sin, and re-endorses Moses's continued leadership.

The march to the "land flowing with milk and honey" resumes (Exodus 33:3).[46] God is afraid to put himself any longer in the midst of the Israelites at this stage of the journey because he is too afraid of succumbing to the temptation to destroy his infuriating chosen people (Exodus 33:3 and 33:5). Even Moses distances himself from the people by pitching the tabernacle outside the camp (Exodus 33:7).[47] Moses, rather audaciously, asks to see God's glory, but God refuses: "Thou canst not see my face" (KJV, Exodus 33:18 and 33:20).[48] Chapter 34 begins with YHWH offering to replace the two stone tablets that Moses in his fury had smashed. YHWH then commits himself to all-out war against a variety of enemy peoples, warning against letting those peoples "become a snare among you" and sanctioning comprehensive destruction of their religious totems.[49] Once again, Moses spends forty days and forty nights in the presence of YHWH. Once again, he descends Mount Sinai with "the two tablets of [divine] Testimony." On this second descent, the skin of Moses's face "was radiating," as a consequence of his converse with YHWH (Exodus 34:29).[50] To attenuate the effect of the skin of his face constantly radiating in this fashion, Moses begins to cover his face with a veil – a veil duly removed whenever he resumes his meetings with YHWH (Exodus 34:33–5).[51] The balance of the book of Exodus (chapters 35–40) is devoted to minute description of the tabernacle. Exodus concludes (40:34–8) with "the Glory of YHWH" inhabiting the tabernacle and God once again guiding the people of Israel on their journey by appearing to them alternately as fire and cloud.[52]

As we've already seen, some of the stories in Exodus get retold in Numbers in slightly different (and in some instances, crucially different) versions. Notably, in the Exodus version of the story of the waters of Meribah, Moses very clearly follows God's instructions, whereas in the Numbers version of the same story, Moses apparently diverges sufficiently from God's instructions as to bring serious divine punishment down upon himself (and upon Aaron). The book of Numbers commences with a comprehensive census of the Israelite camp, followed by very detailed and intricate ritual instructions, together encompassing nearly nine whole chapters of Numbers. Hence the Moses saga basically resumes at Numbers 9:15 with a continuation of the march through the

Sinai wilderness in pursuit of the Promised Land. Hobab had presumably been included in the camp, but expresses a desire to return to Midian (Numbers 10:30: "Rather to my land and to my kindred I will go").[53] However, it seems that Moses is successful in persuading him to stay with the camp and help in guiding the march (Numbers 10:31: "You shall be for us as eyes!").[54] But as the march resumes, so do the revolts against Moses's leadership.

Complaints provoke a fire ignited by the anger of YHWH, a fire that consumes some of the complainers (Numbers 11:1–3). Again, the people are griping about the poor quality of the fare, compared with the much better cuisine in Egypt.[55] The manna supplied by God seems less than desirable (Numbers 11:6). YHWH is still angry, and Moses complains to God that his burden of leadership is too onerous. God suggests creation of a council of seventy elders with whom Moses can share his load (Numbers 11:16–17). This time God does promise to supply the Israelites with actual meat, but the meat is promised more in a spirit of spite than in a spirit of generosity (Numbers 11:20: they will be eating meat "until it comes out of [their] nostrils and becomes for [them] something-disgusting.")[56] It is reported to Moses that two members of the camp, Eldad and Medad, are engaging in prophet-like behaviour. This alarms Joshua, but it doesn't seem to bother Moses (Numbers 11:26–29). Then the meat arrives in the form of vast quantities of quail. But the chapter begins as it started, with another blast of burning wrath from YHWH, striking "a very great blow against the people."[57]

Numbers chapter 12 begins with a challenge to Moses's authority from an unlikely source: Moses's own siblings![58] The pretext for this revolt is a complaint about "the Cushite wife" that Moses had married.[59] Is this Cushite wife Zipporah, or some other wife? It's not clear. Miriam and Aaron ask why they can't share equal standing with Moses as mouthpieces of God (Numbers 12:2). The next verse, rather oddly, asserts a claim about the superlative humility of Moses: "more [humble] than any person on the face of the earth."[60] YHWH then, appearing as a column or pillar of cloud, summons the three siblings to the tabernacle. Miriam and Aaron are called out and given a stern chewing-out by God, condemning their hubris and making clear Moses's pre-eminent status as God's "servant."[61] YHWH vents his anger by striking Miriam with what appears to be a kind of temporary leprosy (Numbers 11:10; Alter calls it "skin blanch").[62] Aaron does his usual routine of pleading for mercy and gets Moses to beg God for the healing of Miriam. The net punishment is seven days of exile from the camp for Miriam, and apparently no punishment for Aaron.[63]

Numbers chapter 13 narrates the episode of the scouts.[64] Twelve scouts, including Joshua, are chosen in order to suss out what awaits the Israelites in Canaan. The scouts come back confirming that the land "is flowing with milk and honey" (Numbers 13:27), but they also give an exaggerated account of the formidable enemy peoples inhabiting Canaan; hence the net effect of their reconnaissance mission is to discourage the Israelites from attempting to take possession of the land that YHWH has promised them. In chapter 14 we again get grumbling, and mutterings that the escape from Egypt was a big mistake. Two of the scouts, Joshua and Caleb, give a more positive account of the prospects of success and urge the community not to lose faith (Numbers 14:6–9). Numbers 14:10 hints at an intention among the whole community to murder Moses and his brother.[65] God once again loses his patience with the Hebrews, threatens to "strike [them] down with pestilence and dispossess [them]," and offers, just as he did in Exodus 32:10, to recreate a new chosen people based on a purely Mosaic lineage (Numbers 14:12).[66] Moses responds with the counter-argument that is already familiar to us: that God will be embarrassed in the eyes of Egyptians for having liberated this people from Egyptian servitude, only later to execute them for being unworthy of his exertions on their behalf (Numbers 14:13–19). YHWH concedes the reasonableness of Moses's argument and hence yet again spares the Israelites. YHWH is clearly very upset by the disappointing performance of the scouts and is determined to punish the whole people for their reluctance to seize the land that he had designated for them. God declares that no Israelite composing the existing community will live to enter the Promised Land – with the exception of the two faithful scouts, Caleb and Joshua (Numbers 14:30, 14:38, and 26:65). The mission of the scouts had lasted forty days, and YHWH ordains that the failed mission will be punished with forty years of wandering in the desert (Numbers 14:34). This is clearly a shockingly harsh penalty – each day of unsatisfactory scouting punished with one year in the wilderness! The people, realizing the dire consequences of their foot-dragging, are now suddenly keen to invade Canaan, but it's too late. They have already alienated YHWH, who allows them to be struck down by the Amalekites and Canaanites (Numbers 14:40–5).

The next major episode is the significant revolt of Korah in chapter 16. Korah is joined by two other rebels, Dathan and Abiram, and they are in turn backed up by 250 prominent leaders of the community (KJV at Numbers 16:2 calls them "princes of the assembly … men of renown"). The rebels implicitly appeal to the conception of Israel conjured up in Exodus 19:6 as "a kingdom of priests, a holy nation." If that is what Israel is supposed to be – a people whose "entire community, the entirety of them, are holy" – why, they ask Moses and Aaron, "do you exalt yourselves over the assembly of YHWH?" (Numbers 16:3).[67] Moses responds that it is up to YHWH to decide the issue of ultimate authority. Numbers 16:1 informs us that Korah is a Levite, so this is in an important sense a revolt of Levites against Levites. Moses emphasizes the Levite character of the revolt in Numbers 16:7–10, repeatedly referring to the rebels as "Sons of Levi" and underscoring their subordinate function in relation to full priests. In 16:9 he characterizes them as dissatisfied, merely performing "the serving-tasks of the Dwelling of YHWH," merely "attending" the community, and in 16:10 he highlights their ambition to "seek the priesthood as well."[68] The whole implication of this speech is that the revolt is not about political authority but rather is driven by resentment on the part of the Levites with respect to their inferior religious status vis-à-vis full priests. Dathan and Abiram, for their part, engage in the standard grumbling about the wilderness not being the land of milk and honey that had been promised, but also discharge a more directly political challenge: they accuse Moses of lording it over them (Numbers 16:13).[69] The two sides then await YHWH's judgment.

YHWH is clearly not well-disposed toward this revolt, any more than he was well-disposed toward earlier revolts, including the one by Moses's two siblings. As happens on other occasions, YHWH threatens to obliterate the whole of Israel ("Separate yourselves from the midst of this community, that I may finish them off in an instant!"), but Moses and Aaron do what they can to persuade him to focus on the actual instigators (Numbers 16:20–2).[70] The punishment is harsh, as it usually is. "There split the ground that was beneath [the rebels]; the earth opened its mouth and swallowed up them and their households, all the human beings that belonged to Korah and all the property … and they perished from the midst of the assembly" (Numbers 16:31–3).[71] Moreover, the 250 elders supportive of the rebellion perish in a consuming fire let loose by YHWH (Numbers 16:35). Following the revolt, YHWH reinforces the authority of Aaron within the tabernacle by means of a stunt involving Aaron's staff (it turns into a kind of almond tree).[72] This has the effect of giving further emphasis to the fact that the Korah revolt was arguably more a challenge to Aaron than to Moses insofar as it was (at least according to Moses's account) centrally a revolt of Levites against full priests. Numbers 18:23 refers to the Levites as being required to "bear their iniquity" in perpetuity, suggesting that the denial of a grant of land uniquely to the tribe of Levites is part of their punishment for the Korah episode.[73]

It's in Numbers chapter 20 that we witness the repetition of the waters of Meribah episode that leads to Moses's and Aaron's exclusion from the Promised Land (Numbers 20:12; cf. 20:24). The chapter begins with what Alter calls an "isolated obituary notice" for Miriam (Numbers 20:1),[74] and by the end of the chapter, Aaron too will be dead.[75] YHWH emphasizes in Numbers 20:24 that Aaron's death prior to the entry into Canaan was a punishment, and it is clear that a similar fate awaits Moses: Aaron "is not to enter the land that I am giving to the Children of Israel – since you (both) rebelled against my orders at the Waters of Meribah."[76] Fox rightly comments, "The question of why exactly Moses and Aaron received such a terrible punishment for a moment of indiscretion will not go away. Can it really be that the towering figure of Moses, liberator and lawgiver, parent and prophet, is to be done away with in the blink of an eye, over a fit of justifiable temper?"[77] It's even more of an enigma because so little explanation is given of what exactly was Moses's "indiscretion." And why does Aaron share in the punishment? It remains mysterious what here constituted "rebelling" against YHWH's orders, but if there was such a betrayal of YHWH's "trust" (Numbers 20:12), surely it was Moses who was the relevant offender.[78] Franz Kafka famously wrote, "Not because his life was too short does Moses not reach Canaan, but because it was a human life."[79] But this is not the biblical view. The biblical view is that Moses fails to reach Canaan because he has sinned, though the exact nature of the sin is extremely obscure.

Much of the remainder of Numbers consists of harsh and cruel wars against the enemies of Israel, a harshness and cruelty consistently incited by both Moses and YHWH. In Numbers 21:2, Israel pledges a "herem" against the Canaanites.[80] With God's blessing, "not a survivor was left" in the encounter with Og, king of Bashan, at the end of chapter 21.[81] At the end of chapter 25, YHWH urges Moses to "attack the Midianites,"[82] a war that is prosecuted in chapter 31. We are told, first by YHWH and then by Moses, that this will be a war of vengeance (Numbers 31:1–3).[83] The Israelite army kills all males, including various Midianite kings, captures the women and children, takes the Midianite property as plunder, and burns down all their towns (Numbers 31:7–10). One might expect that this is vengeance enough. But in fact Moses is "furious with the commanders of the military" (Numbers 31:14). Astonishingly, he demands the murder of children and non-virgin women, and the taking of virgin women as sex slaves (Numbers 31:15–18).[84] Does YHWH sanction a policy this harsh? The text doesn't say that he does, but also doesn't say that he doesn't. The fact that the campaign begins with the announcement that it is a war "to exact the vengeance of YHWH upon Midian"[85] suggests that Moses's harshness has YHWH's blessing. Also, YHWH is implicated in the outcome by virtue of the fact that he receives a substantial share of the booty via the high priest serving as his stand-in (Numbers 31:28–29, 31:41, and 31:51–4). In anticipation of the actual invasion of Canaan, YHWH orders not only the dispossession of the existing population but complete destruction of the things that define their various cults: "You are to destroy all their figured-objects, all their molten images you are to destroy, all their high-places you are to annihilate, that you may take-possession of the land and settle in it" (Numbers 33:52–3).[86] And these commands come with a potent threat: If the Israelites fall short of total dispossession of the enemy peoples, "as I thought to do to them, so I will do to you!" (Numbers 33:56).[87]

Chapters 1 to 11 of Deuteronomy are devoted to re-chronicling the history that the Israelites have already enacted rather than narrating new action, with lengthy speeches by Moses offering various exhortations and reminding the people how abominably they have tried the patience of YHWH, their god. Chapters 12 to 28 then set out another long set of Mosaic laws. The concluding chapters of Deuteronomy give us more hortatory speeches from Moses, culminating in Moses's poetic blessing of the twelve tribes of Israel in chapter 33. The only real new action in Deuteronomy is the death of Moses, narrated in chapter 34. Moses ascends to the top of Mount Nebo, overlooking Jericho, giving him a view of the Promised Land, to which he has been denied entry. "So there died there Moses, servant of YHWH, in the land of Moab" (Deuteronomy 34:5). "He buried him in a valley in the land of Moab … and no man has knowledge of the site of his burial-place until this day" (Deuteronomy 34:6).[88]

Needless to say, it is impossible to know anything about the historical reality of Moses, or even to know for sure whether such a man existed. Robert A. Paul, in his illuminating book on Freud's Moses, suggests that it was a big mistake for Freud (and his critics) to have gotten so exercised about questions concerning the historical Moses, because "no independent information exists" in regard to "who or what Moses might have been in historical terms."[89] A similar judgment is offered by Daniel Jeremy Silver in his equally helpful book on Moses: "The gap remains, as great as ever, between what the Bible reports of Moses and what we can corroborate on the basis of outside information."[90] Silver, who was himself a rabbi, refers to Moses as "a man whose very existence cannot be proved."[91] In short, all we have is the story, and the story is pretty much as we have sketched it above.

Chapter One

Images of Moses in the Modern Western Theory Canon

My motive [in relating the Moses narrative], I think, was somewhat like that which moved the painters of the Middle Ages to paint over and over again the same old subjects: Madonna and Child, Christ Crucified, etc. There are hundreds of these; every painter did one or more. Each artist and every school of painting put into the same, old, known subjects all that they thought they had learned of art, truth and beauty.

– Lincoln Steffens[1]

For the philosopher, full understanding of a problem is infinitely more important than any mere answer.

– Leo Strauss[2]

The figure or symbol of Moses is a significant presence in much of the history of modern (post-Machiavellian) political thought. Machiavelli casts him as an epic founder – even as a model of the redeemer-prince that is desperately needed by a weak and disunited Italy. John Toland elevates him to iconic status at the top of the frontispiece for his monumental 1700 edition of the works of James Harrington.[3] Rousseau portrays Moses as not only equalling the great legislators of antiquity but as decidedly surpassing them. However, Moses not only has his fans and celebrators within the Western canon; he also has severe critics and detractors. Spinoza emphasizes the coerciveness of the Mosaic regime, probably thinking pre-eminently of the golden calf bloodbath, which can hardly be exemplary for a Spinozistic vision of politics oriented toward enlightenment and liberty of judgment. Thomas Paine presents him as a murderer and criminal. (That image is actually present in Machiavelli's Moses as well, but it doesn't deter Machiavelli from celebrating him.) And so on. In short, the debate among images of Moses as either supremely impressive or supremely unattractive carries us to the heart of important issues defining the history of political thought. One obviously can't hope to exhaust, within the confines of a short book, all interesting images of Moses that figure within the subsequent cultural and philosophical history of the West. However, it may be hoped that the short studies offered in this chapter sketch a sufficient range of such Moseses, or Moses appropriations, to allow for a fruitful and illuminating dialogue within the Western tradition.

It is a legitimate part of the responsibility of political philosophy to raise questions such as the following: Why do leading thinkers of the modern tradition present Moses and the Mosaic tradition as exemplary? In particular, why is Moses elevated to the pantheon of heroes of the republican tradition? And does Moses *deserve* to be in that pantheon? *Are* Moses and the Mosaic regime as exemplary as many thinkers within the tradition of Western political thought take them to be? What are the flaws or deficiencies of Moses as a political leader and of the Mosaic regime as a regime? How do we weigh up Mosaic virtues against Mosaic vices? In short: Why is Moses so warmly embraced by such a diversity of thinkers within the tradition of political philosophy, and is it right for him to be so embraced? Of the many puzzles that the Hebrew Bible poses for political philosophy, a key one is (as I formulate it in chapter 4): Given the radically theocratic foundation of the rule asserted by Moses, why would any theorist not thoroughly committed to a theocratic vision of politics see anything exemplary in Mosaic politics or the Mosaic regime? Yet many within the Western theory canon clearly do. Hence we need to really ponder the profound paradox of a tradition of anti-theocratic theorizing, from Machiavelli to Harrington to Rousseau, that nonetheless elevates Moses to a pantheon of founder-heroes as the modern republican tradition does.

Is there a political philosophy in the Hebrew Bible? I think there must be, because the Hebrew Bible articulates a comprehensive conception of human existence, including an authoritative regulation of life in all its moral, social, and political dimensions. In that sense, it's perfectly natural that major thinkers within the Western tradition of political philosophy would engage the Hebrew Bible in theoretical dialogue, and in many instances appropriate aspects of it in support of their own (obviously quite different) political philosophies. Inserting ourselves into the centuries-long dialogue that is political philosophy thus implicates us as well in the biblical narratives that intersect with, or are picked up and carried further by, the theory canon. The Moses story looms large among such narratives.

Machiavelli's Moses: Redeemer and Imperialist

1. The Prince

The modern republican tradition was inaugurated by Machiavelli, and he certainly contributed decisively to the celebration of Moses taken up by subsequent republican political thinkers, so it is appropriate to begin our sketch of appropriations of the Moses story within the Western theory canon with the Machiavellian depiction of Moses. There are two chapters in *The Prince* in which Moses is discussed; both are crucially important texts with respect to the articulation of Machiavelli's political philosophy. The first is the all-important chapter 6, specifying what counts for Machiavelli as *virtù* in the highest sense.[4] Machiavelli says that "the most excellent are Moses, Cyrus, Romulus, Theseus, and the like."[5] I interpret "and the like" (*e simili*) as a reference to Mohammed. Not by accident, all of those on Machiavelli's list are founders of *civilizations*, not merely of polities, and by this criterion, Mohammed obviously belongs on the same list.[6] Machiavelli says that Moses is "mere executor" of God's commands and suggests that a fair portion of Moses's greatness is owed to what God contributes as his "tutor."[7] But if God is the real agent, Moses's greatness as a prince would be the product of *fortune*, namely the fortune of having been chosen by God, whereas the theme announced in the chapter's title suggests otherwise: "new principalities that are acquired *through one's own arms and virtue.*" A prince as dependent on God's favour as the Hebrew Bible makes Moses out to be could in no way be classed under the rubric of relying exclusively on "one's own arms and virtue." When God chooses him, Moses is a mere shepherd tending flocks for his father-in-law; he certainly possesses no arms; and it is only with great reluctance that he is willing to accede to YHWH's call for him to assume leadership of the oppressed Israelites. Surely an important part of what Machiavelli means, in *Discourses on Livy*, book 3, chapter 30, by a "judicious reading" of the Bible is an account that factors out the supposed agency of God. (Interestingly, Fox points out a telling discrepancy, in the so-called episode of the spies or scouts, between the version in Numbers 13:1 and the version in Deuteronomy 1:23.[8] In the former version, the key decisions are made by God. In the latter version, they are made by Moses. This could be read as a concession, on the part of the Hebrew Bible itself, that what are presented as commands of YHWH are really commands of Moses.)

What is in common between Machiavelli's truly exemplary founder-princes is their shared capacity "to introduce any form they please" in shaping the human material given to them. Yes, fortune has to present them with an *opportunity* to do so, but they must rely on their own surpassing virtue if the opportunity is not to go in vain. The enslavement of the Israelites in Egypt is Machiavelli's first example of such an opportunity: Moses's people are desperate to be liberated from oppression; hence where he will lead, they will follow – though the Five Books of Moses present us with repeated episodes of backsliding and regret, which Machiavelli leaves out of his account. Machiavelli claims that in the case of founder-princes of this stature, who become prince "by the paths of virtue," the principality is acquired with difficulty but held "with ease."[9] Of course, that *isn't* the case with Moses, who never ceases having to put down rebellions; but again, Machiavelli doesn't highlight this aspect of the story. It's in this context that Machiavelli introduces his all-important conception of "new modes and orders," which again I interpret as the founding of civilizations or whole dispensations – creations much grander than mere principalities or republics.[10] What follows is the famous account of the superiority of armed prophets to unarmed prophets. Because of the scale of what is being founded, one unavoidably must "use force." If one's followers don't believe, or believe with insufficient zeal, "one can make them believe by force."[11] There is obviously no lack of force backing up Moses's new modes and orders, as is illustrated throughout the books of the Hebrew Bible that convey the Moses saga. "Moses, Cyrus, Theseus, and Romulus would not have been able to make their peoples observe their constitutions for long if they had been unarmed." The concept of the armed prophet is to be interpreted in the most literal sense: Moses is a prophet backed up by an army, just as Mohammed is a prophet backed up by an army.[12] Machiavelli omits to mention who is the obvious exemplar of the *unarmed* prophet: namely, the founder of the civilization inhabited by Machiavelli himself. Machiavelli's thesis is that unarmed prophets necessarily fail, but if that were true, it would be obvious that Christian civilization would never have come into existence. That in turn tells us that Machiavelli's preference for Moses over Christ (or Mohammed over Christ) is a *normative* (= philosophical) preference, not merely a question of what it takes to prevail in a world of cruelty and ruthlessness.

Machiavelli tellingly returns to Moses in the very last chapter of the book (chapter 26).[13] The theme here is redemption. Italy needs a redeemer-prince, just as ancient Israel, Athens, and Persia did. The more enslaved, oppressed, and dispersed the people is, the more we appreciate the virtue of their liberator. This typical Machiavellian theme of "the greater the adversity, the greater the demonstration of virtue" is actually reminiscent of a similar theme in Exodus: God repeatedly "hardens the heart" of Pharaoh so that when Pharaoh eventually relents, the glory of the liberator-god will be all the more manifest. The exemplary "virtue of Moses" (*la virtù di Moisè*) is visible precisely because his people were so utterly subject to the Egyptian yoke. In this sense, the promise of emphatically displayed virtue is truly great for the coming Italian Moses, for the Italy of Machiavelli's day, he claims, "is more enslaved than the Hebrews, more servile than the Persians, more dispersed than the Athenians ... Beaten, despoiled, torn, pillaged, and having endured ruin of every sort." More enslaved than the Hebrews? *Really?* Machiavelli then refers to an unnamed potential redeemer of Italy: a glimmer shone that he (who?) was elected by God for Italy's redemption, just as Moses was for Israel's redemption/liberation, although "later it was seen that in the highest course of his actions, he was repulsed by fortune." Who was this failed redeemer? Cesare Borgia? Machiavelli himself? Machiavelli doesn't say. In any case, the key point here is that "Mosaic virtue" is for him the appropriate standard by which to judge the politics of Italy's salvation – a very high standard indeed. And Machiavelli continues on in the same vein when he turns to addressing Pope Leo X as a possible redeemer-prince, urging him to seize the opportunity at hand in directly Mosaic imagery: "The sea has opened; a cloud has escorted you along the way; the stone has poured forth water; here manna has rained; everything has concurred in your greatness."[14] Machiavelli is telling future great princes of Italy, or better, future founders of a united Italian republic, that they should read the book of Exodus alongside his own book and model themselves on the hero of the Hebraic epic!

2. Discourses on Livy

There are four references to Moses in this work, which obviously repay close attention. In book 1, chapter 9, under the rubric of "be[ing] alone if one wishes to order a republic anew or to reform it altogether outside its ancient orders," Machiavelli (consistent with the suggestion in chapter 6 of *The Prince*) elevates Moses to the highest class of princes, alongside Lycurgus, Solon, and other founders of kingdoms and republics who were able to form laws for the purpose of the common good because they had one authority attributed to them.[15] Machiavelli claims that he needn't elaborate on this because it is "a thing known." In Moses's case, arguably, the singularity of the founder is less than unambiguous. In fact, there's plenty of ambiguity in the biblical narrative. Was Moses exercising a solo authority? There are different ways of reading this. The surface suggestion is that he is a kind of regent for God, who is the real political actor, through the instrumentality of Moses (and Aaron). In some sense it is a dual regime, with Moses in an unspecified office and Aaron as high priest (though the authority of Moses as supreme prophet clearly trumps the authority of Aaron as high priest). And eventually the rule of seventy elders becomes an "institutionalized" part of the regime, though it's possible to imagine, on a Machiavellian view, that this represents a transition from Mosaic monarchy or principality (the authentic founding) to Mosaic or post-Mosaic republicanism once the foundational business of founding the Hebrew state has been completed.

Book 3, chapter 30 is a key Machiavellian commentary on what he sees as Moses's impressive insight into the harsh imperatives of rulership, and it is an interpretation in considerable tension with the biblical account. The heading of the chapter refers to the necessity of eliminating envy ("It Is Necessary First to Eliminate Envy"). Machiavelli writes, "Whoever reads the Bible judiciously will see that since he wished his laws and his orders to go forward, Moses was forced to kill [countless] men who, moved by nothing other than envy, were opposed to his plans."[16] Harvey C. Mansfield Jr. and Nathan Tarcov, in their accompanying note, cite the episode of the golden calf.[17] To be sure, this biblical text fits the theme of having "to kill countless men." However, the theme of envy is much better illustrated by the story of the Korah revolt (and perhaps also by the story of the mutiny by Aaron and Miriam).[18] John H. Geerken helpfully points out that *the Bible itself* identifies envy as being at the root of the Korah rebellion. The relevant text is Psalm 106:16: "They envied Moses also in the camp, and Aaron the saint of the LORD" (KJV).[19]

Machiavelli's suggestion in this chapter is a remarkable reading of the story of the revolts against Moses's authority. Typically, the Hebrew Bible presents the rebelliousness and disloyalty of the Hebrews as a series of tales of sin and idolatry. The Bible's version of these stories revolves not around realpolitik but around the threat of backsliding away from monotheism. Machiavelli's "judicious reading" turns the Mosaic saga into a thoroughly political narrative: one must consolidate one's authority in order to establish a virtuous regime and purge that regime of rivals who resent the authority seized by the "one citizen" (flagged in the chapter title) responsible for replacing corruption with virtue. The Mosaic story offers lessons about the hard necessities of founding a constitutional order oriented toward republican virtue. Moses is the prince who founds a virtuous Mosaic republic, and God is absent from that story. It should be pointed out that this Machiavellian narrative crucially anticipates the Freudian narrative upon which

I draw in chapter 4 of *Civil Religion*. Freud's narrative focuses on the resentments directed at Moses and the desire to kill him as an authority figure. In Freud's story, they actually *do* kill him, though the Hebrew Bible doesn't report this, or (Freud thinks) represses memory of it. Machiavelli and Freud in effect agree that when primordial authority is at stake, it's kill or be killed![20]

With respect to the imperative of "killing countless men," which Machiavelli endorses, we shouldn't omit to mention Hobbes's memorable response to the story of the golden calf, as we have it on the authority of John Aubrey's *Brief Lives*. For Hobbes, the story offers a sad commentary on the bottomless barbarity of human beings. He apparently told Aubrey that "the Crueltie of Moyses" – Moses's "putting so many thousands to the Sword" – illustrated the principle that but for the laws threatening murderers with the gallows, there are human beings who "are of so cruell a nature as to take a delight in killing men more than I should to kill a bird."[21] There's a striking contrast between Machiavelli's and Hobbes's very different responses to the evident fact of Mosaic ruthlessness. For Hobbes, it depicts the human potentiality for evil. Machiavelli exposes the realpolitik motivation, namely the necessity of eliminating rivals jealous of a newly founded political order; but because Machiavelli fully embraces the game of realpolitik, with all its horrors and joys, he doesn't condemn Moses as a practitioner of this deadly game. Near the end of *Leviathan*, Hobbes does seem to justify the execution of idolaters, including the three thousand slain by Moses, as "not Private Zeale, but Publique Condemnation"; that is, as a matter of "formall Judicature."[22] This is obviously very far removed from the "delight in cruelty" view reported by Aubrey. One wonders why Hobbes should, in this text, go out of his way to defend the law of Moses as it applies to idolatry, and one wonders also whether it expresses what he really thinks on such issues. When Hobbes famously said to Aubrey that Spinoza "had outthrowne [me] a bar's length,"[23] he was surely confessing that all the displays of piety that seem implied in Hobbes's laborious biblical commentaries are in no way to be taken at face value.

The references to Moses in *Discourses on Livy*, book 1, chapter 1 and book 2, chapter 8 are related. In the first, Machiavelli cites Moses as an example of a "builder of cities" constrained to take possession of a "new seat" on account of being driven out of the Hebrews' "ancestral country."[24] It's not clear what counts as the ancestral country of the Hebrews: Is it Israel or is it Egypt? Machiavelli doesn't clarify it. In any case, he emphasizes "the virtue of the builder," and Moses is surely exemplary in this regard from a Machiavellian perspective.

The result is the possibility of inhabiting a new country that has been "acquired." But what is the meaning of such an acquisition? Machiavelli doesn't tell us here but does tell us in book 2, chapter 8. Here's his commentary:

> Such peoples go out of their countries, as was said above [seemingly a reference back to book 1, chapter 1], expelled by necessity; the necessity arises either from famine or from a war and oppression inflicted on them in their own countries such that they are constrained to seek new lands. When they are a great number, then they enter with violence into the countries of others, kill the inhabitants, take possession of their goods, make a new kingdom, and change the province's name, as did Moses and the peoples [Goths, Vandals, etc.] who seized the Roman Empire ... [Moses] called that part of Syria seized by him Judea.[25]

"Seized by him" is not quite accurate; the actual seizing, of course, was done by Joshua after Moses's death. But it would be consistent with the biblical narrative to consider this as Joshua's execution of the Mosaic project. This business about changing names is an implicit citation by Machiavelli of Numbers 32:38 and 32:42, when the Israelites were occupied with seizing territories other than Canaan while still under the direct leadership of Moses. In fact, the question of whether names endure or are obliterated is a persistent theme in the Five Books of Moses: see also, for instance, Deuteronomy 7:24, 9:14, 12:3, and 25:19. Let me add: Machiavelli may well have had other sources than these biblical texts in mind when ventilating this particular theme. Josephine Quinn, in a review essay entitled "Caesar Bloody Caesar," quotes the following from Julius Caesar's *Gallic War*: we will "destroy their stock and name."[26]

At the end of the paragraph, Machiavelli cites an inscription where the Maurusians identify themselves as a tribe obliged to flee "before the face of Joshua the robber son of Nun."[27] Joshua was obviously grabbing their land as the completion of the project of imperial conquest set in motion by Moses. Machiavelli doesn't repudiate this as illegitimate; he sees it as a "hard necessity" of the politics of founding. But he acknowledges the theft as theft. This too is a clear departure from the biblical account, which emphasizes notions of divine gift and divine promise, as if God's donating this land to his chosen people doesn't involve *confiscating* it from *other* peoples. Machiavelli pretty clearly sees this as a "theological cover" for what was really a strictly political (or we might say geopolitical) act. It's possible to think of this as Machiavelli's sketching in what the Bible leaves unspoken, though it's implicit in the narrative; and this, surely, is what he means by "reading judiciously."

Hobbes's Moses: Sovereign of the Hebrew State

What is Moses's "office" (= political office)? The Hebrew Bible doesn't tell us. Three possible titles immediately come to mind: prophet; revolutionary leader; messiah. (And according to Exodus 18:26, Moses also functions as a kind of one-man Supreme Court.) It's relatively easy to think of Moses as the Che Guevara or the Ho Chi Minh of the Israelite nation. Michael Walzer calls him "a proto-messiah."[28] Hobbes advances a very different image of Mosaic politics, encapsulated in the title of this section. In this context, it's worth pointing out something highlighted by Walzer in chapter 4 of *In God's Shadow*, namely that the Hebrew Bible never suggests that the Mosaic regime was a monarchy. Kingship was introduced only with the revolt against theocracy in the transition from Samuel to Saul. If Moses had been king, a son of Moses would have been his successor. Yet if Moses is a combined prophet, high priest, and in effect prime minister in a "kingship of God," then it might be reasonable to say that he exercises a kind of sovereignty superior to merely monarchical sovereignty. On the other hand, as we discuss toward the end of our commentary on Hobbes and Moses, Exodus 40:35 presents a tricky problem for the view that Moses's authority, on whatever basis it rests, trumps Aaron's authority in all respects.

Rousseau is absolutely right that what is of utmost concern to Hobbes as a political philosopher is the question of how to "reunify the two heads of the eagle."[29] The two-headed eagle has for very many centuries been an imperial emblem adopted by a wide variety of states, ancient, medieval, and modern, including the Holy Roman Empire, Austria, Germany, Russia, Serbia, and many others. The problem with a two-headed eagle is that it can't fly straight, because each head wants to go in a different direction. This is the fundamental reason why Hobbes insists on unitary sovereignty. And as both he and Rousseau grasp with particular incisiveness, the problem of divided sovereignty – which is a problem in all political orders where political authority and priestly authority are bifurcated – becomes dramatically worse under a Christian dispensation, because Christian theologians and priests situate the true city (Augustine's City of God) in a radically otherworldly location. This problem does not apply to Moses, because political authority and priestly authority are not bifurcated under his theocratic regime (or at least they aren't bifurcated as long as political authority and priestly authority are fused together in his own personal rule), and because the yearnings that animate Mosaic politics are worldly rather than otherworldly. For Hobbes, solving this problem of how to get the spiritual/otherworldly eagle's head to defer to the temporal/political eagle's head is the number one job of a political philosophy, and all viable solutions will in some sense involve a "back to Moses" scenario.

What the figure of Moses represents for Hobbes is the image of a political order where the eagle has only one head. Admittedly, it is not effortless to determine what defines that singular head in the case of the Hebrew "commonwealth" (= *res publica*), as Hobbes insists on calling it.[30] Can the Hebrew state be both a monarchy and a republic? Hobbes seems to suggest that it can. Walzer, on the other hand, asserts that there is no such thing as a "Hebrew commonwealth" or "Hebrew republic," because "insofar as the biblical writers think politically, they do so from the vantage point of the king."[31] What is the nature of the regime? Hobbes refers to it as the "Kingdom of God." He means that quite literally – as indeed the Hebrew Bible itself does! In fact, Hobbes's scriptural hermeneutics are always overwhelmingly literalist, and no one can ever accuse him of opting for metaphorical interpretations of what's in the Bible. "Kingdom of God" means that Israel is in the strictest sense a theocratic monarchy, with God as the reigning monarch, until it becomes a *non*-theocratic monarchy with the people's embrace of normal kingship in the transition from Samuel to Saul (1 Samuel, chapters 8–9). But there is one key text where Hobbes makes clear that a regime where "God truly reigns" really means rule by priests, namely the text in *On the Citizen*, chapter 16, where he refers to "God's rule, i.e., the government of the *Priest* by whom God ruled."[32] In any case, Hobbes says of the kingdom of God that "God truly reigns where the laws are obeyed for fear of God, not of men," and amazingly adds, "And if men were as they should be, that would be the best form of commonwealth"![33]

Hobbes insists that both during Moses's life and subsequent to his death, this required *singular authority* – so that one had certainty about how to interpret God's laws and about how to distinguish between true prophets and false prophets. During Moses's lifetime, this singular authority was held entirely by Moses. "It is clear that while Moses was alive this authority lay wholly with him."[34] Mosaic sovereignty was, as Hobbes relates, tested twice in the book of Numbers: by Korah, Datan, and Aviram (in chapter 16) and by Aaron and Miriam (in chapter 12). In both cases God sided with Moses and punished the rebels (though as usual, Aaron somehow gets off scot free). In the former case, the argument had been made that God intended for the whole of Israel to be a holy nation; hence it was illegitimate for Moses to elevate himself to a supremely privileged status. "What God thought of this point may be seen from the fact that" the rebels were promptly swallowed into hell.[35] "Moses alone was the messenger of God's word ... Moses was the sole interpreter of God's word and also held sovereign power in civil matters."[36] One eagle's head. Although Aaron was notional high priest, Moses's status as singular prophet obviously meant that any authority held by Aaron was entirely subordinate to Moses's. As Hobbes points out, if this weren't the case, it would have made no sense for Aaron to have joined Miriam in rebelling against the rule of Moses.[37] Once again, "it is clear [from the outcome of this revolt] that this Authority did not lie with the high Priest Aaron."[38] As regards this revolt by Moses's two siblings in Numbers chapter 12, Hobbes's acerbic gloss informs us that the rebellion "was not started for the safety of their souls but from ambition for kingdom over the people,"[39] which makes it even more puzzling that Aaron evades punishment for his mutiny.[40] One could say that Hobbes is showing that he, no less than Machiavelli, knows how to engage in a "judicious reading" of the Hebrew Bible!

The situation changes when Moses dies and Joshua succeeds him. Then it becomes clear who the real sovereign is: the *high priest* (Eleazar). But this doesn't mean a contest of rival sovereignties between civil magistrate and priest: "Interpretation of the laws and of God's Word was in the hands of Eleazar, the high Priest, *who was also the King*, absolute under God."[41] Because Israel was a *theocratic* monarchy, kingly sovereignty belonged to whoever held supreme authority to interpret God's word and God's laws, and subsequent to the death of Moses, that had to be the high priest. Joshua clearly possessed diminished authority relative to Moses, as Hobbes makes explicit,[42] yet sovereignty remained unitary. "It is clear that even in the time of Joshua sovereign civil power and authority to interpret God's word belonged to the same person [namely Eleazar]."[43] "The right of the Kingdom instituted by God stayed with the Priest" until the termination of the theocracy with the kingship of Saul. "When kings were appointed, there is no doubt that civil authority was in the hands of the Kings. For when the Kingdom of God by Priests had come to an end at the Israelites' request and with God's consent, the right by which the kings governed was grounded in the people's actual cession [= popular acknowledgment of kingly vs. priestly/theocratic authority]."[44] "Throughout the period from King Saul to the captivity in Babylon, Priesthood was, *as in Moses' time*, a ministry, not a magistracy."[45] Priesthood was a mere "ministry" under Moses presumably because the authority of Aaron was decidedly subordinate to his brother's authority. Return from foreign captivity involved restoration of "the Priestly kingdom": the state that the Hebrews then re-established "was a Priestly Kingdom, i.e., supreme authority, civil and sacred, was united in the Priests." "During that period authority to interpret God's word was not separate from supreme civil authority."[46] In other words, at some points in the history of Israel, sovereignty was held by priests; at other points it was held by kings. But at no time was priestly authority and civil authority anything other than an inseparable unity. So on Hobbes's reading of the history of Israel, there was never a time when sovereignty was in any sense divided: "Just as in merely human Kingdoms one must obey the subordinate magistrates in everything … so in God's Kingdom obedience had to be given to the princes Abraham, Isaac, Jacob, Moses, and the Priest and the King, each in his time."[47] That is, when priests held sovereignty they subsumed civil authority, and when kings held sovereignty they subsumed priestly authority. In neither case was there a two-heads-of-the-eagle problem.

Life under the Christian dispensation is a different story. Hobbes's version of Christianity is intended to solve the two-headed-eagle problem by eliminating the otherworldliness of Christianity. Presumably, this is what Rousseau has in mind when he states that Hobbes grasps both "the evil and the remedy,"[48] though Rousseau doesn't spell out what defines Hobbes's remedy. For Hobbes, Christ is not the sovereign of an otherworldly kingdom. On the contrary, he is (or rather will be) the sovereign of a this-worldly kingdom in exactly the same sense as Moses was. He, no less than Moses, will unify the spiritual eagle's head and the temporal (political) eagle's head. So awaiting the Second Coming of Christ means awaiting the resumption of the original Mosaic theocracy. The Christian covenant exactly replicates the original Hebrew covenant, which means that the former is understood as offering this-worldly redemption just as the latter did. The two heads of the eagle will become one, and the problem of divided sovereignty (between kings and grasping priests) will be conjured away. In the meantime, it's the kings who sit in "Moses's seat," and Christ's injunctions to respect temporal authority ought to delegitimize clerical bids to grab a share of sovereignty. This far-fetched "theology" seems such a strained interpretation of a religion that *really is* otherworldly in its basic vision of salvation that it's a little hard to believe that Hobbes himself actually considered it a valid rendering of the meaning of Christianity. Yet what Hobbes's theological convictions were (if he had any) seems beside the point. What he cared about was a politics of authoritative sovereignty that wasn't undermined by clerical scheming and power grabs, and appeal to the figure of Moses, as well as a re-imagining of Jesus as if he were Moses, was clearly in the service of that political vision. Bishop Bramwell hits the nail on the head when he complains that Hobbesian politics requires the sovereign to "approve or reject all sorts of Theologicall doctrines, concerning the kingdome of God, not according to truth or falsehood, but according to that influence which they have upon political affaires."[49]

In a helpful contextualist treatment of Hobbes's polemical deployment of the image of Moses in his mature political thought,[50] Alison McQueen refers to Hobbes's "elevation of Moses as the scriptural exemplar of a Leviathan sovereign" as Hobbes increasingly "came to focus on the early history of the Mosaic polity in the book of Exodus."[51] The starting point for McQueen's study is the oddness of this choice of exemplar, given that it was precisely the Mosaic regime that was seized upon as an intellectual model by parliamentarian and republican radicals of the time. The argument that McQueen ultimately develops is that "Hobbes's use of Moses [as opposed to Davidic kingship, which, on the face of it, would have more naturally served his purposes] is best seen as a rhetorical and polemical move that appropriates the images and narratives of parliamentarians and republicans and subversively redirects them in the service of absolutism."[52] McQueen persuasively argues that this is a game that can be played in both directions (i.e., on behalf of both staunchly pro-monarchist and staunchly pro-republican political visions) and that Hobbes is willing to embrace this "politically risky strategy"[53] in engaging republicans in a high-stakes contest over the political meaning of Moses. Given Moses's status as a mere "intermediary" of God as civil sovereign of the pre-monarchical Hebrews, and not as a sovereign himself in the proper sense, "Hobbes's decision to appeal to Moses and not one or more of the Davidic kings as the central biblical exemplar of sovereign power remains [on Hobbes's own account] a puzzling one."[54] McQueen endeavours to solve the puzzle by noting Hobbes's common ploy of taking over modes of argument from his republican adversaries and turning them, "subversively," in an opposing direction. Moreover, she indicates various ways in which Hobbes tries to shift sovereignty from God to Moses, although his arguments are far from stable. The fact remains that God is civil sovereign prior to the kingship of Saul, whereas Moses is mere "Lieutenant" or "Viceregent," as Hobbes calls him in chapters 40 and 41 of *Leviathan*,[55] and McQueen is right to point out that this fact poses, or ought to pose, "a serious problem for any attempt to use Moses as an exemplar of Leviathan sovereignty, which, as Hobbes is at pains to insist, must be both unified and supreme."[56]

One further point: Leaving aside the non-trivial question of God's status within the Mosaic regime, it may still be necessary to qualify somewhat the view of Moses's ultimate sovereignty as suggested by Hobbes's interpretation in light of something pointed out by Walzer.[57] Walzer underscores the text in Exodus 40:35 according to which Moses didn't have authority to enter the inner sanctum of the tabernacle; only the high priest could do that, and for these purposes Moses was *subordinate* to "Aaron and his sons" (Exodus 40:31).[58] That seems a rather shocking attenuation of Mosaic sovereignty, and one has to wonder how Hobbes would deal with this particular text. Walzer writes, "The crucial act of sovereignty in the priestly kingdom was the entrance of the high priest into the [literal] presence of God. Here he was alone and supreme." It's true that Hobbes writes in chapter 42 of *Leviathan*, "The High Priest (next and immediately under God) was the Civill Soveraign; and all Judges were to be constituted by him."[59] But it's difficult to believe that it was therefore Hobbes's view that Aaron was superior to Moses as regards civil authority. One is tempted to say that although Aaron was notionally high priest, the true high priest was actually Moses, although again that raises the problem posed by Exodus 40:35. And it's no less difficult to believe that the Hebrew Bible itself intends to teach the ultimate sovereignty of Aaron.[60] In fact, if one consults the corresponding argument in *On the Citizen*, Hobbes there too declares the doctrine of the supreme sovereignty of the high priest ("Royal power [was] understood to be in the hands of the [high] Priest").[61] However, he argues that this doesn't apply to the Moses-Aaron relationship, because Moses was the founder of the regime and the founder always retains sovereignty for himself. Moreover, as Hobbes rightly points out[62] and as we have already discussed, the fact that God sided with Moses against Aaron and Miriam when Aaron and Miriam rebelled against his authority proves beyond dispute that it was Moses who held ultimate sovereignty.

While McQueen is certainly right to raise the interesting question of why Hobbes chooses Moses rather than Davidic kings as exemplary of sovereignty, I'm inclined to think that the puzzle she presents admits of a simpler solution than the one offered in her interpretation. If Rousseau is right that the fundamental problem being wrestled with by Hobbes is how to have a commonwealth ruled by a one-headed eagle rather than a two-headed eagle, then it makes perfect sense to appeal to Moses as a privileged image of this political aspiration, since (notwithstanding all the intriguing complications in the biblical account) Moses basically unites in himself the two roles of civil magistrate and high priest. The Mosaic regime existed prior to the fatal bifurcation of political unity that occurred with Joshua as civil magistrate and Eleazar as high priest, generating a problem that still awaited a reliable solution as late as 1652 (although, as discussed above, Hobbes in *On the Citizen* depicts the problem as far more severe under the Christian dispensation than it ever was under the Hebrew dispensation). Viewed in that light, McQueen's puzzle starts to appear as less of a puzzle.[63]

James Harrington's Moses: Founder of the First Democratic Republic

The three most important theorists of the modern civic-republican tradition are a sixteenth-century thinker, a seventeenth-century thinker, and an eighteenth-century thinker. It's fairly obvious who the first and third are. The middle figure, mediating between Machiavelli and Rousseau, so to speak (though it's unclear whether Rousseau ever read him), is less obvious. He's James Harrington, all of whose works were written and published during the decade when England was a republic – that is, the Cromwellian "commonwealth." He, no less than Machiavelli before him and Rousseau after him, celebrates Moses as an iconic hero of the republican tradition. He, no less than Machiavelli and Rousseau, appropriates the Moses of the Hebrew Bible as a symbol of the civic-republican vision. Harrington is one of a substantial number of sixteenth- and seventeenth-century political thinkers who idealize "the Hebrew Republic" (or "Hebrew Commonwealth"), as it gets dubbed in the early seventeenth century by Petrus Cunaeus, as a privileged model for secular politics.[64]

In 2014 I published an article sketching Harrington's preoccupation with the Mosaic commonwealth.[65] Harrington's conceptualization of this is an essentially democratic one, which quite possibly qualifies him as the first unqualified champion of democratic principles within the Western canon. If there is another candidate, it would be good to know who that theorist might be. (Milton?) In any case, here is a summary, drawn from my article, of the basic institutions of Moses's regime as conceived by Harrington:

1. The kingship of God founded on a (revocable) covenant with the people – that is, on popular consent. (This seems dubious! If the covenant were revocable, it would be revoked every time that the Israelites revolt against either divine or Mosaic authority, which they do again and again. With every revolt on the part of the people, either God or Moses or both express thunderous wrath, which hardly indicates a principle of revocability!)
2. The supremacy of Moses as a Solon-like or Lycurgus-like founder.[66]
3. The subsequent institution of the Sanhedrin (the Israelite senate, more divinely inspired than other aspects of the regime), which becomes (so Harrington claims, though the biblical evidence is weak) an *essential* pillar of the regime and in effect acquires co-sovereignty with Moses.
4. The subordination of Aaron as high priest specifically to the Sanhedrin, not to Moses. Hence: the strict subordination of priestly

power. (Again, it's hard to see the biblical warrant for such a claim, especially since the 250 elders join the revolt of Korah and are incinerated for their efforts.)

5. God, or Moses, or the senate is conceived by Harrington as a *proposer* of the law, but *the people* are depicted as "resolvers" (i.e., genuine decision-makers). This, of course, puts democracy at the centre of Hebrew republicanism. Harrington is right that in Exodus 19:7–8, the laws of YHWH are presented to the assembled people for their consent.[67] The idea here is that with respect to the original covenant, God and/or Moses is merely "proposing" the Mosaic laws; "resolving," that is, acceptance or rejection of what is proposed, is strictly up to the people. Harrington refers to this as a "suffrage" of the people. But Harrington's suggestion that the Mosaic laws are dependent on popular will almost certainly overstates the reciprocity between God and the people in this "covenant." When God "proposes" the Ten Commandments, for instance, is it imaginable that the Hebrews could respond, "Sorry, we're just not interested"?[68]
6. An agrarian law. This, like the senate, carries a special divine seal, so to speak. (That is, Harrington wants to confer a privileged status upon this aspect of the regime.)
7. Rotation of offices.
8. Civic norms that render the national religion consistent with religious toleration. (We will address in our final chapter whether the regime laid out in the Hebrew Bible makes allowance for a diversity of cults within the state. On the face of it, it seems counterintuitive, to put it mildly.)

The various institutions appearing on this list (religious toleration; an agrarian law, rotation of offices; a senate; and above all, the model according to which laws proposed for popular consideration become law only on the basis of popular ratification) are presented by Harrington as exemplary, and much of what is laid out in the political theory sketched in *The Commonwealth of Oceana* is consciously modelled on these "Hebraic" institutions, whether they actually existed in ancient Israel or were merely imagined by Harrington to exist. Of these eight basic principles, the central one is surely number five: popular will as the foundation of the regime. This quote from book 2 of Harrington's 1658 work, *The Prerogative of Popular Government*, conveys the core of his account: "Moses introduced the *chirotonia* ... All ordination of magistrates, as of senators, or elders of the Sanhedrim, of the judges, or elders of inferior courts, of the judge or *suffes* of Israel, of the king, of the priests, of the Levites, whether with the ballot or *viva voce*, was performed by the *chirotonia* or suffrage of the people."[69] This is a very ambitious claim! It asserts that the Hebrew commonwealth as founded by Moses was at the very least a representative democracy, and quite possibly a radical democracy along the lines of a Rousseauian general will. As McQueen nicely puts the point, "in Harrington's hands, the Mosaic polity became a Roman commonwealth."[70] Is this really the impression we get of Mosaic politics from reading the Five Books of Moses? It's telling that in the first instance Harrington cites not actual biblical texts but rather Philo. Here's the text that he has in mind:

> These things Moses, wise here as ever, considered in his soul and does not even mention appointment of rulers by lot, but determines to institute appointment by election. Thus he says "thou shalt establish a ruler over thyself, not a foreigner but from thy brethren," hereby indicating that there should be a free choice and an unimpeachable scrutiny of the ruler made by the whole people with the same mind. And the choice will receive the further vote and seal of ratification from Him who confirms all things that promote the common weal, even God who holds that the man may be called the chosen from the race, in which he is what the eye is in the body.[71]

Philo in this quotation does indeed float the notion that so excites Harrington of the people choosing rulers and Moses/God confirming or ratifying the choices. But it is worth noting that the single biblical text cited by Philo in support of this conception, namely Deuteronomy 18:15, refers to *God* as doing the choosing of a suitable ruler. In fact, the King James Version and the Fox and Alter translations all refer in this text not to a "ruler" but to a prophet. In any case, the emphasis in Deuteronomy 18:15 is not at all on popular election but on the Hebraic identity of the prophet elected by God. Hence textual support for the idea drawn by Harrington from Philo is at best extremely meagre, whether cited by Harrington or by Philo.

The fundamental pivot of Harrington's analysis is a crucial distinction that he offers between *chirotonia* (a bottom-up popular election) and *chirothesia* (a top-down "laying on of hands"). The Harringtonian theory is that the "people's republic" as Moses intended it to be was founded on the former conception, whereas Israel later became a priestly regime based on *chirothesia* that directly subverted the Mosaic intention.[72] What is worse, this priestly subversion of Hebrew republicanism became a fatal precedent for millennia of anti-republican "priestcraft," which Harrington targets as the chief obstacle to his own republican theory in

England of the 1650s.[73] His project is to overthrow oligarchical *chirothesia* and return to the archetypal model of Mosaic *chirotonia*.

I don't want to suggest that Harrington offers *no* biblical texts for his radically democratic interpretation of Mosaic politics. But the text he offers is an incredibly slender support for an enormously ambitious claim. In Numbers chapter 11, God had instructed Moses to establish a senate of seventy elders. Moses puts this instruction into execution in Deuteronomy 1:13 as follows: "Provide yourselves with men, wise, understanding and knowledgeable, for your tribes, and I will set them as heads over you."[74] (Harrington quotes the King James Version, which renders the text as follows: "I will make them rulers over you"; Harrington changes "make" to "constitute.") For Harrington, the decisive feature of this process is that the people appoint the seventy senators; they are not chosen by Moses but merely confirmed ("constituted") by him according to the popular will. The emphasis on confirmation or ratification of what the people choose is obviously drawn directly from the Philo text quoted above. Harrington then seems to extrapolate from this one text that *everything* is decided according to popular will and then "constituted by Moses."[75] Conceived in this way, "suffrage of the people" takes logical precedence over "the constitution of the legislator," and this defines the very essence of "the constitution of Moses."[76] Harrington concedes only a single exception to the principle that the people choose and Moses merely "constitutes" (i.e., confirms) what they have "decreed," namely Moses's appointment of Joshua as heir to Moses's civil authority.[77] The explanation offered by Harrington is as follows: "The commonwealth of Israel, when Moses did this, was neither seated nor planted, nor indeed a commonwealth, but an army designed to be a commonwealth." This argument is a little strange since the same would have been true of Moses's constitution of the senate of seventy elders before Israel had crossed the Jordan – and would be equally true, of course, of *anything* enacted by Moses, since Moses did not live to witness the founding of Israel on the basis of Joshua's conquests. It would be much too big a task to start examining all the aspects of the Mosaic narrative that are in tension with this theory, according to which the Hebrew regime was a form of popular government – indeed an archetype of the kind of republican constitution for which Harrington yearns in mid-seventeenth-century England – but let me merely register my scepticism. One wonders where one might locate a biblical warrant for the suggestion that, for instance, Aaron's appointment as high priest was decreed by the people rather than by Moses himself. Or what biblical texts would indicate that any of the countless laws set out in Leviticus, Numbers, and Deuteronomy had in any sense a popular or democratic foundation. No less than is the case with Machiavelli or other staple theorists of the republican tradition, it is difficult to see the depiction of the Mosaic regime by Harrington as anything other than a *myth* intended to supply republican theorizing with a form of legitimization as unimpeachable as possible.

Let me flag another interesting aspect of Harrington's story. Again and again, he refers to Jethro (the Midianite father-in-law of Moses) as the one who inspired the basic institutions of (as Harrington views it) republican Israel.[78] To borrow the formulation I offer in "James Harrington on the Hebrew Commonwealth": "In chapter 6 of *The Prince*, Machiavelli referred to God as the 'great tutor' of Moses, but in Harrington, Moses's great tutor is Jethro."[79] Why does he do this? There are a couple of related reasons. First, it allows Harrington to place Israel, paradoxically, under the rubric of a "heathenish" (i.e., pagan) commonwealth, since the figure who essentially designed the Mosaic institutions was himself "an heathen."[80] As Harrington puts it in the conclusion to book 2 of *The Art of Lawgiving*, the "orders and courts of Israel," as instituted by Moses, "were transcribed out of another government, though heathen."[81] This in turn makes it more legitimate to align Moses with other legendary founders of ancient republics such as Lycurgus and Solon – contrary to it being, "as some say," "irreverent or atheistical" to do so.[82] And once Moses is safely elevated to the pantheon of classic republican lawgivers, Harrington ups the ante with the further provocative claim that the Mosaic regime, no less than the pagan regimes, was "instituted upon *principles of human prudence*," not divine providence.[83] The opposition between a "judicious" reading of the Hebrew Bible that privileges human prudence (i.e., *secular* political wisdom) and a pious reading that privileges divine providence is of course lifted straight from the pages of Machiavelli, as should be evident to any reader of Harrington. The institution of the Israelite senate is an especially interesting case with respect to these two opposing readings because the *Hebrew Bible itself* offers two conflicting accounts: on the one hand, Exodus 18:14–27, where the institution is attributed to Jethro; on the other hand, Numbers 11:16, where the same institution is attributed to God. Was it Jethro or God? Secular wisdom or divine wisdom? Harrington pretty clearly opts for the secular account.

Harrington tends to write as if there is a singular authoritative biblical regime: a Hebrew republic or Hebrew commonwealth founded by Moses (with helpful guidance from Jethro) and erected on basically democratic foundations. As encapsulated by Gary Remer, Harrington's view is as follows: "Kingship was not God's desired government; popular rule was." Hence, in demanding the institution of a monarchy in the transition from Samuel to Saul, "the Israelites rejected not only God but also their republican government."[84] Contrary to this thesis, the following claim made by Walzer seems quite plausible.[85] There are basically four biblical regimes, none of which is privileged as authoritative. They are: (1) the kingship of God; (2) the kingship of (Davidic) kings; (3) the priestly kingdom instituted in post-exilic Israel when the Hebrews, subject to foreign imperial hegemony, were unable to reinstate a sovereign monarchy; and (4) a mixed regime, headed by a king, sketched in Deuteronomy 16–18. A few further comments are in order. First, it should be pointed out that the first regime can be divided into two phases: the first, under which Moses is God's appointed prophet and lawgiver (or at least oracle or mouthpiece of divine law); and the second, the regime of "judges" (the last being Samuel) appointed by God to fight various wars on an ad hoc basis. Secondly, both Harrington and Spinoza despise the third of these four regimes, because in a good regime the priests are subject to higher civil authority. The third and most important point: If these regimes are all basically kingships, then there was no Hebrew republic or Hebrew commonwealth. Moreover, Thomas Pangle and Timothy Burns persuasively suggest that the unhappy fate of Korah in Numbers chapter 16 stands as a decisive refutation of any notion that either God or Moses respects the principle of Harringtonian popular sovereignty.[86]

Spinoza's Moses: Debunking the Chosenness of the Hebrews

Much of what defines Spinoza's concern with the figure of Moses in the *Theological-Political Treatise* has to do with the question of whether Moses is the author of the text that Jewish tradition calls "the Five Books of Moses." Why is this question so important to Spinoza? Clearly, the Hebrew Bible has a *very* different character if it is the product of collaborative editorial work by historians many centuries after the deeds narrated in the Bible, as compared with being written down by the very prophet and spokesperson of God who actually founded (or is said to have founded) the religion of the Hebrews. The Bible starts looking much more like any other human book. For a culture that took the claim of Mosaic authorship at face value, this work of philology was obviously received as profoundly subversive. Spinoza was not the first debunker of Mosaic authorship: he was building on the groundwork laid by Hobbes in chapter 33 of *Leviathan*.[87] This philological project looms large in relation to what makes the *Theological-Political Treatise* of such notable historical importance. Still, few today would contest the claim that ancient historians and redactors, not God-inspired prophets, were responsible for the biblical text; hence we don't need to go into those particular arguments of Spinoza's.

Of much greater interest, for our purposes, is Spinoza's subversion of what chosenness means in the context of the Five Books of Moses. For it raises questions of truly philosophical proportions. Can a religion be addressed to a particular tribe or group of tribes, to the exclusion of the other peoples and nationalities that compose humankind? Spinoza is very strongly of the view that any true religion must be a religion universally relevant to all human beings alike. But if that is true, then the Hebrew self-understanding, as inculcated by Mosaic religion, is radically flawed. That indeed is Spinoza's view; and if one has that view, then one's appraisal of Moses as the founder of a religion based on an idea of a special divine destiny appointed for a particular national entity will be mixed at best.

The core issue is stated very powerfully in chapter 4 of the *Theological-Political Treatise*: Although he concedes that the Mosaic law was "sanctioned by prophetic insight," the law of Moses falls dramatically short of constituting genuine divine law, which Spinoza characterizes as "natural Divine Law."[88] What are the essential features of natural divine law? Spinoza sets them out in a way that renders unmistakable the deficiencies in the Mosaic law. Natural divine law "is of universal application, or common to all mankind." "It does not demand belief in historical narratives of any kind whatsoever." "Belief in historical narratives cannot afford us the knowledge and love of God." "The law of Moses," by contrast, "was not of universal application but specially adapted to the character and preservation of one particular people."[89] Mosaic religion was built almost exclusively on historical narratives, and Spinoza's evident distrust in the reliability of those narratives means that belief in the veracity of the stories narrated in the Five Books of Moses renders Mosaic religion dependent on what are very probably fictions. "The love of God arises from the knowledge of God, a knowledge deriving from general [= universal] axioms that are certain and self-evident," which these unreliable ancient stories certainly aren't. "Natural Divine Law does not enjoin ceremonial rites, that is, actions which in themselves are of no significance and are termed good merely by tradition ... Those things whose goodness derives only from authority and tradition ... are mere shadows."[90] But what is enjoined by the Mosaic law is almost entirely composed of these shadows! Taken as a whole, this presents itself as a pretty damning indictment of Mosaic religion as virtually a pseudo-religion.

The far-reaching critique of a religion built so predominantly on "ceremonial observance" is pursued further in chapter 5:

> The observance of ceremonies has regard only to the temporal prosperity of the state and in no way contributes to blessedness ... For ceremonial observance [Scripture] promises nothing but material advantages and pleasures, while blessedness is promised only for observance of the universal Divine Law. In the five books commonly [= wrongly] attributed to Moses the only promise made ... is worldly success – honours or fame, victory, riches, life's pleasures and health. And although these five books contain much about moral teaching as well as ceremonial observance, these passages are not set forth as moral teachings of universal application to all men, but as commands particularly adapted to the understanding and character of only their state.[91]

It seems almost certain that Spinoza didn't believe in an afterlife. But he *did* believe in spiritual excellence as an intrinsic reward for virtue, over against mere material prosperity, mere faring well in the goods of material existence. The religion founded by Moses is from his point of view focused to much too great an extent on the latter: having a state, triumphing over one's enemies, reaping the material benefits of such political and military victory, and so on. This is what the promise of a Hebrew messiah promises: self-government in a prosperous ("milk and honey") independent state. Exactly the same point is rightly made by Hobbes in *On the Citizen*: "The Jews expected a Christ, a King to be sent by God, to redeem them and what is more to rule all the nations,"[92] although Hobbes is surely more sympathetic than Spinoza is to the privileging of material aspirations over spiritual aspirations.

One should not fail to note that in chapter 3, Spinoza goes out of his way to assert that Hebrew claims to uniqueness are spurious: "There is no doubt that other nations, like the Jews, also had their prophets."[93] "The Hebrew nation was chosen by God before all others not by reason of its understanding nor of its spiritual qualities, but by reason of its social organization and the good fortune whereby it achieved supremacy and retained it for so many years ... Their election and vocation consisted *only* in the material success and prosperity of their state ... In return for their obedience the Law promises them nothing other than the continuing prosperity of their state and material advantages."[94] Scripture itself instructs us "that other nations also had their own state and their special laws by God's external guidance."[95] As the "good fortune" of the Hebrews wanes (they lose their state, they are brought back to a condition of national servitude) and that of other rival nations waxes, the chosenness of the Hebrews in effect gets transmitted to those other nations. Hebrew monotheism, at bottom, means that only *they* have a god who gives them prophets; only *they* have a god who cares about their national welfare. But these defining articles of faith, Spinoza insists, are false. That is, what essentially defines Hebrew monotheism lacks validity. (But of course, as should be obvious, all monotheisms assert similarly spurious claims.)

Let me put the core issue in my own terms. The question is: Is the Mosaic religion a religion or a civil religion? For they're not the same – at least not the same given how Spinoza conceives the meaning of a genuine religion. Spinoza addresses this issue very powerfully in the following text:

> It is not as a teacher or a prophet that Moses forbids the Jews to kill or steal; it is as a lawgiver or ruler that he [not God!] issues these commands. He does not justify his precepts by reasoning, but attaches to his commands a penalty, a penalty which can vary, and must vary, to suit the character of each single nation ... So, too, his command not to commit adultery has regard only to the good of the commonwealth and state. If he had intended this to be a moral precept that had regard not merely to the good of the commonwealth but to the peace of mind and the true blessedness of the individual, he would have condemned not merely the external act but the very wish, as did Christ, who taught only universal moral precepts. It is for this reason that Christ promises a spiritual reward, not, like Moses, a material reward.[96]

Christ's more spiritual teaching was directed against the Pharisees, who, in their "ignorance," associated blessedness with the observation of "the laws of the commonwealth, i.e., the law of Moses, whereas, in fact, this law concerned only public good, and its aim was to coerce the Hebrews rather than instruct them."[97] This basic conception receives another very powerful formulation in the following text: Moses "taught [the Israelites] in the same way as parents teach their children who have not reached the age of reason. It is therefore certain that they had no understanding of the excellence of virtue and true blessedness."[98]

And if what Moses offered was predominantly a civil religion for a particular national commonwealth, rather than a universally valid moral teaching, how are we to judge it normatively? Consider the following important passage from chapter 17:

> The basic principles of the [Mosaic] state ... must have kindled such an ardent patriotism in the hearts of the citizens that it could never enter

> anyone's mind to betray or desert his country; on the contrary, they must all have been of such a mind as to suffer death rather than a foreign yoke. For having transferred their right to God, believing that their kingdom was God's kingdom and that they alone were God's children, while the other nations were God's enemies for whom they felt an implacable hatred (for this, too, they believed to be a mark of piety),[99] they could conceive of nothing more wicked and abominable than to betray their country, that is, the very kingdom of the God whom they worshipped. Indeed, it was regarded as utterly disgraceful even to emigrate, for the religious rites which it was their constant duty to practise could be performed only on their native soil; it alone was held to be holy ground.
>
> Therefore the patriotism of the Hebrews was not simply patriotism but piety, and this, together with hatred for other nations, was so fostered and nourished by their daily ritual that it inevitably became part of their nature. For their daily worship was not merely quite different, making them altogether unique and completely distinct from other peoples, but also utterly opposed to others. Hence this daily invective, as it were, was bound to engender a lasting hatred of a most deep-rooted kind, since it was a hatred that had its source in strong devotion or piety, and was believed to be a religious duty – for that is the bitterest and most persistent of all kinds of hatred. And this was reinforced by the universal cause of the continuous growth of hatred, to wit, the reciprocation of hatred; for the other nations inevitably held them in bitter hatred in return.[100]

There are two ways of characterizing what is going on in this text. One interpretation is to say that Moses deserves credit for cultivating a form of piety that generated such intense "patriotism" and loyalty to the national community. The opposing interpretation is that Moses deserves intense blame for constructing his religion in a way that erected such rigid and unbridgeable boundaries between nation and nation, tribe and tribe. Which of these corresponds to the ultimate Spinozistic judgment? I think it's fairly clear. He begins by praising Israelite patriotism, but ends by condemning the "lasting hatred of a most deep-rooted kind" stoked up by this kind of "piety." Patriotism and piety, for the Hebrews, were inseparable; but no less inseparable were piety and intertribal hatred. How can Spinoza in the end approve of a religion that would have these (intended and not merely accidental) consequences? The short answer is that he can't and doesn't. In other words, qua civil religion (= foundation for civic solidarity and devotion to the national community), the religion of Moses is praiseworthy; qua religion (= "natural Divine Law"), it merits harsh critique and condemnation. The text I have quoted from chapter 17 is so damning that

Seymour Feldman, who contributed annotations to the Samuel Shirley translation, felt compelled to insert a note defending the Hebrew Bible against Spinoza's ultra-harsh indictment![101]

Spinoza's depiction of the Hebrew commonwealth in chapters 17 and 18 of the *Theological-Political Treatise* is extremely complex. Structurally, it replicates the two-sided account one gets in Harrington's three most salient works of the late 1650s (*Pian Piano, The Prerogative of Popular Government*, and *The Art of Lawmaking*): The Hebraic regime is a model of superlative republican virtue, *and* it succumbs to wholesale corruption engineered by a hegemonic priesthood. Corresponding to the standard discourse of civic-republican theory, it is a tale of *virtue and corruption*, and as is typical of such discourse, the corruption is in large measure priestly corruption. As regards the positive aspects of Hebrew republicanism, it appears unlikely that Spinoza ever had the opportunity to read Harrington, but it seems probable that both drew upon Cunaeus as a shared source.[102] This complicated narrative is one that I seek to disentangle in chapter 11 of *Civil Religion*, and it's obviously not possible to redo that large exercise here. Let it suffice to say that like Rousseau, Spinoza has a pretty hefty measure of admiration for Moses's gifts as a legislator – and especially so in light of the fact that the *religion* founded by Moses is one for which Spinoza, as we've seen, has profound critical reservations, to put it mildly.[103]

In short: What is being played out in Spinoza's political philosophy are two different standards that are very much in tension with each other. Spinoza does belong to the tradition of civic-republican discourse, shaped by Machiavelli, Harrington, and Rousseau, that hails the genius of Moses as a founder of the Hebrew commonwealth, inventing a civil religion that secures virtue and "patriotism" within this solidary political community. But these theoretical ideals are trumped by Spinoza's powerful normative commitment to (Christianity-inspired) moral universalism. The civic virtues cultivated by Moses as a civic-republican legislator are relevant to a *particular* moral and political community and intensify bonds within that particularistic community. But a rational religion of the kind associated by Spinoza with "natural Divine Law" must pertain to a community of all humankind, and "apply universally." It's the latter standard that Moses fails, and fails monumentally, to satisfy. This is why Moses is for Spinoza to some extent the kind of civic-republican hero that he is for Machiavelli, Harrington, and Rousseau. But it's also why the religion that constitutes the substance of the Mosaic founding is subject to severe critique by Spinoza. It is impossible to affirm civic-republican patriotism of a robust kind without violating the universalism to which Spinoza is philosophically committed.

Spinoza affirms both the republican vision and the vision of a universal moral and rational community, but ultimately it is the latter that represents the far deeper commitment. Hence Moses's exemplary achievements as legislator for Israelite virtue and patriotism pale in relation to his inscribing a highly particularistic (= tribal) view of life for the Hebrews.

One can make the same point in slightly different terms, as follows. Spinoza's stance toward Moses is essentially tension-ridden. He seems respectful of Moses's achievements as a "civil religionist," that is, as a legislator successful in harnessing piety in the service of national solidarity and public order. On the other hand, as I discuss in chapter 9 of *Civil Religion*, Spinoza consistently aligns himself with Saint Paul with respect to Paul's being the one chiefly responsible for the repudiation of ritual law within Christianity as the successor religion to Mosaic religion.[104] Spinoza affirms Paul's principle that the spirit takes absolute precedence over the flesh, and hence a religion of ritual practice cannot be the true religion.[105] In this sense, Spinoza's philosophy is decisively anti-Mosaic. There are Spinoza scholars who affirm that Spinoza's view of Judaism is a non-"supersessionist" one – that is, according to them he's not of the view that the validity of Judaism is philosophically or normatively "superseded" either by Christianity or by some secular religion inspired by the Enlightenment. This reading of Spinoza is clearly not one to which I subscribe.

Rousseau's Moses: True Legislator

1. On the Social Contract

Apart from the allusions to Moses at the end of book 2, chapter 7 of *On the Social Contract* indicating that Moses fully qualifies as the kind of Rousseauian "legislator" that it is the purpose of that chapter to sketch, there is only one reference to Moses in *The Social Contract*. It occurs, of course, in book 4, chapter 8 (the civil religion chapter). Here is the text:

> The Gods of the pagans were not jealous Gods. They divided dominion over the world among themselves. Moses himself and the Hebrew people accepted this idea sometimes when speaking of the God of Israel. It is true that they regarded as nothing the Gods of the Canaanites, a proscribed people destined for destruction, and whose land they were to occupy. But notice how they spoke of the divinities of neighboring peoples whom they were forbidden to attack! *Is not the possession of what belongs to Chamos your God*, said Jeptha to the Ammonites, *legitimately yours? By the same token, we*

> *possess the lands that our victorious God has acquired.* It seems to me that this was a clear acknowledgment of parity between the right[s] of Chamos and those of the God of Israel.[106]

What Rousseau suggests in this text is exactly right. There are two kinds of gods: *national* gods, who retain full authority within the boundaries of their own national community but assert no such authority outside it; and *jealous* gods (= monotheistic gods) who claim *universal* authority and hence provoke wars of religion between peoples.[107] Just to be clear: The jealousy of YHWH *mainly* relates to the question of the loyalty of the Hebrews and the imperative binding on them not to be tempted by other gods. But this jealousy *also*, though to a lesser extent, extends to the annihilation of cults practised by those peoples whom Rousseau rightly characterizes as "voués à la destruction," slated for destruction.[108] God chooses which cults are to be tolerated and which ones are to be eradicated. Rousseau's phrase seems drawn from a similar formula in, for instance, Deuteronomy 13:16–18, which Fox renders as "devote it to destruction"/"what is devoted-to-destruction," and Deuteronomy 20:16–17: "devote-them-to-destruction."[109] Fox interprets the phrase as: destroy them by way of a devotion (= sacrifice) to God.[110] Interestingly, such phrases are absent from the King James Version, which renders 20:17 simply as "utterly destroy them." The New Oxford Annotated Bible simply has "You shall annihilate them." Rousseau uses the Vulgate (Latin) translation, where, one suspects, this phrase is translated in a way that is closer to the original Hebrew.[111]

Rousseau is right that there is consistent vacillation within the Hebrew Bible about whether YHWH is in this sense a national god (a god of the Hebrews) or a jealous god (a god who enforces his authority beyond the limits of Hebrew nationhood). Sometimes he's one and sometimes he's the other. (Hence Rousseau correctly writes that "sometimes" [*quelquefois*] Moses himself and the Hebrew people expressed a conception of their god closer to the pagan idea of divinity.) "*Our* victorious God," as referred to in the text from Judges, is clearly a national god in a sense identical to the national gods of the pagans. But the Hebrew Bible is not consistent about this; in fact, it's blatantly inconsistent. Although I think it's true that "Moses himself" sometimes does treat YHWH as a national god respectful of the jurisdiction of other gods, I'm inclined to say that the dominant image of YHWH over the course of the Mosaic narrative is Rousseau's *jealous god* who demands that the Canaanite cults be erased from the face of the earth.[112] Without question, Rousseau (quite reasonably) sees the national pagan gods as normatively superior to the monotheistic jealous god with his catastrophic wars of religion, and to that extent (though this certainly isn't the full story), the civil religion chapter is a brief for paganism.[113]

2. The Government of Poland, *Political Fragment 24 ("About the Jews"), and John Toland's "Two Problems Concerning the Jewish Nation and Religion"*

Let me start by quoting two texts from chapter 2 ("The Spirit of Ancient Institutions") of *The Government of Poland* that frame the discussion of Moses as legislator before zeroing in on the substance of what Rousseau says about Moses himself:

> I gaze out over the nations of the modern world, and I see numerous scribblers of laws, but not a single legislator. But among the ancients I find no less than three legislators so outstanding as to deserve our special mention: Moses, Lycurgus, and Numa, all of whom concerned themselves with matters that our doctors of learning would deem absurd. Yet each of them achieved a kind of success which, were it not so thoroughly supported by evidence, we should regard as impossible.[114]
>
> All these legislators of ancient times based their legislation on the same ideas. All three sought ties that would bind the citizens to the fatherland and to one another. All three found what they were looking for in distinctive usages, in religious ceremonies that invariably were in essence exclusive and national, in games that brought the citizens together frequently, in exercises that caused them to grow in vigor and strength and developed their pride and self-esteem; and in public spectacles that, by keeping them reminded of their forefathers' deeds and hardships and virtues and triumphs, stirred their hearts, set them on fire with the spirit of emulation, and tied them tightly to the fatherland.[115]

Moses "conceived and executed this astonishing feat: he founded the body of a nation, using for his materials a swarm of wretched fugitives who possessed no skills, no arms, no talents, no virtues, and no courage, and who, without an inch of territory to call their own, were truly a troop of outcasts upon the face of the earth. Moses made bold to transform this herd of servile emigrants into a political society, a free people."[116]

> Determined that his people should never be absorbed by other peoples, Moses devised for them customs and practices that could not be blended into those of other nations and weighted them down with rites and peculiar ceremonies. He put countless prohibitions upon them, all calculated to

> keep them constantly on their toes, and to make them, with respect to the rest of mankind, outsiders forever. Each fraternal bond that he established among the individual members of his republic [*sa république*] became a further barrier, separating them from their neighbors and keeping them from becoming one with those neighbors.[117]

It's extremely telling that the entire emphasis in this passage is on *Mosaic agency* ("*Moses* devised for them customs and practices"). There's no mention at all of divine agency. The laws, customs, and rites that confer peoplehood on the Hebrews are all the brainchild of Moses, not of God.

The celebration of Moses in *The Government of Poland* is supplemented by a political fragment (number 24: "On the Jews") that, if anything, has the effect of elevating Moses even higher than the texts already quoted:

> It is an amazing and truly unique spectacle to see an expatriate people, without either location or land for nearly two thousand years; a people that has been modified, oppressed, and mingled with foreigners for even longer [than other nations]; perhaps without a single offspring of the first races; a scattered people, dispersed over the earth, subjected, persecuted, scorned by all nations, and yet preserving its customs, its laws, its morals, its patriotic love, and its initial social union when all its links appear broken. The Jews give us this amazing spectacle. The laws of Solon, of Numa, of Lycurgus are dead; those of Moses, far more ancient, are still alive. Athens, Sparta, Rome have perished and have no longer left any children on the earth. Zion, destroyed, did not lose hers; they are preserved, they multiply, spread throughout the world, and always recognize each other. They mingle among all peoples and never become confounded with them. They no longer have leaders, and are still a people; they no longer have a fatherland, and are still citizens.
>
> How strong must a legislation be to be capable of producing such marvels; capable of facing conquests, dispersions, revolutions, centuries; capable of surviving the customs, laws, dominion of all nations; which promises, finally, through the trials it has sustained, to sustain them all, to conquer the vicissitudes of human things and to last as long as the world? ... All men, whoever they may be, ought to acknowledge it to be a unique marvel, the divine or human causes of which certainly deserve the study and admiration of wise men in preference to all that Greece and Rome offer that is admirable in political institutions and human establishments.[118]

The overwhelming emphasis in Rousseau's account of Moses is (as he sees it) the spectacular Mosaic accomplishment of enforcing national exclusivity, and the placing of permanent cultural "barriers" serving to keep the Hebrews segregated from non-Hebrews.[119] The purpose is not to honour God as God demands to be honoured. The purpose is a *civic* one: to forge a profound sense of distinct nationhood or peoplehood such that membership in one's "fatherland" is at the core of one's being, and members of other nations are felt to be enduringly alien. Citizenship is grounded in patriotism, and patriotism is grounded in a sense of unbridgeable otherness. Permeable boundaries between peoples is the destruction of citizenship (hence, from Rousseau's perspective, the *essentially* anti-civic character and legacy of Christian universalism), and the standard by which we measure the greatness of different legislators is the extent to which their legislated customs and mores (including, not least, laws of religious observation) erect boundaries of sufficient rigour. No modern politician, Rousseau tells us, meets this test. Not only does Moses meet it but, as we are informed in political fragment 24, he meets it *to a greater extent* than do his three peers (Solon, Lycurgus, and Numa).[120] That's because his laws, his attempt to keep the Hebrews separate from all other peoples, have proven themselves to be of superior enduringness, relative to the laws legislated for Athens, Sparta, and Rome.[121] Not only is Moses *a* bona fide legislator but he is, measured according to the Rousseauian standards articulated in these texts, the *supreme* legislator, superior to all successors, ancient and (especially) modern. If one thinks of a comprehensive ranking of Rousseauian legislators (although it's a very small club to begin with), Rousseau is saying that Moses is the all-time number one! Here's a question that one may ask: Why doesn't the fact that Moses is in effect the originator of the imperialistic monotheism that is the source of the wars of religion (= holy wars) that Rousseau condemns put a dent in Rousseau's celebration of Moses? How does Rousseau reconcile his superlatively positive judgment of Mosaic politics with the following very different judgment offered in the "Letter to Beaumont"? "The Jews were born enemies of all other Peoples, and they began their establishment by destroying seven nations according to the express order they had received to do so."[122] And it is no less obscure how he reconciles his praise of Moses with his clear denigration of Mosaic morality, in *Emile*, relative to the higher morality of Jesus.[123]

Interestingly, the striking claims about the unique superiority of the Mosaic founding asserted in Rousseau's "About the Jews" are also to be found, in almost identical terms, in an appendix to *Nazarenus* by Harrington's disciple, John Toland; the appendix is ostensibly a 1709 letter written by Toland, but the letter may be a fiction, as is much of what composes *Nazarenus*. In this text Toland notes that the Mosaic religion continues to be observed by the Jews, despite their dispersion and persecution, whereas the civilizations of the Egyptians, Babylonians, Greeks, and Romans are all long vanished.[124] This staying power of the Hebrews bestows upon Moses "a rank in the politics farr superior to" all the other great legislators of antiquity.[125] In fact, Toland's claims on behalf of the superiority of Moses go even beyond Rousseau's. He claims to "admire infinitely" the Mosaic republic "above all the forms of Government that ever yet existed," surpassing not only historical republics like those of Sparta, Rome, and Venice but even philosophical utopias such as "the Atlantis of Plato, Sir Thomas More's *Utopia*, and such like."[126] Toland goes even further: If the Hebrews had implemented "the Plan given by Moses" precisely as the Mosaic imagination had designed it, it would have become the kind of "Government immortal" conjured up by Harrington.[127] One other noteworthy aspect of this remarkable text: Toland emphasizes that the Mosaic religion has the character of a *civil religion*, citing the judgments of Strabo and Diodorus Siculus that the Mosaic regime was "purely [Moses's] own contrivance … father'd upon God, to procure it the easier reception and the greater veneration."[128]

Thomas Paine's Moses: Impostor and Genocidaire

We now turn from the most extravagant celebration of Moses to the most uninhibited vilification of him. The harshest account by far of Moses and the Hebrew Bible within the Western canon comes from Thomas Paine, in *The Age of Reason*. It's scathing: he has literally nothing good to say about either the Hebrew Bible or Moses. What's of interest, for my purposes, is whether the celebrations of Moses within the civic-republican tradition survive Paine's indictment. I don't think that they do.

Here are some representative texts that give one a sense of how Paine reacts to the Hebrew Bible:

> Whenever we read the obscene stories, the voluptuous debaucheries, the cruel and torturous executions, the unrelenting vindictiveness, with which more than half the [Hebrew] Bible is filled, it would be more consistent that we called it the word of a demon, than the Word of God. It is a history of wickedness, that has served to corrupt and brutalize mankind; and, for my part, I sincerely detest it, as I detest everything that is cruel. We scarcely meet with anything, a few phrases excepted, but what deserves either our abhorrence or our contempt, till we come to [the Psalms, the Proverbs, and especially the book of Job].[129]

> There are matters in [the Hebrew Bible], said to be done by the express command of God, that are as shocking to humanity, and to every idea we have of moral justice as any thing done by Robespierre ... in France, by the English government in the East Indies, or by any other assassin in modern times. When we read in the books ascribed to Moses, Joshua, etc., that they (the Israelites) came by stealth upon whole nations of people, who, as the history itself shews, had given them no offence; that they put all those nations to the sword; that they spared neither age nor infancy; that they utterly destroyed men, women and children; that they left not a soul to breathe; expressions that are repeated over and over again in those books, and that too with exulting ferocity ... To believe therefore the [Hebrew] Bible to be true, we must unbelieve all our belief in the moral justice of God ... And to read the [Hebrew] Bible without horror, we must undo every thing that is tender, sympathising, and benevolent in the heart of man.[130]
>
> The character of Moses, as stated in the [Hebrew] Bible, is the most horrid that can be imagined. If those accounts be true, he was the wretch that first began and carried on wars on the score or on the pretence of religion; and under that mask, or that infatuation, committed the most unexampled atrocities that are to be found in the history of any nation.[131]

Paine illustrates this claim with what is indeed one of the most horrifying passages in the Mosaic narrative: Numbers chapter 31, on the war against the Midianites (the nation to which Moses's own wife and father-in-law belong!). He cites 31:15, in which an enraged Moses orders the massacre of all women who are not virgins, and 31:18, in which he sanctions the retention of virgins as sex slaves. Paine offers the following commentary: "Among the detestable villains that in any period of the world have disgraced the name of man, it is impossible to find a greater than Moses, if this account be true. Here is an order to butcher the boys, to massacre the mothers, and debauch the daughters."[132] He then cites Numbers 31:35, according to which "the number of women-children consigned to debauchery by the order of Moses was thirty-two thousand," saying that a story like this is "too horrid for humanity to read, or for decency to hear."[133] Somehow people revere the sacred books and fail to see the wickedness: "Brought up in habits of superstition, they take it for granted that the Bible is true, and that it is good." But on the contrary, "it is a book of lies, wickedness, and blasphemy: for what can be greater blasphemy, than to ascribe the wickedness of man to the orders of the Almighty!"[134] Paine takes up the book of Joshua and describes it as follows: "It is horrid; it is a military history of rapine and murder, as savage and brutal as those recorded of his predecessor in villainy and hypocrisy, Moses; and the blasphemy consists, as in the former books, in ascribing those deeds to the orders of the Almighty."[135]

What can we learn from Moses as seen through the eyes of Thomas Paine? I would say that we learn that if a people claims to be divinely favoured in relation to all other peoples, and especially if they make territorial claims supposedly backed up by divine wrath, no good will come from that. The closest equivalent that we have had to that in recent politics is, it pains one to say, the politics of the Islamic State. Its claims were roughly on a par with the kinds of claims asserted throughout the books of the Bible with which we are concerned. As it grabbed chunks of Iraq and Syria, it believed that it was entitled to a territorial land mass occupied by other peoples, and it claimed that Allah wanted those peoples to be dispossessed of that land and for it to be placed in the hands of Allah's chosen instrument. That in itself surely tells us that we are in extremely dangerous territory with respect to the kind of politics that is ventilated in the Hebrew scriptures. Or consider what happens when priests of the Russian Orthodox Church get mixed up with Russian imperialists, as they sometimes do.[136] The world was able to see just how dangerous this kind of theocratic politics can be when Patriarch Kirill gave his full support to Vladimir Putin's brutal February 2022 invasion of Ukraine. In any case, here's what I think is a plausible hypothesis with respect to the interpretation of Paine's thought: Given his view of the Bible, and the Hebrew Bible especially, he had no choice but to embrace deism – in order to distance himself as far as he could from what he saw (not unreasonably) as the horror and atrocities of politics in the ancient Hebraic age. "It is," he writes, "a duty incumbent on every true deist, that he vindicates the moral justice of God against the calumnies of the [Hebrew] Bible"[137] – calumnies because they portray God as the mastermind behind Israel's imperialism and ruthlessness.

I suppose that one can put the following question to Paine: Why single out Israel, as if this kind of genocidal politics were unique to Moses and his monotheistic God among ancient peoples? As I have noted elsewhere,[138] there is a long tradition (predating Rousseau's discussion of YHWH as a "jealous god" in his civil religion chapter) of associating polytheism with religious toleration and associating monotheism with the kind of holy-war mentality that led to the Hebrew genocide of the Canaanite nations. But Walzer has made the important point that this isn't fair to monotheism – because the polytheistic Moabites were equally capable of holy-war-motivated genocide.[139] That is, the slaughter of a rival nation can just as readily be set in motion by appeal to what a national god supposedly commands as by appeal to what a monotheistic god supposedly commands. And we should not fail to mention that the victims of this Moabite genocide were in fact Hebrews.[140]

Before leaving Paine, there's one other thing I'd like to highlight in *The Age of Reason*. At least three times in chapter 1 of part 2 of the book, Paine refers to the Hebrew prophets as "impostors."[141] He also dismisses the New Testament as "fable and imposture."[142] This had become a significant trope in modern political thought, culminating in the inflammatory depiction of the three Abrahamic religions in the notorious radically Spinozist text *The Treatise of the Three Impostors*, which suggested that the "three impostors," Moses, Jesus, and Mohammed, were tricksters and con men. Apparently, there is no conclusive way of demonstrating who wrote it and when, although there are a variety of speculative theories concerning authorship and when and where it was composed.[143] The same trope is anticipated in a notable text near the end of book 2, chapter 7 of Rousseau's *Social Contract*.[144] Rousseau starts by sketching the image of a figure like Moses as someone capable of performing conjuring tricks: "Any man can engrave stone tablets … or find other crude ways to impress the people." Yet he hastens to insist that the view of Moses and Mohammed as "lucky imposters" (*heureux imposteurs*) is not his own but on the contrary one deriving from "proud philosophy or blind partisan spirit." Mere conjuring tricks like this would certainly not have sufficed to found a whole civilization or an entire cultural and political dispensation, he assures us, which was indeed the achievement of a Moses or a Mohammed. First he plants the idea of Moses as an impostor or trickster, then he aligns himself on the side of piety. This double-sided rhetoric can be found again and again in Rousseau's writing. In fact, this kind of double-edged rhetoric (simultaneously subversive and pious or supposedly pious) tends to run throughout modern political thought. One finds it even in Paine, since he claims that his own philosophical deism is a kind of superior piety (and in Spinoza too, obviously).

John Locke and Joseph de Maistre on the Exceptionality of the Mosaic Regime

In my book on civil religion, I present Maistre and Locke as polar opposites within the tradition of Western political philosophy. Locke is a paradigm case of tolerationist liberalism, committed to a firm separation of church and state. Maistre is a paradigm case of theocratic political philosophy, committed to a robustly enforced subordination of politics to orthodox religion.[145] Yet strangely enough, there is a peculiar kind of parallel in the problem that the Mosaic regime presents for both of them, which we will endeavour to set out in this section.

In his "Essay on the Generative Principle of Political Constitutions and Other Human Institutions," Maistre asserts the following principle: *"Man cannot create a constitution, and no legitimate constitution can be written.* The collection of fundamental laws which necessarily constitute a civil or religious society never has been or will be written *a priori."*[146] Like Burke, Maistre thinks that unwritten constitutions are valid in a way that written constitutions are not, and the decisive difference is that unwritten constitutions flow from a given nation's historically evolved practices and norms, whereas written constitutions try (impossibly) to legislate a political existence in advance. That is, the sort of founding documents on which, one would think, the United States as a civic republic erected its institutional existence are some kind of mirage: they have no right to exist, and the reality of the political community for which (according to its own self-understanding) these constitutive documents provide a foundation are a kind of pseudo-reality. "*Never has been or will be*": that's a pretty strong thesis. But as Maistre knows, "the legislation of Moses" directly violates this Maistrean thesis, or so it would appear. Having announced his seemingly categorical principle, he promptly qualifies it: "We know but one exception."[147] How can a pre-political constitution be utterly illegitimate in every case, and yet a pre-political constitution in the case of the Mosaic regime be legitimate? Maistre is obliged to address the legitimacy, according to his political philosophy, of the laws set out (in writing!) in the Five Books of Moses.

Here is how Maistre characterizes the exceptionality of the Mosaic legislation: "This alone was cast, so to speak, like a statue and written even to the smallest details by an extraordinary man [Moses, presumably] who said, FIAT! Without this work ever after needing corrections, additions, or modifications by himself or anyone else. This alone has withstood time, from which it borrowed and expected nothing. It survived fifteen hundred years."[148] Even the dispersion of the Jewish nation did not entirely annul Moses's laws: "We see it enjoying a second life and still binding, with some nameless and mysterious bond, the various scattered families of a people dispersed but not disunited. Like magnetism, and with a similar force, it operates at a distance, making one whole of many widely separated parts. Evidently, to intelligent minds, this legislation surpasses the limits of human capability and is a magnificent exception to a general law which has yielded once, and then to its Author. And it singlehandedly manifests the divine mission of the great Hebrew lawgiver."[149] In a note attached to the next paragraph, Maistre cites a theocratic text from Plato's *Laws*, which he describes as "an admirable and wholly Mosaic passage."[150]

Once again, Maistre presents the laws of Moses as an "exception" (a *unique* exception) to "a general law" whose "Author" is obviously God.[151] Constitutions should never be written; yet Moses, commanded to do so by God, *did* inscribe a comprehensive political constitution for the Hebrews. The point, presumably, is that political constitutions legislated by mere human beings (that is to say, sinful creatures like us) cannot be viable; hence *secular* constitutions, like that of the American founding, are doomed to fail. And since the theocratic regime of Moses was *not* a secular founding, it's exempt from the "general law." But in fact, for Maistre *all* legitimate constitutions are theocratic constitutions, so in that crucial respect, paradoxically, the Mosaic constitution turns out *not* to be exceptional. Hence we encounter a significant tension in Maistre's argument. The exceptionality of the Mosaic constitution, it had appeared, was that the laws of Moses were, uniquely, a direct emanation from God. However, Maistre goes on to inform us that "the principle of *every* constitution is divine."[152] That is, the *apparent* exceptionality of the Mosaic regime rests, one would have assumed, upon the fact that its true founder was God, whereas all other regimes are legislated by fallible human beings. But since Maistre's actual view is that all political institutions – and in fact all institutions full stop[153] – have a theocratic foundation, the basis for deeming the theocratic Mosaic constitution as exceptional in relation to a secular norm collapses. Again, *all* polities, on Maistre's view, are ultimately theocratic.

There are definitely echoes, in Maistre's account, of Rousseau's similar celebration of the temporal staying power of the Mosaic founding.[154] But is the legislation as flawless as Maistre makes out? Is it really in need of no subsequent revision? Is Maistre really suggesting that Jews (or anyone else) in the early nineteenth century should still be executing people who violate the Sabbath or stoning to death adulterers and idolators? For instance, here is the punishment meted out to someone who was caught gathering wood on the Sabbath (Numbers 15:35–6): "YHWH said to Moses: The man is to be put to death, yes, death, pelt him with stones, the entire community, outside the camp!"[155] Would Maistre really affirm the eternal validity of Deuteronomy 25:12's legal requirement to chop off the hand of a woman who had grabbed the genitals of her husband's assailant? Or Deuteronomy 25:9's command that one spit in the face of a man who refuses to marry his dead brother's widow? Moreover: If it was really the Divine Author who gave the Hebrews their perfect and timeless laws, why shouldn't all other peoples embrace the same perfect and timeless laws? If God considered these laws perfect and eternally binding for this particular ancient people, why would God not require the same perfect laws for all other nations? Maistre doesn't tell us.

Let us turn now to Locke. The purpose of Locke's *Letter Concerning Toleration* is to make a convincing philosophical/theological case for religious toleration. But as we'll see in more detail in chapter 4, the existential horizon of the Hebrew Bible does not provide for religious toleration. On the contrary, the God of the Hebrews on certain occasions directly prohibits religious toleration. The Hebrew God certainly wants to prevail over rival gods, and he wants his people to abstain from any intertribal mixing that might attenuate their loyalty to him. This is not a tolerationist regime! Yet the Hebrew Bible, as one of the two Testaments that compose the Christian Bible, is authoritative for Christians. So how does Locke, presenting himself as a committed Christian addressing himself to fellow Christians, cope with a set of scriptural texts that clearly run contrary to the political-philosophical conclusion at which he aims?

It turns out that the Mosaic regime is, for Locke, as much an exception to *his* general principles as that same regime is, for Maistre, an exception to his (hence the parallel I'm trying to sketch). It surely would have been open to Locke to argue that the civil punishment of idolators is normatively unjustified for all societies, and hence was so no less for ancient Israel. But that's not the argument that Locke makes. Instead, he makes an exceptionality argument parallel to Maistre's. If God chose to apply (severe) sanctions to idolators among the Hebrews, who is Locke to say that that's normatively off-limits? So Locke deploys a far more modest line of argument: Mosaic laws were binding on the Hebrews but not binding on non-Hebrews (including modern Christians). "The Law of *Moses* … is not obligatory to us Christians. No body pretends that every thing, generally, enjoyned by the Law of *Moses*, ought to be practised by Christians."[156] Moses instituted a positive law – that is, a law binding only on his own people. Christians are subject to a moral gospel preached by Jesus, who legislated no commonwealth. Moreover, the character of the Mosaic constitution is *theocratic*. Participation in God's covenant with the Hebrews is what defined *citizenship* in Moses's state, and turning one's back on the Hebrew God constituted apostasy. By virtue of their apostasy, the people committing this sin amounted to "Traytors and Rebels, guilty of no less than High Treason."[157] "The [religious] Laws established [in Israel] were the Civil Laws of that People, and a part of their Political Government; in which God himself was the Legislator."[158] Hence in the case of "an absolute *Theocracy*" like that of the Mosaic state, there neither was nor could be "any difference between that Commonwealth and the Church." In fact, *there are no other such cases*: "The Common-wealth of the Jews [was] different in that from all others."[159] If theocracy is in general an impermissible basis for political community, as it surely is for Locke, why should an exemption be made for this one particular commonwealth?

There's an astonishing text in the *Letter on Toleration* in which Locke goes so far as to assert the idea of the Hebrew God as precisely a *national* god: "God [was] in a peculiar manner the king of the *Jews* ... in the land of *Canaan*, which was his Kingdom ... His Dominion ... was perfectly Political, in that Country."[160] Because Israel was a theocracy ruled by God, capital punishment applied to pagan worship of other gods was legitimate because it constituted "properly an Act of High Treason against himself."[161] Would Locke apply this kind of principle to any other "king"? And finally, Locke offers not a single word of criticism of Mosaic imperialism, which one might have expected in light of the severe critique of European imperialism directed against Indigenous populations in America merely a few pages earlier ("the pretence of Religion [serving as] a Cloak to Covetousness, Rapine, and Ambition"[162]). Does Locke really think that the imperialism of Israel under Moses's and Joshua's leadership was anything other than "Covetousness, Rapine, and Ambition" under the cloak of religion?

Before concluding this section, let us return to the Maistre-Locke parallel. It's true that Maistre declares the Mosaic laws to be perfect and timeless (an absurd claim!), and Locke never makes such a claim. On the other hand, the laws concerning idolatry are in such glaring violation of Locke's political principles (which is obviously why Locke took up this problem to start with) that Locke in effect judges the Mosaic regime to be sacrosanct and hence beyond normative judgment. That's an extraordinary move for a philosopher who believes in the normative truth of liberal principles. It's worth pointing out in this context that there's a key vacillation in the quotations I cited from Maistre with respect to the source of the Mosaic legislation. He refers to it as the work of "an extraordinary man," presumably Moses. But he also refers to it as composed by a divine "Author": God. This is relevant to Locke. If *Moses* (a mortal human being) is the true author, why not simply say that the impermissibility of idolatry is an illegitimate subject for political legislation? But Locke doesn't say this. Again, why should one set of principles apply to the ancient Israelites and another, opposing set of principles apply to all other nations, ancient and modern? He's implicitly conceding that the Mosaic laws were really commanded by God and hence can't possibly be de-legitimized at the level of philosophic principles. Actually, it's explicit rather than implicit: "God himself was the Legislator."[163] But does Locke actually believe this?

Freud's Moses: Tyrant-Father of the Primal Horde

The extent of Freud's obsession with Moses is beyond dispute. In a letter to Lou Andreas-Salomé dated 6 January 1935, he wrote that the problem of how to solve the Moses riddle "has pursued me throughout the whole of my life."[164] Or consider what Freud wrote to Arnold Zweig: "The man, and what I wanted to make of him, pursues me incessantly."[165] But precisely what design Freud was pursuing in "what he wanted to make of him" is far less clear. Moreover, Freud's many critics may be entirely right that his arguments concerning Moses in *Moses and Monotheism* are pretty weak and unpersuasive.[166] Still, he offers a picture of how Moses stands in relation to the national community that he led that is highly charged with political implications and therefore impinges fairly directly on the business of political philosophy.[167] As Bluma Goldstein rightly observes, Freud's anti-biblical Moses is presented as a "liberator [who] does not promise to prepare his flock for any kind of democratic life or self-determination"; on the contrary, Freud presupposes an unbridgeable "distance between a vastly superior leader and his subaltern followers."[168] Why does Freud sketch Moses according to *Totem and Taboo*'s template of the primal horde ruled by a tyrannical father? No doubt, *Moses and Monotheism* is an extremely strange and inscrutable book. As Goldstein again highlights, it's incredibly hard to make out what Freud's purpose is or why he might have thought that his particular way of re-describing the Moses myth would be helpful to Jews like himself facing a potentially genocidal onslaught even worse than the centuries of persecution that had preceded it. (It was "potentially genocidal" while Freud was writing the Moses book; it became *actually* genocidal soon thereafter.) According to Goldstein, Freud claims that "it was current attacks on Jews that once again aroused his interest in Moses. [Yet] Freud's inquiry into antisemitism, though apparently motivated by prevailing Nazi persecution, reaches into the remotest past and the most inaccessible regions of the psyche, indeed into the psyche of the victim … In *Moses and Monotheism*, the victims of persecution are asked to explore their own unconscious for traces of a prehistoric repressed murder and to seek liberation in the recesses of their psyche, while anti-Semitic perpetrators, be they individuals or the state, are spared the full moral responsibility for their acts."[169] We are unlikely to decipher the abundant enigmas that suffuse this curious book. Still, with all its oddness (of which Freud himself was acutely aware), *Moses and Monotheism* retains a significant place within the tradition of intellectual appropriations of the figure of Moses.

Freud begins the book by acknowledging that Moses continues to be a man whom the Jews "take pride in as the greatest of their sons" and by more or less apologizing for "depriving" this people (Freud's own people) of their iconic progenitor.[170] The Jews are said to be threatened with the loss of Moses because – Freud devotes the first two essays that compose *Moses and Monotheism* to this "hypothesis" – the figure presented by the Bible as a hero of the Hebrews was in fact Egyptian – "probably an aristocrat," Freud adds.[171] However, far from this being an especially novel theory, it has been thoroughly documented by Jan Assmann in *Moses the Egyptian* that this sort of speculation has had a long historical lineage.[172]

The core of Freud's thesis in the second essay is that the God of the Hebrews is actually a fusion of two distinct non-Hebrew gods: the Egyptian "sun god, Aten," and the Midianite "volcano god," YHWH.[173] Equally, the putative founder of the Hebrew nation is a fusion of two non-Hebrew Moseses: an Egyptian Moses devoted to Aten and a Midianite Moses beholden to YHWH. The Egyptian Moses is "domineering, hot-tempered and even violent"; the Midianite Moses is "the mildest and most patient of men."[174] As regards the former Moses: he belonged (Freud speculates) to the inner circle of the monotheistic Pharaoh Akhenaten, and when Akhenaten's revolutionary overturning of Egyptian polytheism foundered, the ambitious Moses conceived "the plan of founding a new kingdom, of finding a new people to whom he would present for their worship the religion which Egypt had disdained," in order to keep the monotheistic flame from being extinguished.[175] "In order to solder the two figures together, tradition or legend had the task of bringing the Egyptian Moses to Midian,"[176] which basically runs parallel to the task of "fusing" or "soldering together" Aten and YHWH. It has to be conceded to Freud that this theory of two distinct Moseses does go some way toward accounting for discernible oddities in the biblical Moses's surprising metamorphosis into a Midianite shepherd deferential to his priestly father-in-law (and naturally does the same for palpable inconsistencies between universalistic and particularistic aspects of the Hebrew God's nature and personality). Disentangling the threads that the Bible weaves together, Freud conjectures that Moses, the Egyptian notable, led the exodus out of Egypt with no help from YHWH ("it was [Moses] and not the volcano god who had liberated the people"), and on the other side it was the Midianite priests, not Moses, who designed the religion that eventually became Judaism.[177] On Freud's creative rendition of the story, the law-giving Midianite

Moses is basically an invention to "compensate" the Egyptian Moses (= the real Moses) for getting less than full credit for the exodus.[178]

Freud's account of the Midianite YHWH cult as the point of origin for what became Mosaic religion is largely drawn from Eduard Meyer, and the main challenge for Freud is how to synthesize Meyer's theories with Freud's own theory of an Egyptian Moses. The linchpin of Freud's interpretation is what he calls in one place the *fact*, discovered by Ernst Sellin, that the Jews "rose against Moses one day, killed him and threw off the religion of the Aten which had been imposed on them,"[179] even though Freud elsewhere acknowledges repeatedly that this is not a "fact" but merely a theory.[180] Sellin's hypothesis crucially assists Freud in integrating the story of the Akhenaten-inspired monotheism of the Egyptian Moses with the volcano-god cult that figures centrally in Meyer's theory. It does so by allowing Freud to theorize that Moses was murdered, and his monotheistic religion jettisoned, *before* the Hebrew refugees from Egyptian bondage rejoined other kindred tribes in the vicinity of Midian and together with them definitively adopted their shared religion.[181] The Sellin-Freud theory also makes an appearance in Moses's lament to God in Thomas Mann's 1943 novel, *The Tables of the Law*: "What should I do with these people? They don't want to eat manna anymore. Just wait, You'll see. Before long they'll be stoning me."[182]

Following Meyer, the oasis of Kadesh is specified as the location where this new national religion was conjured into existence. After the assassination of Moses, his memory and his doctrines were preserved by his loyal retinue, the Levites, who struck a deal with "the priests of Midian" in negotiating the terms of the new religion.[183] Perhaps the strangest aspect of the narrative as Freud presents it is that even though Moses had been murdered before the Hebrews adopted YHWH as their god, and even though the form of monotheism that he brought with him from Egypt perished with his own demise, "the original religion of Moses" made a later comeback, probably thanks to the exertions of the Levite followers of the Egyptian Moses.[184] (Freud speaks of "the final victory of the Mosaic god over Yahweh.")[185] This is a complicated story, and Freud is clearly alert to the fact that it barely sustains a coherent narrative thread. Moreover, Freud constructs his theory of Moses in complete independence of the biblical account because it is, he declares, "a pious piece of imaginative fiction" driven by "its own tendentious purposes."[186]

Why was Moses murdered? Freud tells us that the Jewish people, upon whom Moses "forced his faith" – just as Akhenaten before him had forced his faith upon the polytheistic Egyptians – were unable to tolerate "such a spiritualized [*Vergeistigte*] religion." Freud speaks of this Mosaic theology as a "burden" that the people were desperate to throw off. Hence: "Moses, like Akhenaten, met with the same fate that awaits all enlightened despots."[187] But in fact, we learn, Moses's fate was *not* the same as Akhenaten's. Akhenaten's people, "tame Egyptians" that they were, waited for him to die, whereas "the savage Semites" took active measures to "rid themselves of their tyrant."[188] The next stage of the story is "when people began to regret the murder of Moses and to seek to forget it"[189] – an aspect of the story that comes to loom large in Freud's third essay. What happens is that "in the course of centuries," the more crass YHWH religion gradually ebbs within the synthetic creed fashioned at Kadesh, and the portion of the Israelite nation that had imbibed "a more highly spiritualized notion of god" from the Egyptian Moses gains the upper hand (likely under the guidance of the Levites).[190] That is, despite Moses's murder and despite the initial dominance of the volcano god, there was a sufficient residual Mosaic tradition such as would allow "this other god," "the forgotten god of Moses," namely Aten, to prevail eventually over the parochial Midianite god.[191] Freud concludes his narrative in the second essay by suggesting that only this unexpected "victory" of Aten over YHWH can account for the miraculous endurance of the people of Israel over the centuries. No merely "local god" could have accomplished that.

These inventive but fairly wild speculations (for that is what they are) are certainly not without interest, and they receive further elaboration in the third (much longer) essay – something closer to a full treatise, drawing more directly on characteristically Freudian modes of theorizing. It might be said that the purpose of the third essay is to convert the postulated historical narrative of the first two essays into the technical conceptualization of Freud's psychology. The third essay displays a fair bit of repetition of theses already ventilated in the first two essays, but there are also new emphases given to certain aspects of the previously laid-out narrative. Notably, Freud draws a straight line between "Sellin's suspicions about the end of Moses," and the speculations about archaic religion advanced in *Totem and Taboo*, with that text's schematized depiction of the primal horde led by the tyrannical father until his overthrow by the patricidal band of brothers. The murder of the Egyptian Moses (the "father" of their religion) by his own people (i.e., "the sons") is a classic Freudian trauma, and as we all know, it is a central feature of Freudian psychology that such traumas are not lost to the past but rather burrow their way into the unconscious, where they continue to inflict damage in the present. At least at the unconscious level, these patricidal sons experience "remorse for the murder of Moses."[192] The guilt is, according to the standard Freudian pattern, *repressed*, and this in turn elicits an inevitable "return of the repressed," to invoke Freud's famous conception.[193] But the trauma of having murdered the primal father is not limited to the immediate doers of the deed; the crime and its repressed memory somehow get passed on to the whole of the Jewish nation, this remorse or guilt thereby coming to pervade the totality of Jewish experience. According to Freud, it is "plausible to conjecture" that continuing remorse on the part of the Jews was what generated the fantasy of a reborn Moses in the guise of a redeeming Jewish Messiah.[194] However, the suggestion that this hypothesized remorse insinuates itself into Jewish history, from biblical times until the present, is far from plausible. "According to Sellin the tradition of the murder of Moses was always in the possession of priestly circles till eventually it found expression in writing which alone enabled Sellin to discover it."[195] But if the memory of Moses's murder was a closely guarded *esoteric* tradition, how would it have come to engender guilt among the Jewish people as a whole? Freud is quick to acknowledge that this is indeed a puzzle, but his response to the puzzle is vague and unsatisfying.[196]

"A growing sense of guilt had taken hold of the Jewish people."[197] Guilt for having murdered Moses? Guilt for having murdered the father of the primal horde? Why does Freud seem so keen to pile guilt onto the Jews? Revealingly, in a brief discussion of Islam, Freud remarks that "the murder of the founder of their religion" (again stated as if it were a historical fact) had conferred "depth" on the Jewish psyche.[198] He also claims that by virtue of recognizing the need for absolution by Christ as a redeemer, Christianity embodied an *avowal* of the crime of killing the primal father, an avowal that the Jews stubbornly refused to make.[199] Despite this avowal, Christianity represented "a cultural regression" relative to the preceding Mosaic civilization.[200] Clearly, then, Freud sees the guilt of the Jews as part and parcel of their cultural superiority (their superior *Geistigkeit*) – a cultural superiority jealousy of which helps to spur historic anti-Semitism.[201]

Perhaps the key line of the book, certainly the most striking, is when Freud writes, "The distortion of a text resembles a murder: the difficulty is not in perpetrating the deed, but in getting rid of its traces."[202] Sellin's hypothesis provides Freud with the central drama that matters to him; Freud picks up that ball and runs with it. But one big problem is that the traces that he says are difficult to get rid of are in fact not nearly as easy to detect as he suggests. What exactly are these traces? (Given the importance of the murder drama to Freud's whole narrative, it is truly remarkable that he doesn't cite any of the texts or evidence on which

Sellin based his theory.) Basically, what Freud is referring to are just psychological traces supposedly inhering in a collective psyche widely dispersed and extending over millennia, the existence of which have validity only if one fully buys into Freud's highly speculative psychology. As Robert A. Paul rightly pinpoints, the insurmountable problem with Freud's construction is that the theory "makes untenable assumptions about collective memories enduring across generations in the unconscious and operating in a civilization the same way a traumatic repressed memory does in an individual."[203] There are all kinds of reasons to be sceptical of Freud's account of individual psychology; but even if one thought otherwise, one would be entirely justified in saying, following Paul, that Freud's "analogies" drawn from the realm of individual psychology add zero plausibility to his story about Moses unless it could be demonstrated that an entity such as "the Jewish people" is in possession of a collective psyche subject to the same psychic dynamics that Freud claims are at work in neurotic individuals and to a significant extent in all individuals.[204]

Let us return to the two weighty issues raised by Goldstein that were quoted near the start of this section. Both merit further consideration. One is whether Freud wrongly shifts blame for persecution of the Jews (including what became genocidal persecution) onto the victims. The other is whether Freud erects a chasm between "the great man" and the demos that is politically harmful. Both pose serious normative challenges to Freud's vision of politics arising from his reflections on Moses, and *Moses and Monotheism*'s third essay does supply plenty of ammunition for both challenges. Let's start with the first of Goldstein's challenges. Somewhat shockingly, Freud actually *bolsters,* in his own weird fashion, the traditional charge against the Jews of being deicides. Killing the "father" of their religion while "stubbornly" refusing to acknowledge their responsibility for his murder is tantamount to killing God; hence the historic reproach put to the Jews by their enemies of being God-killers "is true, if it is correctly translated."[205] How is *this* supposed to help the Jews in their moment of peril as they confront the dire menace posed by Hitler?

Assmann, at the end of chapter 5 of *Moses the Egyptian,* makes a rather feeble attempt to justify Freud's strategy of responding to anti-Semitism by analysing the Jewish psyche going back to Moses: "Not the Jew but monotheism [qua religion of the father] had attracted [the anti-Semite's] undying hatred. By making Moses an Egyptian, he deemed himself able to shift the sources of negativity and intolerance out of Judaism and back to Egypt."[206] This is a particularly far-fetched suggestion, even if Assmann is right that Freud somehow did have ideas along these lines. And indeed, Freud does deploy an argument to the effect that it's animus *against monotheism in general* that drives the most ferocious Jew-haters: Really, Freud suggests, they are still Teutonic pagans under the skin who "have not got over a grudge against the new religion which was imposed on them [namely Christianity]; but they have displaced the grudge on to the source from which Christianity reached them [namely Judaism]." "Their hatred of Jews is at bottom a hatred of Christians."[207] Yet this thesis is easily refuted by the fact that when the Nazis proceeded to set up extermination camps, it was specifically Jews who were the intended prey. One suspects that Freud was simply too enamoured of his own theories to acknowledge that his ideas about Moses were not a helpful response to fascist anti-Semitism.

Goldstein's second challenge promises to put another serious dent in whatever trust we may be inclined to confer on Freud as a source of normative instruction. It's quite clear that a major source of Freud's Moses obsession is his image of Moses as a prime example of "the transcendent influence [on human history] of a single personality,"[208] towering over the lowly masses. Freud himself gives huge emphasis to this aspect of his picture of Moses by including a section specifically devoted to a theory of "the great man." Such was Moses, with his extraordinary power to "form a people out of random individuals and families, [to] stamp them with their definitive character and determine their fate for thousands of years."[209] Freud's image of Moses as a great man shaping the malleable masses is a direct function of his patriarch-centred psychology, as Freud himself spells out very clearly: "We know that in the mass of mankind there is a powerful need for an authority who can be admired, before whom one bows down, by whom one is ruled and perhaps even ill-treated. We have learnt from the psychology of individual men what the origin is of this need of the masses. It is a longing for the father."[210] Goldstein seems right to worry that one is not likely to put much store in a democratic culture if one's thought is so dominated by the idea of human beings as children yearning for (but also cowering in fear before) the absolute authority of the mythical patriarch. With a psychology so preoccupied by an image of "the autonomy and independence of the great man, his divine unconcern which may grow into ruthlessness,"[211] is it likely that one will be able to cultivate respect for the democratic autonomy of ordinary human beings?[212] On the other hand, it is important to bear in mind that the core of Freud's story about Moses is not submission to authority but on the contrary revolt against the father figure. The Hebrews don't defer to Moses; they kill him!

It doesn't seem the least bit unfair to think of the Freudian depiction of Moses as an elaborate Freudian myth.[213] But, it has to be asked, what is the point of the myth? In reading *Moses and Monotheism,* as with reading Freud's other work, one feels a very strong impulse to psychoanalyse Freud.[214] Freud clearly conceived himself to be a heroic liberator and saw the psychoanalytic movement as a tribe as difficult to manage as the stiff-necked nation of Israel. Frederick Crews points out that Moses as presented by Freud is "a 'Freud figure,' as every reader has noticed."[215] The truth of this observation is fully borne out by something that Freud himself wrote in a letter to Carl Jung dated 17 January 1909: "You will as Joshua, if I am Moses, take possession of the promised land of psychiatry, which I am only permitted to glimpse from afar."[216] We stand by our earlier suggestion that there is, if not an overt political philosophy, then at least a latent political philosophy in Freud's speculations about Moses, particularly in relation to the primal-horde scenario originally sketched in *Totem and Taboo;* but we have good reason to take with a grain of salt an account of Moses and his relevance for normative reflection penned by someone who was himself clearly in the grip of a kind of Moses complex.

Chapter Two

The Question of a Mosaic Regime: A Perennial Debate

The regime [*politeia*] is an arrangement of a city with respect to its offices, particularly the one that has authority over all [matters]. For what has authority in the city is everywhere the governing body [*politeuma*], and the governing body *is* the regime.

– Aristotle[1]

Is there such a thing as a Mosaic regime? In our discussion of Harrington in the previous chapter, we briefly considered, and quickly – perhaps too quickly – dismissed Harrington's views with respect to this question. After all, Harrington is hardly unique within the history of political thought in believing ancient Israel to be the first real example of a regime erected on democratic normative foundations[2] – although this view is by no means uncontested. This is a sufficiently important question within the history of political philosophy that it deserves more concerted attention than we gave it in chapter 1; hence the following attempt to do somewhat greater justice to the question in the discussion that follows.[3]

Let's resume where we left off last time, namely, with a restatement of the Harringtonian position. At the beginning of the chapter of *The Commonwealth of Oceana* entitled "The Preliminaries, showing the Principles of Government," Harrington writes the following: "Giannotti, the most excellent describer of the commonwealth of Venice, divideth the whole series of government into two times or periods. The [first ended] with the liberty of Rome, which was the course or empire, as I may call it, of ancient prudence, first discovered [i.e., revealed] unto mankind by God himself in the fabric of the commonwealth of Israel, and afterward picked out of his footsteps in nature and unanimously followed by the Greeks and Romans."[4] That is:

history's original instance of a self-ruling republic was the regime instituted by Moses. The Greeks and the republican Romans did not discover a new kind of politics. Rather, they followed in "God's footsteps" by refounding a kind of regime that the Israelites, thanks to Moses, had experienced many centuries before them. This view of the history of republican politics is expressed even more emphatically when Harrington refers to the Hebrew commonwealth as "that original whereof all the rest of the commonwealths seem to be copies."[5] On the same page, Harrington also affirms that rather than relying on Hobbes for one's understanding of the meaning of a parliament, the honour is "better due unto Moses."

A mere fourteen years after the publication of *Oceana*, Spinoza, in the *Theological-Political Treatise*, offered views about the Hebrew republic and what he claimed to be its originally democratic nature that are strikingly similar to those of Harrington. According to Spinoza's view, as stated in chapter 17 of the *Theological-Political Treatise*, the *original* form of the Mosaic regime (although it fairly rapidly became a Mosaic monarchy) was full-blown democracy. Following the counsel of Moses, the Israelites "resolved to transfer their right not to any mortal man, but to God alone."[6] "Since the Hebrews did not transfer their right to any other man, but, as in a democracy, they all surrendered their right on equal terms, ... it follows that this covenant left them all completely equal." "They all had an equal right to consult God, to receive and interpret his laws; in short, they all shared equally in the government of the state."[7] But one wonders, on this account, at what moment divine democracy was succeeded by Mosaic "monarchy." Spinoza refers to Exodus 20:18 and Deuteronomy 5:22–33 and 18:15–16,[8] suggesting a transition from the original democracy to de facto rule by Moses at a pretty early stage of the story. Spinoza claims that it was the people's terror in the presence of God (fear that "this great fire will consume us," that "we shall surely die," if they continued to converse in an unmediated fashion with God) that induced them to transfer effective authority to Moses. "By this they clearly abrogated the first covenant, making *an absolute transfer to Moses of their right to consult God and to interpret his decrees*."[9]

It's widely assumed, probably correctly, that both Harrington and Spinoza drew heavily on Petrus Cunaeus in forming their respective conceptions of ancient Hebrew republicanism.[10] That gives us good reason to attend carefully to Cunaeus's account of the Mosaic regime. This chapter will go on to canvass a few other notable treatments of the regime question available in the history of political thought; but let us start with Cunaeus.

Petrus Cunaeus

On what basis can one consider the polity founded by Moses as a "republic"? Its status as a republic is presumably put in question by the undoubted fact that the Hebrews were ruled monarchically from the appointment of King Saul[11] until, first, the destruction of the kingdom of Israel circa 722 BC, and then the destruction of the kingdom of Judah circa 587 BC. But did the Hebrews have a kind of "republican" regime, or a regime at all, during the pre-Saul dispensation? And did defining aspects of the original regime survive into the era of Hebrew kingship? It's reasonable to hope for answers to such questions from Cunaeus's *The Hebrew Republic*. The book, drawing heavily on Flavius Josephus's *Jewish Antiquities* and *Against Apion* as well as Moses Maimonides's *Mishneh Torah*, was published in 1617. In it, Cunaeus assumes (as the title of his book makes clear) that Moses founded something that can rightly be called a "republic," and that notwithstanding Israel's adoption of kingship in the transition from Samuel to Saul, this form of Mosaic republicanism in some sense remained the principle of Hebrew/Jewish political existence until the Jewish state was definitively terminated by the Romans in 70 AD.[12]

His topic, Cunaeus tells us, is "the ancient republic and the pristine institutions of the nation."[13] First of all, it's evident that Cunaeus presents the Mosaic polity as absolutely exemplary – an exemplarity that on his view includes, not least, its relevance as a guiding star for Cunaeus's contemporary Holland. He writes to his fellow Dutch citizens, "For your inspection ... I offer a republic – the holiest ever to have existed in the world, and the richest in examples for us to emulate."[14] The Mosaic law "was greater than any of the institutions and laws of the gentiles; and it was certainly more distinguished, since its author was God."[15] Secondly, Cunaeus endorses Josephus's classification of the regime as a "theocracy (as one might call the sort of state whose chief and ruler is God alone)."[16] He refers to it as "the holy state – founded by Moses at the command of God."[17] "Its creator and founder was not some man sprung from mortal matter, but immortal God Himself."[18] Thirdly, Cunaeus, somewhat in tension with his description of the regime as a theocracy (God-ruled state) in the strict sense, identifies Moses as the authoritative lawgiver for this "republic." "The Republic of the Hebrews was founded by Moses."[19] Moses "was the first to write and publish laws so that the people might learn what was right and what was wrong, and which sanctions might steady the state Almighty God had ordered to be set up in Palestine. Before the time of Moses the world knew nothing of written law."[20] "Flavius Josephus the Jew has made this overblown nation [the Greeks] swallow its pride ... Flavius proves that the Greek lawgivers are, when compared with Moses, scarcely ancient at all, and seem to have been born yesterday or the day before."[21] "Moses, a man of God, had given [the Hebrews] very sound laws about religious rites and practices, and about justice and the rights of citizens."[22] Hence the Mosaic legislation served to constitute both a religion and a state: "Nothing held Moses' republic together more than his religious teachings."[23] The vivid tension between the Hebrew republic viewed as a strict theocracy and the same state conceived as the product of Mosaic law-giving is captured in the following text: "Because [Moses] wanted to found a republic that would be the most sacred in the world, *he handed supreme authority over to God*." Moses realized "that it would be utter madness to enter into a joint reign with Him."[24] That is, it was *Moses*, not God, who determined that God should have sole and sovereign authority within the Mosaic regime. Cunaeus of course never clarifies how the idea that the absolute sovereign of the Mosaic republic was God, "not some man sprung from mortal matter," is consistent with the image of Moses as the singular source of the laws.[25] Finally, the Hebrew state, on Cunaeus's account, is distinguished from all other states by virtue of "the permanent stability of the [Mosaic] laws" over time, not admitting of any addition or subtraction.[26]

But again: By virtue of what is it appropriate to call this a "republic" (*republica Hebraeorum*)? Or is Cunaeus simply using "republic" as a generic term for "state" (like "polity"), as Hobbes was later to do in calling his Leviathan-state a "Commonwealth"?[27] To be sure, Cunaeus states that the Hebrew nation "defended with great passion the people's liberty";[28] but liberty here probably means liberty vis-à-vis rival nations rather than an internal organization of the political community. However, Cunaeus's statement that Moses "wanted his magistrates to be not the masters of the laws, but their guardians and servants"[29] perhaps suggests that it is the supremacy of law that characterizes the Mosaic regime as a "republic." Moreover, in a discussion that likely contributed to later republican discourse (notably in Harrington and Spinoza), Cunaeus praises the highly egalitarian Mosaic agrarian law (as described by Maimonides), both with respect to its original equality-promoting distribution of land and the fact that this original distribution got restored every fifty years with the institution of the Jubilee.[30] And in a discussion quite reminiscent of Machiavelli's in book 1, chapter 1 of the *Discourses on Livy* (though Machiavelli is never cited), Cunaeus affirms that Moses's purpose with these laws was above all to cultivate virtue in the citizenry.[31] Similarly, in book 1, chapter 4, Cunaeus insists that the Hebrew economy was predominantly an agricultural one, which contributed crucially to its being a virtuous republic, quoting Aristotle's judgment that a political community where the citizens are always busy farming provides the best foundation for a republican way of life: "Such states govern themselves and their affairs according to laws; for they have by their own efforts as much as they need to live on, and yet they have no time to be idle."[32] All of these themes clearly fit Cunaeus into a broader republican tradition, or at least explain why a bona fide theorist of republican liberty like Harrington would see Cunaeus's book as a resource for republican theorizing.

The breadth or elasticity of what Cunaeus might associate with a republic finds striking expression in a quite odd text in book 1, chapter 8. The context is a challenge posed to Maimonides's apparent attempt to interpret Jacob's declaration in Genesis 49:10 that "the sceptre shall not depart from Judah" in such a way that "communal authority" is transferred to the exiled Hebrews in Babylon. Cunaeus rejects that interpretation, insisting that the "sceptre" (sovereign authority) can be located nowhere but Palestine: "The scepter about which the prophecy spoke can only be the Jewish Republic, i.e., that priestly kingdom whose rites and practices were ... its very soul and spirit."[33] Still, he concedes to Maimonides "that the Jews of Babylonia took part *in a sort of republic*, and that they made laws for the others of their nation who lived in Palestine."[34] Notwithstanding the strange suggestion in this text that the Babylonian Hebrews participated in "a sort of republic" (whatever that might mean), he makes quite clear in the next chapter (book 1, chapter 9) that republicanism presupposes a state where a particular people is sovereign: "The sceptre can only represent sovereign power, namely that which lies in the very republic itself."[35] When the citizens of the northern kingdom were exiled from Palestine, the Judeans of the southern kingdom became the repositories of popular sovereignty, so that the "Hebrew republic" became a "Jewish republic."[36] But the principle that made the former a republic remained no less operative in the latter: "Sovereignty belonged to the people."[37] Contrary to those who associate sovereignty with kingship, "any people that has its own state and lives under its own laws can quite properly take pride in its authority and its sovereignty."[38]

Overall, the argument is largely stipulative. Moses founded a republic. Republics are ultimately based on popular sovereignty. Hence the Hebrew republic gave expression to the will of the people via political institutions that were in some sense representative of that popular will, although the exact mechanism by which the citizenry was consulted is left fairly vague. There's one further theme in Cunaeus that clearly fed into later republican political thought (certainly that of Harrington and the thinkers influenced by him), namely, Cunaeus's emphasis on the importance of the Hebrew Sanhedrin or senate. This is unquestionably conceived by Cunaeus as an aristocratic aspect of the Mosaic regime, and praised as such.[39] Cunaeus refers to the general populace as a "mob," so no one should imagine that he is partial toward democracy any more than were the classical sources, such as Aristotle, to whom he appeals in developing his idea of a republic.[40] Still, Cunaeus claims that the Sanhedrin, in reaching its decisions on "the highest matters of state" (such as questions of war and peace, and the selection of kings), "called assemblies" in order to "consult with the people": "Decrees about kings and wars were ... passed at the people's initiative, while the senators of the Sanhedrin took care of everything else by themselves."[41] It is easy to see how a text like this would contribute to Harrington's vision of a republic as a dialectical synthesis of aristocratic wisdom and popular consent. Yet Cunaeus offers no specific evidence that the elders composing the senate relied upon popular input, let alone that this process of consultation is traceable back to Moses.

Thomas Aquinas

It's in a work of thirteenth-century theology/philosophy, namely Aquinas's "Treatise on Law," that we get a more intellectually disciplined (though still problematic) reflection on the regime question than we ever get from Cunaeus.[42] The relevant text is the *Summa Theologica,* first part of the second part, questions 104–5.[43] Aquinas's basic position is well summarized by Graham Hammill as follows: "In the *Summa Theologica,* Aquinas reads the Mosaic constitution through the lens of Aristotle's *Politics,* arguing that Moses instituted a mixed constitution, a form of government that was part monarchy, in that he and his successors ruled over all the people; part aristocracy, since he chose seventy-two elders and gave them governing responsibilities; and part democracy, since the rulers were chosen from among all of the people. Since it was ordained by divine law, the Mosaic constitution affirms mixed constitution as the best available."[44] Douglas Kries, in a very helpful and thorough commentary on Aquinas's philosophical account of the Mosaic regime, goes so far as to claim that what we have here is an attempt by Aquinas "to recover the wisdom of the politics of the Old Testament for Christian political thought."[45] This is not exactly easy to do within the boundaries of Catholic theology, given Saint Paul's clear affirmation that the authority of the Mosaic law was terminated with the arrival of the Christian dispensation.[46] It's obviously impossible for Aquinas to deny entirely that the New Testament had abrogated the laws of Moses.

Kries explains that Aquinas gets around this by emphasizing that it's mainly continued adherence to the *ceremonial precepts* that is sinful for Christians, whereas "the possibility of retrieving the judicial precepts for Christian politics" is left open.[47]

Hammill, in his short discussion of Aquinas, offers the intriguing suggestion that the Thomist account of the Mosaic government "helped to lay the foundation for a secular understanding of government" because it posited judicial precepts as "purely political."[48] Kries's much fuller account helps clarify the sense in which Aquinas, seeking to bridge reason and revelation as he does, might be seen as offering a proto-secular theory of politics. On the revelation side of the equation, "the precepts of the Old Law," for Aquinas, "reflect the wisdom of the divine intellect." But on the other side, Aquinas is equally committed to the proposition "that a rational understanding of the judicial precepts is attainable by the unaided human intellect, and he spares no effort in attempting to grasp the inherent reasonableness of the Mosaic regime."[49] This, notwithstanding the fact that "according to the Bible itself, the basis for the legislation of Moses is not reason but faith."[50] Kries calls the Thomist account "an encounter between the revelation of Moses and the reason of Aristotle."[51] As he rather colourfully puts it: "We can imagine Thomas composing his articles on the judicial precepts with the revealed, supernatural politics of the Pentateuch at his right hand and the reasonable, natural politics of Aristotle at his left, carefully comparing the two on the question of the best political regime."[52]

Let's turn now to the actual texts. Aquinas defines "judicial precepts" as those "which derive their binding force … from some institution, divine or human." That is, they are precepts "that are directed to the ordering of one man in relation to another, which ordering is subject to the direction of the sovereign as supreme judge." Moral precepts, by contrast, "derive their binding force from the dictate of reason itself," without the mediation of political-legal structures of authority.[53] Question 104, article 3 turns to the interesting puzzle of how it should come about that the authority of laws imbued with divine authority should lapse. The article's third objection cites Saint Paul's declaration of "the weakness and unprofitableness" of the Hebrew laws (Hebrews 7:18) but interprets this judgment as applying only to the ceremonial precepts. By contrast, the judicial precepts, so the objection asserts, "still retain their efficacy" because these precepts "were useful and efficacious in respect of the purpose for which they were instituted, viz., to establish justice and equity among men."[54] As flagged in the Kries commentary, Aquinas himself accepts a strong distinction between the ceremonial precepts and the judicial precepts but, in opposition to the objection, accepts that the judicial precepts "were annulled by the coming of Christ."[55] The judicial precepts are indeed dead in the sense that "they have no binding force." But whereas the observance of the ceremonial precepts is prohibited after the arrival of the Christian dispensation, it is open to a given sovereign "to order [the] judicial precepts to be observed in his kingdom," provided that the sovereign doesn't legislate them "as though they derived their binding force through being institutions of the Old Law."[56] Hence Kries's argument that the Mosaic regime can be legitimately resurrected if a basically *secular* argument for their utility comes to be embraced by Christian rulers.

If what originally gave these laws their authority was that they enjoyed divine sanction, why are sovereigns still to come allowed to reactivate the laws only on the condition that they confer merely secular political authority on the same laws? Aquinas's explanation is a rather strange one. The purpose of the Mosaic legislation was not to establish a political-legal ordering of eternal validity but merely to "shape the state of [the Jewish] people" in such a way that they would be fitted to receive Christ: "The Law was a pedagogue, leading men to Christ." Christ arrived, and thus this particular purpose (the defining purpose of the Hebrew legal order according to Aquinas) became redundant. Continuing to observe "the Old Law" as before would be a mode of asserting "that the former state of the people still lasts," which would amount to a culpable failure to recognize the arrival of the saviour whom those laws were meant to "foreshadow."[57] In other words, the purpose of the laws, as intended by God, was not to supply an ideal ordering of the social-political existence of the Hebrew nation as an end in itself, but instead simply to prepare the Jews, "pedagogically," for the providential event by which "the state of that people" would be utterly transformed. "The judicial precepts established by men retain their binding force forever, so long as the state of government remains the same. But if the state or nation pass to another form of government, the laws must needs be changed."[58] This is a particularly curious argument since it treats the lapsing of the Hebrew legal order as if it were an Aristotelian change of *regime* rather than what it really is for Aquinas (as for all Christians): a change of dispensation.

The standpoint from which Aquinas evaluates the Mosaic regime in question 105 is a radically different one since it focuses on the regime qua regime rather than the regime qua "pedagogy." Aquinas takes it on the authority of Numbers 24:5 that Israel is distinguished by "the beauty of its order": "The beautiful ordering of a people depends on the right establishment of its rulers," from which Aquinas draws the ambitious conclusion that "the Law made right provision for the people with regard to its rulers."[59] So the first article of question 105 very directly engages the regime question, with Aquinas directly endorsing the established rulership of the Hebrews. The way in which the objections structure the analysis is of course as interesting as Aquinas's replies to the objections. Article 1's first objection complains that "the Law contains no precept relating to the institution of the chief ruler" – which, it has to be said, seems to be a valid complaint since the biblical text never really spells out any such institution. According to the objection, the Mosaic law focuses instead on "prescriptions concerning the inferior rulers," namely the seventy elders composing the Sanhedrin.[60] The second objection appeals to the authority of Plato's *Timaeus* in asserting that *kingship* constitutes "the best ordering of a state," approaching "nearest in resemblance to the divine government." But rather than categorically mandating monarchy, the Hebrew Bible seems to render its eventual embrace of a kingly regime conditional on popular will, as if Aquinas were anticipating Hobbes or Harrington. (The people "should not have been allowed a choice in the matter.")[61] And objection 5 claims that when God did eventually confer monarchy upon Israel as its authoritative regime, it was in fact a tyranny rather than a proper kingship.[62]

As we already know from the Hammill summary quoted at the start of this section, Aquinas, rather than repudiating the "popular" element in the regime, such as it is, affirms this aspect of democratic self-rule as part of his account of the mixed regime as a best regime.[63] Aquinas invokes the Aristotelian principle in *Politics*, book 2, chapter 6, according to which "all should take some share in the government, for this form of constitution ensures peace among the people, commends itself to all, and is most enduring." While kingship of some form is indeed best, "the people have the right to choose their rulers," and an ideal form of government should be "partly kingdom, ... partly aristocracy, ... partly democracy." "A government of this kind is shared by all," with all being "eligible to govern" and the rulers being "chosen by all." Moreover, this is in fact "the form of government established by the divine Law."[64] Similar to the later accounts in Cunaeus and Harrington, the seventy-two members of the Sanhedrin, being "elders in virtue," are held to compose the aristocratic element of the regime, and the fact that Exodus 18:21 and Deuteronomy 1:13–15 provide for these rulers being both "chosen from all the people" and "chosen by the people" is said to constitute the aspect of "democratic government."[65] Kries points to a subtle ambiguity within Aquinas's argument about Moses's Israel as the notional best regime: "He seems to argue in the body of [article 1] for the superiority of the mixed regime, whereas in responding to the objections he seems to argue for the superiority of monarchy, as he does in certain other works."[66] The explanation, as plausibly elaborated by Kries, rests on Aristotle's own distinction, in the *Politics*, between the best regime in ideal circumstances (virtuous monarchy) and the best practicable regime (the mixed regime).[67] However, one might perhaps put the point slightly differently. It could be said that Aquinas *exploits* an ambiguity or equivocation in Aristotle's own account of the best regime in order to reconcile Aquinas's commitment to the superiority of kingship with his attempt to vindicate as best a regime that is obviously not strictly a monarchy (and certainly not so at the time of the commencement of the regime).

As regards objection 1's point about the Mosaic law's failure to specify a "chief ruler," Aquinas replies that "the Lord reserved to himself the institution of the chief ruler."[68] And given the ever-present possibility of the best regime sliding into the worst regime (namely tyranny), and given that "the Jews were inclined to cruelty and avarice, which vices above all turn men into tyrants,"[69] God rightly postponed the inauguration of a monarchy governed by a human king until the people demanded it: "From the very first the Lord did not set up the kingly authority with full power, but gave them judges and governors to rule them."[70] But this insistence on God's supreme authority as "chief ruler" introduces significant tensions into Aquinas's account, since it has the effect of attenuating, or perhaps simply contradicting, the earlier assertions about the choice of their rulers residing in the hands of the people: "The Lord did not leave even the choice of a king to the people, but reserved this to Himself."[71] This can't help but have the effect of blurring the nature of the regime – an outcome that is perhaps inevitable given the tensions or inconsistencies in the biblical text itself (as well as in Aristotle).

In question 104, article 4, Aquinas had divided the judicial precepts into four categories: (1) laws governing the relation "of the people's sovereign to his subjects"; (2) laws governing the relations among members of the polity; (3) laws governing relations between citizens and aliens; and (4) laws regulating relations within the household (namely, the relation of the head of the household to his wife, children, and servants).[72] This four-fold division structures Aquinas's endeavour to scrutinize the reasonableness of the Mosaic precepts in the four articles comprising question 105. Rather than affirming the laws simply because they had been willed by God, Aquinas undertakes the monumental task of meticulously weighing the various elements of the Mosaic legal order according to the standards of philosophic reason. This is indeed a reason why one might regard Aquinas's project as a move in the direction of "a secular understanding of government." In question 105, article 4, he quotes Psalm 19:9: "The judgments of the Lord are true, justified in themselves."[73] But if the laws are "justified in themselves," why do we require the torrent of words flowing from Aquinas's pen in order to rationally justify them? It would be much too onerous to review all of Aquinas's detailed arguments for the reasonableness of the Mosaic laws, on topics ranging from whether women can inherit property, to the permissibility of divorce, to whether a man ought to marry his widowed sister-in-law. Let's zero in on two salient discussions (one in article 2 and one in article 3) in order to illustrate the apologetic character of Aquinas's commentary.

Article 2's ninth objection points out, perfectly reasonably, that the Mosaic law requires "certain slight offences" to be "severely punished." The two examples the text cites are the stoning to death of a man "for gathering sticks on the Sabbath day" (Numbers 15:32–6) and the stoning to death of an "unruly son … because of certain small transgressions" (Deuteronomy 21:18–21).[74] How can there be proportionality between vice and penalty in the Jewish law when a bit of youthful carousing is punishable with death? Objection 9 poses a particularly interesting challenge since, whereas many of the objections take up a position harsher than what's in the Mosaic law (e.g., the laws prescribing forgiveness of debts during the Sabbath year), in this case the objection (rightly) condemns the Old Law for being unduly harsh. Aquinas endorses the Mosaic law's punitiveness because "men are not easily deterred from such sins unless they be severely punished," although the hope of "curing" someone of their sins obviously isn't relevant in the case of someone who has been executed.[75] Aquinas also refers to the necessity of severe punishment "in order to deter others from committing such sins."[76] Aquinas informs us that the most culpable crimes occurred "when a man sinned from stubbornness or obstinacy; and then he was to be utterly cut off as a rebel and a destroyer of the commandment of the Law." Clearly, the two examples of excessive harshness cited in objection 9 fall into this category: "The unruly son was slain, not because he ate and drank, but because of his stubbornness and rebellion, which were always punished by death … As to the man who gathered sticks on the Sabbath, he was stoned as a breaker of the Law, which commanded the Sabbath to be observed, as a witness to the belief in the newness of the world … And so he was slain as an unbeliever." Aquinas evidently has no problem assenting to the Mosaic law's principle that unbelief warrants capital punishment (as does "irreverence towards one's parents"),[77] and if some latter-day Moses were to decide to bring back the Old Law, gathering sticks on the Sabbath would once again become legitimate grounds for death by stoning.

Our second example is located within the sphere of "international relations." Article 3, objection 4 takes issue with the divine command in Deuteronomy 20:13–19 that the chosen people "utterly destroy" various enemy nations. The basis of the objection is that, according to the next two verses, only the trees shall be spared. The puzzle is why the trees should be treated more mercifully than the men, women, and children who compose these cities.[78] Aquinas declares, "The Law contained suitable precepts."[79] But as Kries observes, Aquinas's admission that these suitable precepts mandate *herem* (uninhibited massacre of the population) at least in certain cases is very much in tension with what Aquinas otherwise sees (surely fairly implausibly) as precepts promoting a policy of "just war."[80] The law "commanded that war should be declared for a just cause," and "it enjoined that [the Hebrews] should use moderation in pursuing the advantage of victory, by sparing women and children."[81] That's what Aquinas asserts in the main body of the article; but in the reply to objection 4 he concedes that in the neighbouring cities listed in Deuteronomy 20:17, "*all* were ordered to be slain."[82] Why was it acceptable in these cases to set aside the moderate policy of sparing women and children? Aquinas says that it was "because of their former crimes, to punish which God sent the Israelites as executors of divine justice."[83] Was it "divine justice" to slaughter children because their parents happened to be idolaters? It's hard to avoid the conclusion that Aquinas's view is that the Mosaic law is never wrong, not just because it was divinely mandated for the ancient Hebrews but also because independent philosophical arguments can be mobilized to vindicate its consistent reasonableness, even if these supposedly "reasonable" considerations look pretty unreasonable to us today.

One of the main pillars of classical political science, including Aristotelian political science, is the notion of a "best regime." This conception of an ultimate normative standard, discernible by human reason, is what helped give us a tradition of political philosophy. It seems extraordinary that Aquinas hits on the idea of reading the Five Books of Moses through this Aristotelian lens,[84] implying that the Bible can be incorporated within the philosophical dialogue animating profane theory and that God's law can be judged by a human yardstick. This Aristotelian interpretation of the Hebrew Bible *at least to some extent* vindicates Hammill's suggestion that Aquinas's fusing of Aristotle and Holy Scripture "helped to lay the foundation for a secular understanding of government." What we *don't* get from Aquinas is any account of why the Mosaic polity, this "best regime," so quickly became corrupted, with unvirtuous leaders, sordid struggles for power, and a woefully unfaithful citizenry.[85] How could a regime that, it is claimed, simultaneously satisfied the standards of both divine and human wisdom – as if these two authorities, reason and revelation, *converged* on a shared vision of an ideal regime[86] – lead to so much vice and impiety (*even during the lifetime of Moses*, let alone subsequently)?

To be sure, Aquinas's attempted synthesis of Aristotelian reason and Mosaic revelation isn't seamless. As Kries rightly points out, "the *Politics* is useful to Thomas only up to a certain point. The *Politics* provides reasonable explanations for many of the judicial precepts, but it cannot provide all the explanations." Despite Aquinas's effort "to downplay [differences between Moses and Aristotle] as much as possible," given the "relatively apathetic attitude toward religion in the *Politics* … Moses and Aristotle simply do not always come to the same conclusions about politics."[87] The point, though, is that whether one justifies the Mosaic polity by reference to Aristotle's *Politics* or by reference to its divine inspiration, either way one is assuming that it represents a constellation of laws that exceeds in perfection all other political communities – an assumption that is hardly likely to survive serious critical scrutiny. If the legal order fashioned by Moses (or by God) was so perfect, how did these laws fail so conspicuously in creating a well-ordered state? Can anyone read Moshe Halbertal and Stephen Holmes's *The Beginning of Politics*, for instance, and think for one moment that the polity established on the foundation of Mosaic laws embodied exceptional virtue, either moral or political? Did Moses himself think that Israel under his rulership constituted a best regime? Did God?

Martin Buber

One thing that's woefully missing from both Cunaeus and Aquinas is a sufficient recognition that the Mosaic regime in the strict sense, whatever one takes it to be, is limited to the period antedating the kingship of Saul. A robust corrective can be found in a twentieth-century text, namely Martin Buber's 1932 book, *Kingship of God*.[88] First, let us recall the Spinozistic vision of an original Hebrew democracy that we quoted earlier in this chapter:

> [The Hebrews] transferred to God all their natural power of self-preservation … and consequently all their right. It was God alone, then, who held sovereignty over the Hebrews, and so this state alone, by virtue of the covenant, was rightly called the kingdom of God, and God was also called the king of the Hebrews … Since the Hebrews did not transfer their right

> to any other man, but as in a democracy, they all surrendered their right on equal terms, ... it follows that this covenant left them all completely equal, and they all had an equal right to consult God, to receive and interpret his laws; in short, they all shared equally in the government of the state.[89]

This is obviously a much more radical view of what the regime was (at least initially) than Aquinas's interpretation of the Mosaic polity as a mixed regime incorporating a democratic aspect alongside monarchical and aristocratic aspects. Buber's narrative is similar to Spinoza's,[90] except that the kingship of God, with its implication of a fully egalitarian community of citizens subject to the unmediated authority of the divine king, is not abrogated quite so quickly. *Kingship of God* is a highly technical work of biblical scholarship, and we are not competent to enter into the many complex and difficult philological debates with which Buber engages. But Buber is also a political philosopher, and theorists have good reason to take an interest in what normative vision is suggested in the book's argument that Mosaic Israel was originally subject to the "kingly rule of God."[91]

Buber takes his point of departure from Judges 8:22–3: "And the men of Israel said [to Gideon], 'Rule over us, you and also your son and also your son's son, for you have rescued us from the hand of Midian.' And Gideon said to them, 'I will not rule over you, nor will my son rule over you. The LORD will rule over you.'"[92] Clearly, Israel is asserted to be, at this stage of its political existence, what Josephus, Cunaeus, and Spinoza all assert it to be: a theocracy. But Buber insists that we not confuse (as we otherwise might) this original Israelite theocracy with "hierocracy" – that is, "rulership of the consecrated ones," namely, direct rule of a priestly caste or "kingship legitimized by a priestly oracle."[93] No; rule by God means rule by God. Buber in effect claims that it was a sense of collective aspiration that found expression in Gideon's affirmation of God's rule. It was historical in the sense that it gave voice to how the people experienced their destiny: as "something welling up out of its depths."[94] Is this the assertion of a "regime" or the denial that there was any real regime prior to the kingship of Saul? Buber's answer is somewhat elusive. At the end of chapter 1, he cites Julius Wellhausen's argument, contra Josephus, "that in ancient Israel a theocracy never existed as a form of government" with clearly defined institutions.[95] Buber makes the seemingly decisive concession that there is indeed no evidence that the pre-Saul theocratic dispensation possessed any fixed or definite institutional shape, yet he nonetheless resists Wellhausen. The Gideon text, he tells us, expresses the historical consciousness of the Israelites that it was their accountability to a divine rather than human king that animated their existence "in the midst of the whirl of political actualities": "a will of a religious and political kind in one." As Buber rather obliquely puts it, it was not a constitution but "a will toward constitution"; not a set of institutions but an "institutional will."[96]

In chapter 2, Buber presents the book of Judges as an implicit dialogue between opposing anti-monarchical and pro-monarchical narratives. On the one side we have a set of narratives articulating a view of the intrinsic perversity of (human) kingship: "It is vain, but also bewildering and seditious, that men rule over men ... No one needs to rule – no one except God alone."[97] On the other side we have the view that this is a recipe for nothing other than anarchy, as pointedly expressed in the final verse of Judges: "In those days there was no king in Israel. Every man did what was right in his own eyes."[98] Buber suggests that pre-monarchical Israel was a kind of noble attempt at "primitive theocracy," but the people "was not 'ripe' to actualize a structure intended for it ... by its spiritual leaders"; hence the attempt failed.[99] So, with respect to the pro-monarchical side of the book of Judges (chapters 17–21, according to Buber[100]), the view is that "kinglessness" (= "direct theocracy")[101] inevitably means anarchy, and "order and civilization" necessarily require human kingship.[102] Buber's remarkable suggestion that Israel fell short of being spiritually equipped for the primitive theocracy or direct theocracy that originally defined it as a religious-political community[103] seems to tell us that whatever Israel was under divine kingship was on a higher plane, humanly speaking, than what it became when it acquired an actual regime, namely human kingship.

In chapter 3 Buber discusses the fact that Israel was hardly unique among ancient societies of the region of the Middle East in conceiving a national god to be "the true king."[104] But Buber asserts that Israel nonetheless introduced something entirely novel: an "immediate, unmetaphorical, unlimitedly real theocracy" as acknowledged by Gideon in Judges 8:23.[105] Yet in the preface to the second edition, Buber states (in answer to a critic) that he is less committed to the "theocracy" label than to that of "kingship of God": "With 'king' I mean precisely the 'primitive' *melekh* which the elders of Israel mean when they (I Samuel 8:19ff.) demand a king."[106] Buber also cites 1 Samuel 12:12, where Samuel reminds the elders that they had already had the king that they had sought, namely YHWH. At the end of chapter 2, Buber goes so far as to refer to the books of Judges and Samuel as a "Biblical *Politeia*"[107] – which obviously suggests that these texts articulate a bona fide "constitution" or "regime." At the end of chapter 5, however, Buber tells us that the fact that YHWH led Israel as *melekh*, as king, until he was succeeded by

Saul doesn't mean that YHWH held this royal status in the context of a Hebrew state. YHWH "had appeared in the early period of the people as the 'King' of Israel – not yet, of course, in the sense of the head of a state, which didn't exist as yet, but in the sense of the head of a land-seeking confederation of tribes."[108] In chapter 6 Buber points out that it was necessary for YHWH to rule Israel *politically* because otherwise his authority would fall short of "rule over the entire actuality of worldly life."[109]

Arguably, it is in Buber's account in chapter 7 of the covenant between God and Israel in Exodus that we can perceive direct implications of his *melekh* theory at the level of regime analysis. Clearly, a democratizing interpretation of the covenant would see popular consent as essential for the validity of God's law. Although he refers repeatedly to the reciprocal character of the covenant, Buber doesn't present it in that way. "The Sinai covenant is a kingly covenant" – "a theopolitical act" establishing YHWH as the "exclusive, political Head" of Israel.[110] "Israel could only come to understand its God as King of the world when it had proclaimed Him as King of the people."[111] What is distinctive about Buber's interpretation is spelled out more directly in a parallel discussion in his later book on *Moses*: the covenant "has the character not of an agreement but of a royal proclamation."[112] It is a *melekh* covenant that YHWH wishes to conclude with the people in the sense that it is presented "as a royal proclamation from above and as an acclamation of royalty from below."[113] While there is indeed popular "acclamation from below" (mediated by elders), the emphasis here is far more on the kingly "proclamation from above." As Buber puts it in *Kingship of God*: it is a "relationship of unconditional super-ordination and subordination."[114] To the extent that the covenant is seen as "a royal proclamation," democratizing interpretations of what transpired at Sinai (such as Spinoza's) will inevitably be undermined or impugned.[115]

Where does Moses figure in all of this? What is perhaps most remarkable in chapter 7 of *Kingship of God*, devoted to the kingly covenant in Exodus chapter 19, is the paltriness of Moses's role in Buber's version of the story. Fairly astonishingly, Buber limits himself to referring to "the strong and 'submissive' mediatorship of a man who ... did not wish to be lord," invoking the description of Moses in Numbers 12:3 as "meek" or "humble."[116] Apart from this one reference to Moses's submissive relationship to Israel's authentic king, Moses is well-nigh invisible in the chapter. It seems obvious that this deliberate sidelining of Moses, for that is surely what it is, is motivated by Buber's determination to keep the spotlight focused exclusively on the theopolitical authority of YHWH.[117] Similarly, Buber begins chapter 8 by arguing that Moses's inability to "transmit power" to his heirs proves his limited authority as mere "emissary"; Buber calls the political office held by Moses and his successors "charismatic" as opposed to "dynastic."[118] Indeed, it's striking that Moses figures in chapter 8 primarily with respect to the *termination* of his office as the bearer of charismatic authority. Buber highlights the fact that "the transfer of the leadership to Joshua is joined to *the rejection of Moses*."[119] That is, Buber's emphasis on the displacement of charismatic rulership from Moses to Joshua precisely in regard to fulfilment of "the great mission" (namely the occupation of Canaan) again strikes me as aimed at an intentional downplaying of the status of Moses.[120] Notwithstanding the fact that Moses is thoroughly subordinated to Joshua in chapter 8, Buber in one place does concede that Joshua, being the military man that he is, "has never felt the theopolitical ardour of his master" (again omitting to identify Moses by name).[121] This would seem to constitute a definite acknowledgment of the preeminence of Moses, something that Buber makes no effort to elaborate in chapter 8 or elsewhere in the book.

What is Buber's purpose (i.e., his normative purpose) in putting as much emphasis as he does on the idea that the Israelites, during the epoch spanning from Moses to Samuel, lived under a "regime" of divine kingship? Paul Mendes-Flohr offers a formulation that helps, I think, to capture a key aspect of Buber's normative impulse. Mendes-Flohr writes that in Buber's view it was the "direct-theocracy" dispensation prior to the entry into Canaan "that witnessed the most pristine expression of the people's relationship to God,"[122] to which we can add that for Buber it at the same time represents a pristine "pre-political" situation offering a utopian glimpse into a political world innocent of the harsh realities of power and domination. The fatal problem with this whole vision, as should be obvious even from a cursory reading of the Bible, is that there is nothing remotely utopian about the political world summoned up in the books of Numbers, Joshua, and Judges. Charles Lesch, in a recent book, spells out what he takes to be the normative subtext of *Kingship of God*:

> Theopolitics, Buber argues, arose as a way to transplant pre-state Israel's "nomadic ethos" – its total rejection of human power – into settled life: When all people are mutually dependent on divine rule, none are dependent on merely human rule.[123]
>
> Human beings, by making themselves mutually and fully dependent on God, become fully and mutually independent of each other ... Under such an arrangement, power, reserved to the deity, cannot be exploited by men for their own aims. When power *is* exercised, it is understood as

> having been done so by God in the form of divine law. Its use is not interpreted as arbitrary ... For a people that has jointly and equally accepted the "yoke" of God's kingship, divine law's coercive force is not recognized *as* coercion.[124]
>
> [Judges 8:23] captures the essence of the theopolitical spirit: *kingship itself*, as an institution, is reserved to God alone. No human being, now or in the future, is entitled to dominion over another human being, for dominion itself is a province of the divine.[125]

Buber never states as clearly as Lesch does that this is the political philosophy underlying *Kingship of God*.[126] But to the extent that Lesch faithfully encapsulates Buber's normative project (which I think he does), it should be clear that this is a thoroughly idealizing or apologetic (i.e., tendentious) depiction of Mosaic Israel.[127]

On Lesch's account, Buber sees the *melekh* dispensation stretching from Moses to Samuel as preventing the unjust dependence of less powerful Israelites on more powerful Israelites; as securing a political order where power is never exercised arbitrarily and coercion is limited to what is prescribed by divine law. But how can one assent to this wholly benign picture of things without addressing the fact (according to the Bible's own narrative) that Moses ordered the mass execution of apostates *on his own authority* (no coercion? no arbitrary power?) during the episode of the golden calf?[128] The equality of all citizens certainly didn't impress Korah, Dathan, Abiram, and the 250 men of renown as a distinguishing feature of the Mosaic regime when they accused Moses and Aaron of unjustly violating Exodus 19:6's principle that Israel would be a holy nation where all would be priests; and as we know, YHWH sided with Moses and Aaron and did so very harshly. Nor does it seem especially reasonable to refer to the transcendent justice of the divine kingship when most of the political action during YHWH's reign revolved around God urging his chosen people to seize the territory of other peoples and sometimes to apply a policy of *herem* to those they dispossessed. Lesch would seem right in claiming that for Buber theopolitics remains the lodestar of Jewish political aspiration: that although the *melekh*-ship of YHWH had lost its hold on the religio-political faith of the Israelites by the end of the period of the judges, the idea was kept alive by the moral appeals of the later prophets; and that it fell into eclipse not because it lost anything of its normative authority but simply because Israel as a nation proved unworthy of it. Our own view, in sharp contrast, is as follows. The fact that Moses – with his resolute exercise of quasi-monarchical power in his own right[129] – is almost completely airbrushed out of the biblical saga by Buber exposes the normative vision of a just and egalitarian kingship presided over by YHWH as little more than an edifying fiction.[130] The Korah episode that is the subject of the next chapter highlights very powerfully the fact that the Moses narrative is not just, as Buber wants us to see it, a story of God's relation to his chosen people, with Moses occupying at most a minor side role. It is, rather, the account of a *regime*, one that was ruled quite heavy-handedly by Moses and that was very much seen that way by the citizens of this regime.[131]

Harrington Once More

Let us conclude this chapter by circling back to where we began, namely with Harrington's *The Commonwealth of Oceana*. Arguably, Harrington actually gives us a more developed account of a putative Mosaic regime than the other sources that we have looked at, ranging from Aquinas in the thirteenth century to Cunaeus in the seventeenth century to Martin Buber in the twentieth century. According to Harrington, "the commonwealth of Israel consisted of the senate, the people, and the magistracy."[132] As regards the people, Harrington appeals to Numbers 10:3 in claiming that the Mosaic constitution made provision for regular "assemblies of the people," summoned by trumpet blasts according to God's direct specifications.[133] Harrington suggests that these assemblies corresponded to what gets referred to in Greek as *ecclesia*, a word that "was also anciently and properly used for the civil congregations or assemblies of the people in Athens, Lacedaemon and Ephesus."[134] In the context of the New Testament, these *ecclesia* are conceived as "spiritual congregations," which, Harrington points out, ought to have conveyed to subsequent Christian tradition that the apostles "intended the government of the church to be democratical or popular."[135] However, a more developed account doesn't necessarily mean a fully convincing account. Numbers 10:3 does indeed refer to a gathering of "the entire community at the entrance of the Tent of Appointment,"[136] but the text doesn't refer to the assemblying of the Israelites for purposes of popular deliberation or democratic decision-making but simply as preparation for "the marching of the camps" (Numbers 10:2).

Harrington rightly acknowledges that "the church or congregation of the people of Israel assembled in a military manner" (citing Judges 20:2), with the implication that the people typically gathered as an army rather than as a popular assembly; but he quickly moves on to his ambitious claim, which we discussed in chapter 1, that the people retained "the power of confirming all their laws," including even the question of whether to confirm or reject God as their "king." It was the fact that ultimate authority rested with the assembled people that obliged "Samuel, being next under [God] supreme magistrate," to depose God as "civil magistrate." If the people had *this* power, then surely they had no less power in relation to the laws in general, "for where the suffrage of the people goes for nothing, it is no commonwealth."[137] "The whole body of the Israelitish laws … being proposed by God, were no otherwise enacted than by covenant with the people, … and so the result of that commonwealth was in the people."[138]

> Nor had the people the result only in matter of law: but the power in some cases of judicature (Joshua, 7:16; Judges 20:8, 9, 10), as also the right of levying war (Judges, 20:8, 9, 10; I Samuel, 7:6, 7, 8), cognizance in matter of religion (I Chronicles, 13:2; II Chronicles, 30:4), and the election of their magistrates, as the judge or dictator (Judges 11:11), the king (I Samuel, 10:17), the prince (I Maccabees, 14), which functions were exercised by the *synagoga magna*, or congregation of Israel, not always in one manner; for sometimes they were performed by the suffrage of the people, *viva voce* (Exodus, 9:3, 4, 5), sometimes by the lot only (Joshua, 7; I Samuel, 10), and all others by the ballot, or by mixture of the lot with the suffrage, as in the case of Eldad and Medad.[139]

To be sure, to give Harrington his due, this is an appreciable collection of textual citations pointing toward instances where Israel's leaders did seem to consult "the people" in some manner.

Harrington then proceeds to the question of "the senate of Israel, called in the Old Testament the seventy elders and in the New the Sanhedrim."[140] According to Harrington, "Moses … sat in the midst of [this senate] as prince or archon."[141] Harrington concedes that the Israelite senate, like "the Areopagites in Athens, … was little more than a supreme judicatory," hence not really involved in determination of the laws.[142] The reason in the case of Israel was "that the legislator of Israel was infallible," with the Hebrew commonwealth in possession of "laws given by God such as were not fit to be altered by men."[143] He cites Deuteronomy 17:9–11 to the effect that unlike the operation of most ancient senates, "the function of this council … was executive, and consisted in the administration of the law made."[144] This seems a significant concession since it is not so easy to conceive of the "senate" or council of elders as a bona fide part of a political regime if it merely administers laws and doesn't contribute to law-making. As for the third pillar in this regime, namely "the magistracy," Harrington omits to say anything about it at all in his summary of the Hebrew constitution. Moses is mentioned "as prince or archon," but there is no elaboration here of his role within the regime. One can speculate that the question of the magistrate is an awkward topic for Harrington because insofar as one regards *God* as the relevant magistrate, the political agency that matters is elevated far beyond the human realm; and insofar as one attends to the moment in I Samuel 8 when God is *displaced* as magistrate, Israel takes on the character of a genuine kingship and to that extent is no longer a "commonwealth" in the strict sense. In any case, one may continue to ponder whether the decisive question has been answered, namely the question of whether all of this adds up to a proper regime in any organized sense and whether it suffices to constitute Israel as a true "commonwealth" with political authority duly divided between a people, a senate, and a magistrate.

Chapter Three

Exodus Betrayed: Korah, Moses, and Class Struggle in the Wilderness

You have gone too far! For all the community are holy, all of them, and God is in their midst. Why then do you raise yourselves above God's congregation?

– Korah, Numbers 16:3

It is true that Jewry has never lacked rebels; the rugged individualism of the majority of Jews assures us an unfailing supply of iconoclasts, be they congeners of Korah, Spinoza, or Trotsky.

– Israel Abrahams, *Pathways in Judaism*[1]

Korah, like his late descendant, Trotsky, was not rehabilitated by a later generation more inclined toward committee rule. The opposition, literally driven under ground, has remained there, its reputation blackened, ever since.

– James H. Meisel, *Counterrevolution: How Revolutions Die*[2]

The Criticism of Moses, Right and Left

Between Exodus and entry into the Promised Land, there is the process of shaping the Israelites into a force for conquest. The current generation must perish before entering Canaan, but even more than that: deviations from the path that YHWH has predestined for His people demand suppression. The various murmurings in the wilderness have their reckoning in Moses's theologico-political purges. The most well-known of these purges is the golden calf episode of Exodus 32, where Moses punishes the Israelites for sliding back into paganism. This purge is a response to a kind of reactionary backsliding. Tired of waiting for Moses's new dispensation and the word of God to arrive, the Israelites ask Moses's brother, Aaron, to fashion them an idol. Aaron reluctantly accepts, making a cultic Apis bull for these wayward children of God.

This golden calf is a hackneyed but comforting and familiar image, worshipped in many other cultures.

YHWH throughout the Bible warns his people to stop thirsting after "strange gods," but YHWH seems like the strangest god of all. He is strange, as Jan Assmann argues in *Moses the Egyptian*, because he wants to be worshipped to the exclusion of all other gods. According to Assmann, the decisive innovation of Moses, contrary to the pluralistic culture of paganism, was the idea that a particular culture can be wrong about theological matters, because the universal truth binding on all peoples is that there is one and only one God.[3]

Some recent postmodern critics of Moses and the Mosaic dispensation, including Assmann himself, the late Bruno Latour, and Peter Sloterdijk, argue that there is a straight line from the politics of truth represented by Moses to contemporary ideologies of intolerance and domination.[4] The horrors of modernity – including even the crisis of climate change – are due to what God revealed to Moses on top of Mount Sinai and what Moses did when he came down the mountain to punish the faithless. This image of Moses as a tyrant is nothing new in political philosophy, and it is perhaps ironic that such a totalitarian image of Moses in postmodern discourse can be partially found in the deistic rationalism of Thomas Paine's *The Age of Reason*. While incarcerated in a French Revolutionary prison awaiting trial (and the possibility of death), Paine had time to vent his resentment against Robespierre's regime with the anachronistic comparison of Moses as an ancient version of the Incorruptible himself.[5]

But Paine's criticism of Moses was not Nietzschean. The problem for him was not Moses's moral universalism but the fact that Moses was not universalistic enough. For Paine the deist, Moses was held back by chauvinism, religious bigotry, the need for conquest, and wholesale xenophobic slaughter. Moses is a figure both appropriated and denounced by secular politics, and there emerged in modernity progressive and reactionary styles of Moses criticism. However, whatever their intentions (including that of Paine), the revolutionary Left continued a tradition of immanent critique of the original Mosaic dispensation. The Exodus itself became a symbol for universal solidarity and liberation, detached from the more problematic and Napoleonic phase of Joshua's conquest of Canaan. This was certainly the case for the experience of Black abolitionism against the Southern slavocracy in the United States, in the biblical imagery of Eugene Debs's anti-capitalism, and for more contemporary examples of liberation theology in Latin America.[6]

There is also the tradition of a left-wing critique of Moses that seeks to out-universalize the Mosaic dispensation. This left-wing critique can be discerned early on within the Torah itself and the wilderness episodes. A current of what Robert Alter calls "spiritual egalitarianism" is found in Korah's revolt in Numbers 16, which challenges Moses's authority as illegitimate and undemocratic. Korah's democratic challenge cannot be refuted logically by Moses but is merely violently suppressed in the manner of an internal purge of the tribe of Levi. It is our purpose here to rescue Korah from centuries of condemnation, from under "a mountain of dead dogs, a huge load of calumny and oblivion."[7] Of course, we cannot in this space completely rehabilitate Korah's left opposition to Moses. But against most commentaries that have accumulated over the centuries, Korah deserves a fair hearing as continuing the universalistic impulses of the Exodus narrative. The suppression of Korah's revolt, we will argue below, is the equivalent to a Thermidorian Reaction à la the French Revolution, where the new privileges of a usurping class had to be defended at the expense of social equality.

The culmination of this Mosaic counter-revolution against the universalistic promise of the Exodus ends with the centralization of the cult in Jerusalem.[8] This is the final consolidation against the murmurings of the Israelites, setting up a rule of obscurantist priests over the Israelite masses. In world history, it is certainly no coincidence that Korah's revolt has come back as a political metaphor for left oppositions within revolutions that fail to live up to their egalitarian promises. This was the case when Levellers during the English Civil War were compared to Korah.[9] And in the twentieth century, we can imagine Leon Trotsky as a carrier of Korah's message of making the universality of the Exodus permanent by overthrowing the Mosaic "bureaucracy."[10] Reading back from Trotsky to Korah, Korah then appears as the Trotsky of the Exodus saga, since it was Trotsky's own politics of "permanent revolution" that fought against the bureaucratization of the Russian Revolution under Stalin.[11]

Korah's Revolt

In Numbers 16, Korah makes his appearance as a rebel against Mosaic authority. He is "Korah son of Izhar son of Kohath son of Levi" and thus a cousin of the Levite troika of Moses, Aaron, and Miriam. Along with Dathan and Abiram, who are sons of the tribe of Reuben, "they [all] rose before Moses" with "two hundred fifty men of the Israelites, community chieftains ... men of renown" (Numbers 16:1–2).[12] This is an internecine struggle for power, equivalent to a factional fight in a political party. The words "took up," according to Alter, signify that Korah is the archetype of the "presumptuous rebel against just authority."[13]

If one perceives something Luciferian in the Miltonic sense – of an angel rebelling against the divine itself – they would not be wrong.[14] Like the demon princes of hell, these rebels are depicted as "princes of the congregation, the elect men of the assembly, men of renown" (Numbers 16:2–3).[15] But like the erstwhile favourites of heaven, this rebellion of Korah's is depicted not only as politically foolhardy but as cosmically misguided.

From the start, the Bible apparently ropes together two different revolts into one. Alter claims that Korah's revolt, as the biblical narrative presents it, is spliced together, illicitly, with the rebellion of the Reubenites. "Two rebellions have been combined, a rebellion of Levites for priestly privilege [that was being stripped away from them] and a rebellion of Reubenites for political power."[16] Thus, in the style of a political amalgam, two different revolts with different agendas are fused. This finds an echo with Stalin's Moscow show trials, where disparate political factions, such as Trotsky's Left Opposition and Bukharin's Right Opposition, were assimilated into one anti-Soviet conspiracy. Prosecution was made easier with a simplified amalgam that could treat all criticism and dissent as one reactionary mass.[17]

It is therefore crucial to distinguish between these two rebellions: Korah confronts Moses in the sanctuary ("before the LORD"; Numbers 16:16),[18] while Dathan and Abiram confront Moses at the entrance of their tents. Korah's revolt is much more doctrinal in quality; this is about everyone's relationship to God and is not a mere power grab, even if it is hard to separate sacerdotal and political power. The rebellion of the Reubenites, on the contrary, is more about clout and being passed over. As Alter explains, "Reuben is the firstborn [of Jacob's sons] who has been passed over in the struggle of political preeminence."[19] This is why the Reubenite rebellion occurs at their tents; the phrase "To your tents, O Israel!," as we know from 1 Kings 12:16, is code for tribalist warfare that threatens the unity of the Davidic kingdom. "Back to the tents!"[20] is then a slogan of tribalist secessionism. Korah's intention, however, is not secessionist, even though it appears schismatic.

According to the rabbinical literature, these are the same Reubenites who in Exodus 2:14 had threatened to betray Moses to the Egyptians for killing a cruel taskmaster. Even before Moses is acknowledged as a deliverer of the nation from bondage, there is a political intuition of what is to come in this early challenge: "And he [presumably a Reubenite] said [to Moses], "Who set you as a man prince and judge over us? Is it to kill me that you mean as you killed the Egyptian?" Thus, unlike Korah, the Reubenites do not present themselves as pious folks. They are wholly, according to Jonathan Kirsch's commentary, secular rebels, upset that Moses has made himself the uncrowned king of the nation.[21]

But in contrast to the tribe of Reuben, what is the essence of Korah's rebellion within the tribe of Levi? What is the main sin this alleged Hebrew Cataline is condemned for? It is his critique, which he states clearly, and with an eloquence and audacity worthy of a Danton: "And they assembled against Moses and against Aaron and said to them, 'You have too much! For all the community, they are all holy, and in their midst is the LORD, and why should you raise yourselves up over the LORD's assembly?'" (Numbers 16:3). This is an immanent critique of what the Israelites are supposed to stand for: that all the people of Israel should be priests, as was communicated to the whole nation in Exodus 19:6. The promise of universal equality (at the level of spiritual power) has not been fulfilled. And one should keep in mind how brave Korah and his clan were in opposing Moses at this time. They had already seen what God did to Miriam and Aaron at the tent of meeting; how Miriam was punished with leprosy after speaking against Moses taking a Cushite wife in Numbers 12. This is not to mention all the afflictions that the camp had suffered at the hands of an angry god. Furthermore, the Israelites had been routed in their initial battles with other nations in the wilderness. The context of Korah's revolt is already fraught with danger.

However, what did Moses and Aaron do specifically to provoke Korah? What was the proximate cause of the revolt? Assmann points to the immediate cause in Numbers 15, right before the Korah episode. There, God via Moses institutes what Assmann calls a "new mnemotechnical institution for preserving the covenant in everlasting memory."[22] These are the "fringes" (or tassels) YHWH orders the Israelites to put on their garments, so that they always see it; they should always "be mindful of all the LORD's commandments … and you shall [remember to] be holy to your God" (Numbers 15:40). But if all Israelites are commanded to be holy, then why do Moses and Aaron enjoy special access to God?

Right after Korah makes his case publicly, Moses is stung speechless. "And Moses heard and fell on his face" (Numbers 16:4).[23] This is not an expression of reverence but, as Alter points out, one of "extreme dismay."[24] And as Kirsch argues, Moses falls on his face because Korah's challenge is theological and not political. Dathan and Abiram, in contrast, accuse Moses of political offences, such as greed and acting like a cruel prince over them. So, unlike how he reacts to Korah, Moses is quick to recover in answering their charges. Before God, Moses exclaims, "I have not taken one ass from them, neither have I hurt one of them" (Numbers 16:15).[25]

In the narrative, Moses soon snaps out of his paralysis and directly addresses Korah's group. The Korahites are treated as a political faction, as the Bible indicates with the Hebrew word "*adato*": they are simultaneously a "legitimate collective organization of Israelites" and a "mutinous break-off group."[26] The language is ambiguous when it comes to legitimation, and Korah's own rebellion is not bereft of communal sympathy. After all, Korah is a member of the Levite aristocracy; he, like his fellow revolutionaries, is a man of renown. In most of the rabbinical literature (i.e., the Talmud and Midrash accounts), he is represented either as extremely wealthy or as a wise man that is head of his family, the Kohathites. According to Numbers 3:27–32, the Kohathites are a sub-tribe of Levi, responsible for vessels and objects in the holy sanctuary. They are the ones who carried the Ark of the Covenant on their shoulders.

Given all these factors, the threat Korah poses to Moses's authority is one of the most important challenges in the wilderness episodes. And due to the justness of his egalitarian claim, it is perhaps the most important one. Moses cannot refute Korah logically; unlike subsequent stories in rabbinical literature, Moses does not denounce Korah as a rich hypocrite or as merely rapacious and power-hungry. Some rabbis in the Talmudic era pointed out how "Korah" means "baldness," something Korah was cursed with due to his rebellious nature.[27] But in Numbers 16:4–5, instead of resorting to ad hominem arguments and red herrings, Moses says the following: "In the morning, the LORD will make known who is His, and him who is holy He will bring close to Him and him whom He chooses He will bring close to Him." This contradicts the spiritual egalitarianism implied in Exodus 19:6, since now Moses admits that God does play favourites and will decide very soon who is privileged and who is damned.

Moses orders the rebels to take pans to where God dwells in the tent of meeting. They will put fire in these pans, along with incense, and offer them to God. "And the man whom the LORD chooses, he is the holy one" (Numbers 16:7). Moses then taunts Korah as already having too much, which elides the difference between Korah's clan and that of the Reubenites, Dathan and Abiram. Given the fact that they already have enough, Moses asks the rebels rhetorically, "Will you seek the priesthood as well? Therefore you and all your community who band together against the LORD – and Aaron, what is he that you should murmur against him?" (Numbers 16:11). Aaron is singled out because it is, as Alter explains, "upon Aaron and his sons that priesthood has been conferred," radically privileging them in relation to the rest of the Levites.[28]

The Reubenites defiantly respond to Moses's call and repeat the murmurings of past episodes. At this point in the saga, these murmurings seem warranted. They say, "We will not go up. Is it too little that you brought us up from a land flowing with milk and honey to put us to death in the wilderness, that you should also actually lord it over us? ... Would you gouge out the eyes of these men? We will not go up" (Numbers 16: 14–15). Alter insists that this claim of the Reubenites is not meaningless: "This complaint is abundantly justified. They [the Israelites] are still stuck in the pitiless rocky landscape of the Sinai Desert, and the effort of the ten scouts to lead an expedition against the high country of Canaan has just been turned back in disastrous defeat."[29]

Moses then calls to God, asking him not to accept the offerings: "Do not turn to their offering. Not a donkey of theirs have I carried off, and I have done no harm to any one of them" (Numbers 16:15). But Alter suggests that this is another textual confusion, since it was Korah who was asked to make an offering and not the Reubenites.[30] Moses finally instructs Korah and his community to bring 250 fire pans to the tent of meeting – 250 pans for the 250 rebels. There, God will render his final (and terrible) judgment about this ethnic-religious-political amalgam of power-hungry Reubenites and renegade Levites.

As the story goes, the Lord appears to the disputants in all his glory; and he speaks to Moses and Aaron as follows: "Divide yourselves from this community, and I will put an end to them in an instant" (Numbers 16:21–2). Unsure about God's meaning, and having been traumatized by God's repeated threats to wipe the nation of Israel from the face of the earth, the brothers bow down on their faces and ask, "El [it is not the storm god YHWH they are speaking to here, but God's other henotheistic personality], God of the spirits for all flesh, should one man offend and against all the community You rage?" (Numbers 16:22–3). God clarifies what he meant and asks Moses to tell the community (which seems to mean the Israelites as a whole) to "move up from around the dwelling of Korah, Dathan, and Abiram." Moses tells the rest of the nation to turn immediately away from these insurgents and their tents – not even to touch anything of theirs, "lest you be swept away in all their offence" (Numbers 16:24–7).[31] But as Alter points out, Korah has disappeared from the scene in front of the tents, because, as discussed, his rebellion is not based in the tents, but based in "the dwelling" or tabernacle.[32] This is the tent of meeting itself, the holiest of holies, and not a mere headquarters for one's tribe.

Gathered with their wives and sons and young children, the Korahites and Reubenites are addressed one final time by Moses. He tells them that he is not responsible for what is about to happen. Even more, Moses insists that "it was not from my own heart" and that God "sent me to do all these things." Either these people will die like all people must one day, demonstrating that God finds them blameless; or, "if a new thing the LORD should create, and the ground gapes open its mouth and swallows them and all theirs and they go down alive to Sheol, you will know that these men have despised the LORD" (Numbers 16:29–31).[33]

As soon as Moses is done pronouncing this either/or, God proceeds to act with utmost celerity. The horrible judgment and destruction of the rebels is worth quoting in full:

> And it happened, just as he finished speaking all these words, the ground that was under them split apart, and the earth opened its mouth and swallowed them and their households and every human being that was Korah's, and all the possessions. And they went down, they and all that was theirs, alive to Sheol, and the earth covered over them, and they perished from the midst of the assembly. And all Israel that was round about them fled at the sound of them, for they thought, "Lest the earth swallow us." And a fire had gone out from the LORD, and consumed the two hundred and fifty men bringing forward the incense.
>
> (Numbers 16:31–5)

As Alter comments, this "justice" is pitiless and "scarcely accords with the discrimination applied to guilty agents elsewhere in the Mosaic Code – everyone associated with Dathan and Abiram [and Korah?] is engulfed, down to the little children." He even goes so far as to write that the "real thrust of the story is not considered justice but monitory spectacle," with all and sundry tumbling down to the underworld of Sheol.[34] While the Judaic conception of hell is not the same as the Christian one, there are elective affinities insofar as Sheol here is depicted as an infernal pit where sinners go to perish. This is also juxtaposed with God hurling fire from the sky. Alter points to the sloppiness of the biblical narrative, since – strictly speaking – it is Dathan, Abiram, and their supporters that tumble into Sheol, while the Korahites at the sanctuary are all consumed by fire. "The consequent confusion is carried into postbiblical Hebrew tradition, where Korah is sometimes represented as having been buried alive, and sometimes as having been incinerated."[35] In terms of the punishment fitting the crime, one can suggest a distinction between merely secular and theological crimes. While the Reubenites are swallowed, fire is needed to thoroughly cleanse the

Korahites. The Reubenites' rapacity was temporal; they wanted the throne and seemed indifferent to the spiritual dimension of the insurgency. But the Korahites went directly after the altar. This makes them more satanic in a Miltonian vein since they are challenging God's decision to favour Moses and Aaron.[36]

The aftermath of this event, as recounted in Numbers 17, is particularly brutal. As Kirsch writes, "the repeated acts of insurrection in the wilderness betray the fact that Moses was perceived as a monarch by the very people over whom he exercised such stern authority, and more than a few resented him bitterly."[37] This resentment is not killed off with the defeat of Korah, and God must suppress more than just 250 rebels in this next chapter. God orders Eleazar, the son of Aaron (and eventually Aaron's successor), to take the fire pans of the dead Korahites and hammer them "into a plating for the altar" (Numbers 17:5). This sight is to be a "remembrance for the Israelites, so that no stranger, who was not the seed of Aaron, should come forward to burn incense before the LORD, and none should be like Korah and his community, as the LORD had spoken to him in the hand of Moses" (Numbers 17:5).

But the community, weary of all this death, starts murmuring against Moses and Aaron, saying, "You, you have put to death the LORD'S people" (Numbers 17:6–7). A new rebellion is sowed, and they turn to the tent of meeting once again. But the masses are mistaken; God is not on their side and clearly aligns with Moses and Aaron. He does not consider Korah and company the "LORD'S People," as demonstrated in the purge. If these stories tell us anything, it is that "the defiance of Moses and the defiance of God are one and the same." As Kirsch opines, the divine right of kings, which Korah tried hard to resist, starts with Moses.[38]

God is ready for these new rebels, and after asking Moses and Aaron to separate from the murmurers, he afflicts the Israelites with an awesome scourge: "And those who died by the scourge came to fourteen thousand and seven hundred, besides those who died because of Korah" (Numbers 17:14–15). Thus God lashes out with multiple massacres in just one day. After this latest massacre, whose numbers approximate the number of people killed during Robespierre's entire Reign of Terror, God orders Moses to take a staff from every tribe. These are twelve staffs in all, with Aaron's name written on the staff that represents Levi. Before the tent of meeting and before the Ark of the Covenant, God tells Moses he will choose a staff, and that staff will flower. God chooses Aaron's staff, and this for God is to "subside from Me the murmurings of the Israelites which they murmur against you" (Numbers 17:21). After all the staffs are gathered, the nation sees Aaron's staff in full bloom: "It had brought forth flower and had burgeoned in blossom and had borne almonds" (Numbers 17:23–4). As Alter explains with stages of plant growth in mind, the accelerated growth and the bearing of fruit (the almonds) attest to the miraculous character of the event: "Divine favor accorded the Levites is figured in this image of agricultural fertility linked with the tribe whose sacerdotal duties in fact removed them from the soil [from work in the fields]."[39]

God wants Moses to bring Aaron's staff before the Ark, "as a sign for rebels." He calls for the murmurings to stop: "Let there be an end to their murmurings against Me, and they shall not die" (Numbers 17:25–6).[40] This does nothing to assure the Israelites. They respond to Moses in utter despair, saying, "Look, we perish, we are lost, all of us are lost. Whoever so much as comes near the LORD'S Tabernacle will die. Are we done with perishing?" (Numbers 17:28).[41] Alter comments that the people are now "gripped with fear that at any time they might step over the line [of the sacred zone] and be struck down."[42] No one apart from Moses, Aaron, and Aaron's descendants can have special access to God anymore, and Korah's proto-Protestant challenge to Moses and Aaron's proto-Catholic priestly supremacy is over.[43] The priests have won as a special elite group. As God makes clear in Numbers 18, Aaron and his sons now hold the priestly supremacy, and he proceeds to address Aaron directly (without Moses): "You and your sons and your father's house with you, you shall bear the guilt of the sanctuary, and you and your sons with you, you shall bear the guilt of your priesthood" (Numbers 18:1–2).[44] The guilt here refers to Aaron and his sons bearing the consequences for any transgressions against the sanctuary, consequences that will trigger God's wrath.[45]

The Case against Korah from Hobbes to Zornberg

It is not only the Bible and rabbinical literature that conflate the Reubenite and Korahite revolts. At a deeper level, such splicing together may not be simply a case of hasty redaction or bad textual analysis. Instead, the fusion of the spiritual and the temporal revolts in these texts intuitively draws out the political implications of Korah's challenge. It is hard not to see the sacerdotal challenge Korah poses to Moses as inextricably linked to the political one, where the Korahite program of spiritual egalitarianism could serve as the theological (theoretical) premise of practical action. This is how the English philosopher Thomas Hobbes understands Korah in his great treatise of political thought, *Leviathan*. There, Hobbes makes no distinction between these clans, merely asserting that God simply opened the earth to swallow them all as a political threat to established sovereignty.[46]

Hobbes's concern about Korah's challenge to right sovereignty was anticipated by the Elizabethan politician Edwin Sandys. In a remarkable passage from his sixteenth-century sermons, he reduces Korah's revolt to "the pride of their hearts" – that is, to illicit ambition. One notices how Sandys links pride and democratic tendencies here: "Corah, Dathan and Abiram in the pride of their hearts sought to displace Moses and Aaron, the chiefe magistrate and the chiefe minister. They set downe a handsome platforme of equalitie, and many of the multitude allowed of it as well pleased with a popular estate; where the worst of them might be as good as the best. But GOD brought their [design] and [themselves] to nought."[47] Korah and his confederates present us with a "handsome" program of modern politics – that is, equality. The multitude, of course, is attracted to this and falters in their vanity. But God puts a stop to this foolishness that goes against the absolutist regime of Moses and Aaron. Sandys was – generally speaking – a supporter of Elizabethian monarchism, but even before the English Civil War and the French Revolution, he was prescient regarding the political modernity to come. In the words of William Kolbrener, it was a modernity that God literally dragged down to hell (Sheol).[48]

Assuming the conception of sovereignty as uniting both the temporal and spiritual, Hobbes perceives Korah's revolt as a challenge to the legitimate monopoly on power held by Moses. According to Hobbes, Moses's authority was gained by the consent of the Israelite nation. He was not directly related to Abraham, nor was he a firstborn (Moses was three years younger than Aaron), so his sovereignty was not based on a hereditary principle. Instead, as Hobbes explains, citing Exodus 20:18–20 from the King James Bible, the Israelite masses "saw the Thunderings, and the Lightnings, and the noyse of the Trumpet, and the mountaine smoaking, removed, and stood a far off. And they said unto Moses, speak thou with us, and we will hear, but let not God speak with us lest we die."[49] The Israelites found themselves in a state of nature, threatened with violent death, so – in good Hobbesian social-contract fashion – they rationally agreed to let Moses be sovereign. They also obeyed Moses since he was favoured by God to speak with him. The rest of the nation did not enjoy such a spiritual-political privilege (and even if they tried to approach God, they would die): "They obliged themselves to obey whatsoever he should deliver unto them for the Commandement of God."[50] And while the kingdom was partly sacerdotal as a kingdom of priests under Aaron, Moses was nonetheless the ultimate authority. As the first founder of the commonwealth, Moses was ultimate sovereign of the Jews. Moses was again the one called up to God – not Aaron and the other priests – and thus the "sole Soveraign under God."[51]

When, according to Hobbes, God "caused the earth to swallow him [Korah]," this illustrated Moses's complete power over the Israelite nation: "Therefore, neither Aaron, nor the People, nor any Aristocracy of the chief Princes of the People, but Moses alone had next under God the Soveraingty over the Israelites: And that not onely in causes of Civill Policy, but also of Religion: For Moses onely spake with God, and therefore onely could tell the People, what it was that God required at their hands."[52] According to Kolbrener, Moses re-establishes the Leviathan in the desert against Korah, who represents a "Spinozistic" threat to the absolute sovereignty of Moses, and Korah's revolt is transformed into sheer egalitarianism when he says that the people of Israel are all holy. Kolbrener thus goes further in interpreting Korah as Spinozistic: if all are holy, then the authority of Moses's law is man-made. Kolbrener then puts the following words into Korah's mouth: "It's your doing Moses; your Torah keeps you in control; your Torah reflects your preferences."[53]

Like the rabbinical tradition of the Talmud before him, Kolbrener reduces Korah's revolt to a merely ideological and political one, where his challenge to Moses masks his own will to power, even if it has a democratic veneer. Ironically, Kolbrener sees this revolt as having a Hobbesian quality too, since Hobbes sees politics only as a conflict of bodies in motion. The Spinozism of Korah partakes of the same logic as Hobbes's secularizing defence of Moses's authority. Or, as Hobbes told Aubrey about Spinoza's *Theological-Political Treatise* – acknowledging how Spinoza was his own philosophical offspring – the heretical Jew had gone much further and outdone him; Hobbes admitted that he would "durst not write so boldly."[54]

Kolbrener wants a more robust defence of Moses and Aaron's authority than Hobbes's own proto-materialism can muster. He finds his position in the Hebrew sages – that is, those committed to the Torah – "and not their own interests or ideologies." As he puts it, "the Houses of Hillel and Shammai learn Torah 'for its own sake,' not Torah as a means to pursue separate and competing agendas." There is a deeper, Spinozistic problem in how Kolbrener valorizes the Torah and presents the will of heaven as infallible – namely, how something so ineffable can sustain a democratic politics. What grounds the judgments of the Torah beyond an authoritarian will that is beyond reason? How does this not lead to its own theological Machiavellianism? But it is clear for Kolbrener that Korah has no real love of Torah; any rationality supporting his case is dismissed as its own secular Machiavellianism. The Talmudic scholar Maharal is cited, and we know that Maharal diagnosed Korah as destructively self-righteous. Korah is thus reduced to a power-hungry Reubenite. "Korah projects a world based upon his selfish desires and political machinations."[55]

Avivah Gottlieb Zornberg defends Moses on postmodernist and Chestertonian grounds. Zornberg's adoption of the perspective of G.K. Chesterton makes sense here, since Korah is seen sometimes as the first Protestant (i.e., "proto-congregationalist" in Donald Harman Akenson's phrase),[56] while Moses and Aaron can represent the unjustified privileges of a proto-Catholic priesthood. Zornberg clearly diagnoses and condemns Korah's revolt as "rationalist," and she gives a sustained critique of its rationalism in her book *Moses: A Human Life*, devoting a whole section to Korah. According to Zornberg, Moses and Korah are mirror images of each other (and it is not a coincidence that they are first cousins). Korah, like a good Hegelian Marxist, speaks in the "rhetoric of totality."[57] And like a Spinozist, his conception of holiness is oceanic. This "oceanic holiness is the condition of the people, without nuance or conflict or difference." Korah's monism threatens to undo and liquidate all these (for him) unjustified dualisms and pluralisms, until one democratic polity is established. But like Kolbrener, Zornberg dismisses all this as "demagoguery."[58]

Zornberg cites a Midrash that stresses the antagonism between Korah and Moses. She puts her deconstructive gloss on it, but it is worth quoting in full because it highlights both Korah's rationalism and Zornberg's postmodern critique of the rebels:

> A famous midrash heightens the drama by suggesting that all the rebels deck themselves out in tallitot she-kulan techelet, prayer-shawls that are entirely made of blue thread. In place of the single blue thread that is commanded and that signifies a slender link with the transcendent (sea, sky, the throne of glory), they stand flaunting a total holiness – heavenly blue as far as the eye can see – and taunt Moses: "Do *these* garments still require a thread of blue?" Their sarcasm is clear: in the face of the oceanic holiness of the people, how can you insist on the *difference* of a particular man, or a particular family, or symbolic object? The image speaks louder than a thousand words in ridiculing and silencing Moses. What can be said in reply to the theatrics of totality? The rebels have, effectively, put an end to language.[59]

Besides reducing language to deconstruction and *différance*, which for Zornberg would protect the mystical sacredness of language from

Korah's rationalist (and levelling) logic, she sees Korah's revolt not just in egalitarian terms or Protestant ones but as a pantheistic revolt. Is Korah not only the first Protestant but the first Spinozist-Hegelian Marxist?

Zornberg goes further in citing the Midrash accounts about Korah. The suggestion is that Moses tried to reason with him: "With all these arguments, Moses tried to win Korach [*sic*] over, yet you do not find that the latter returned him any answer." Why won't Korah answer these unspecified arguments of Moses? As one Midrash reports, Korah was so wicked and selfish that if he did answer Moses, he admitted that "I [Korah] know quite well that he [Moses] is a very wise man, and will presently overwhelm me with his arguments, so that I will be reconciled to him against my will."[60] Zornberg says that for Korah, language itself is treacherous.[61] But as we see in Numbers 16, it is Korah who makes use of language; it is he who brilliantly and eloquently makes his case to Moses, while Moses can only bow his head in dismay. In an act of historical revisionism, worthy of an ecclesiastical whitewash, these accounts invert what happened in the actual biblical text.

Combining Maharal's remarks with Chesterton's critique of modern rationalism, Zornberg claims that Korah suffers from "a kind of manic rationality." It is a rationality that refuses to reduce itself to "metaphor … any indication of the human incompleteness that inspires language." Indeed, Korah is the consummate expression of a rationality that has not assimilated the truths of poststructuralism, since "he represents a resistance to language."[62] She also marshals Walter Benjamin, Jacques Lacan, and Julia Kristeva to condemn Korah as unable to handle ambiguity. He is "allergic to voids." His entire revolt is construed as profound "disorientation" in the face of the messiness of the world. If Korah is the logic of sameness, then Moses and YHWH promote the logic of difference.[63]

Thus, Zornberg enlists an entire postmodern canon to defend the traditionalism of Moses and Aaron against the rationalist impulses of Korah. But she makes it clear that this postmodern logic of difference is not necessarily a friend of democracy. As the young Marx argued, scepticism about reason tends not to be democratic; more likely, it favours conservatism. If there is no basis in reason to criticize the status quo, then one might as well leave the status quo alone.[64] The postmodern position of Zornberg resembles the philosophy of Sextus Empiricus or the Christian Pyrrhonists of the sixteenth century; their respective emphases on incompleteness, ambiguity, and difference made them better patriots (as in the case of Sextus) or better defenders of the Catholic Church (as in the case of Erasmus and Montaigne) against rationalists and Protestants.[65] Thus, as Zornberg shows, one can use sceptical postmodernism to justify the Mosaic Leviathan on deconstructive grounds and to justify the suppression of democratic dissent as represented by Korah. For instance, Zornberg never challenges the swallowing up and incineration of Korah and his clan as unjust, although she cites the rabbinic sages as wondering if Korah's children really died or whether they did not instead become singers in the temple.[66]

Spinoza avec Korah

In his *Theological-Political Treatise*, Spinoza, as a renegade Hobbesian in some ways himself, inverts Hobbes's own pro-Mosaic narrative in *Leviathan*. Spinoza critically takes the side of the Israelite masses against the usurping Levite priesthood. This is clear in certain passages from chapter 17 of the TTP, on the character of the Hebrew state in the time of Moses, which includes the chapter description "on the reasons why this divine state could perish, and why it could scarcely exist without sedition."[67] As Lewis Feuer notes, it is not only Numbers that informs Spinoza's discussion but also Josephus's *Antiquities* with its stress on sedition.[68]

Spinoza traces the seeds of decline of the Hebrew state to the golden calf episode, after which the firstborn Israelites were rejected and declared unclean in favour of the Levites. The latter would take the place of the former in terms of wielding the authority of the "sacred ministry."[69] Spinoza is perplexed that God would want to punish anyone out of a sense of vengeance, or even erect laws "to avenge himself and punish them [the firstborn]." Because the nature of God is no different than nature for Spinoza, and God's decrees are tantamount to the laws of nature, he cannot abide these anthropomorphic deficiencies.[70] Thus, these laws imposed on the Israelites were not real laws, but mere "penalties and punishments." Spinoza anticipates a historical-materialist view (or what Machiavelli once called a "judicious reading") when he argues that these laws are not from God but from the Levite priests, including the laws mandating "all the gifts they [the people] were obliged to donate to the Levites and the priests, their obligation to redeem their first-born and pay a poll-tax in silver to the Levites, the exclusive privilege of the Levites to approach whatever was sacred."[71]

If the Hebrew state was consistently set up "according to its first design, all the tribes would have retained equal right and honour, and everything would have proceeded in complete security." But such structural asymmetries opened the Levites up to constant criticism and protest. Equality would have meant that "all the tribes would have remained far more closely bound to each other, that is, if all had had an equal right to administer the sacred things."[72] Is this not the rhetoric and logic of Korah himself?

Spinoza then switches from the Torah to what he calls the histories, which according to Feuer are Josephus's *Antiquities*. The people who weren't the common folk but from the upper echelons of the Israelites began to resent the "priestly election." They began to "foment the view that Moses was setting up these institutions not by divine command but simply as he pleased, since he had chosen his own tribe over the others and conferred the right of priesthood forever on his own brother."[73] It is worth quoting Spinoza's rendition of Numbers 16 in the TTP: "So they [Korah and company] instigated a commotion and went to see him [Moses], claiming they were all equally sacred and that it was not right that he should be elevated above all the rest. Nor was there any way that he could pacify them; however, via a miracle [in chapter 6 of the TTP, Spinoza argues that miracles are not real] which he invoked as a token of his high standing with God, they were all annihilated."[74] But suppressing Korah's revolt did not end the rebellious nature of the people. There "arose a new and more general sedition of the whole people; for the people believed that those men had been destroyed not by God who was their judge but rather by the craft of Moses." This suppression of revolt, stemming from the violent affirmation of a priestly elect, demoralized the Israelite nation. Moses did not create stability, and the demoralization of the people meant that this suppression was more a "case of sedition lapsing than of harmony being established."[75] Spinoza quotes from Deuteronomy 31:27, highlighting Moses's lament that after his death, the people will stop worshipping God and rebellions will continue.

The decay of the Hebrew state had its seeds in turning itself into a royal court: "All the tribes were no longer fellow citizens under the divine law and the priesthood but under kings. This was a major cause of further subversion, which in the end brought about the fall of the entire state."[76] The Levites forbade the kings or any subjects from handling divine matters, sowing further division and driving the people to worship other gods outside the authority of their priests. This also meant that after a prophet conferred power onto a king, his successor sons would rebel against the priesthood, clamouring for more power. For Spinoza, the Bible shows that the Hebraic monarchy was an unstable institution, exacerbated by its separation from the prophets. New prophets constantly arose and denounced the kingdoms of Judah and Israel as wayward from God, always waiting for new kings to reign.[77] The whole condition of the Hebrew state thus was divided against itself and could not stand: "For what could be more insupportable to kings than to reign on sufferance or have to put up with a state within the state?"[78] This also made the state increasingly vulnerable to foreign attack, inevitably leading to the destruction of Jerusalem by the Babylonians at the end of the sixth century BC.

Marx the Levite

Not all the rabbinical literature puts Korah in such an awful light. Indeed, in one account, Korah's spiritual egalitarianism is united with a conception of social equality. Korah starts his rebellion by connecting his larger project with the socio-economic resentment of the people. Korah remonstrates with the masses, arguing how Moses "has laid upon all the children of Israel heavy burdens and given them laws which are very severe." He calls attention to the fate of a poor widow who is so burdened by God's commandments that she faces starvation. As Kirsch recounts this Kafkaesque story:

> The law of Moses forbids her to sow her field with two kinds of seed or to reap the corners of her field and yet commands her to tithe to the priests, and so she is forced to sell her land in order to meet her obligation. With what is left of the proceeds, she buys two sheep, but then Aaron shows up and demands the firstborn sheep for himself. "All firstlings," he reminds her, citing the Mosaic code, "thou shalt sanctify unto the Lord thy God." When she slaughters the remaining sheep, he shows up again and demands "the shoulder, the two cheeks and the maw as his share." And when she seeks to evade his latest demand by declaring that the animal has already been devoted to God, Aaron seizes both sheep. "If such is the case, then all is mine, for everything in Israel belongs to the priests," says Aaron to the poor widow.[79]

In this tale, Korah sounds like a socialist. He says the following, in a statement worthy of the Hebrew prophets: "Thus, the priests are always despoiling the poor, the widows and the orphans. When the children of Israel are asking them: why are ye acting thus? They reply: because such is the Law!"[80]

Marx himself was no stranger to biblical imagery and was intimately familiar with the Lutheran Bible, as S.S. Prawer makes clear in his book *Karl Marx and World Literature*.[81] Marx's comments about Moses can wax sarcastic; for instance, in *Capital*, the capitalist law of accumulation – that is, the profit motive to accumulate the value produced by the workers themselves – is mocked as a Mosaic commandment: "Accumulate,

accumulate! This is Moses and the Prophets!"[82] One notices the pun here of "Prophets" and "profits." But not all Mosaic imagery is appropriated by Marx as a means of derision. When describing the revolutionary struggle of the proletariat, Marx understands the need for discipline and unity in its ranks and how long such a process can be before the workers are mature enough to take power. As he puts it in *Class Struggles in France* (1848), "the present generation is like the Jews whom Moses led through the wilderness. It has not only a new world to conquer, it must go under in order to make room for men who are able to cope with a new world."[83]

It is also interesting to note that the original surname of the Marx family was Levi and that Marx himself was descended from a long line of rabbis. Mordechai Levi, Marx's paternal grandfather, was an ordained rabbi and served as chief rabbi of Trier until his death in 1804. When Napoleon invaded Germany, French officials started calling Mordechai Levi in their documents "Marcus Levi" or "Marx Levi." Marx's father was called "Herschel Lewy" according to the 1801 census. But with the institution of the Napoleonic Code, Jews could now enter professional mainstream society, and in a document from the Imperial University of Coblenz in 1813, Marx's father was now known as "Henry Marx" or "Heinrich Marx." Shlomo Avineri notes, "It is still intriguing to speculate that had it not been for the French insistence that Jews embrace 'civil' surnames rather than variations on their patronymics, Karl Marx would have been born Karl Levi. Would a theory called 'Levism,' or later 'Levism-Leninism' have the same appeal and resonance as 'Marxism'? The haunting question 'what's in a name' may echo here as well."[84]

As for the class sociology of the wilderness, compared with Spinoza's reconstruction from the TTP, Marx does not have very much to say; we see Marx in the *Grundrisse* comparing Moses's legislation as relatively more humane in terms of landownership than modern agriculture. The Israelite families can at least subsist on the land without having to make it profitable in the capitalistic sense. And while Marx in other texts is critical of theorists who praise traditional societies against modernity wholesale, there is no mention of the persistence of slavery in the Hebrew state.[85] Indeed, before Marx composed this commentary, his friend, the poet Heinrich Heine, even went so far as to call Moses and Jesus socialists, but argued that Moses's socialism was moderate and (unlike the otherworldliness of Jesus) pro-property:

> No Socialist was more of a terrorist than our Lord and Saviour. Even Moses was such a Socialist; although, like a practical man, he attempted only to reform existing usages concerning property. Instead of striving

> to effect the impossible, and rashly decreeing the abolition of private property, he only sought for its moralisation by bringing the rights of property into harmony with the laws of morality and reason. This he accomplished by instituting the jubilee, at which period every alienated heritage, which among an agricultural people always consisted of land, would revert to the original owner, no matter in what manner it had been alienated.[86]

The Russian Marxist Anatoly Lunacharsky in his major work *Religion and Socialism* continued this line of justification from Heine to Marx, arguing that the law of Moses was proto-socialist in terms of wealth redistribution. Lunacharsky insisted that it was this social aspect that informed the writings of the Hebrew prophets.[87]

But neither Marx, Heine, nor Lunacharsky takes up Korah's cause explicitly.[88] However, within Western Marxism, there is an example of a pro-Korah approach in the work of Ernst Bloch. Bloch in his book *Atheism in Christianity* promotes "anti-Yahwism" and argues that there are two different and mutually opposing tendencies in the Bible. One tendency represents a reactionary god who defends inequality and hierarchy, and the other represents a divine avenger who will redeem the masses from oppression. This latter tendency is sometimes anticipated in the coming of a messiah. As the scholar Roland Boer comments, "In *Atheism in Christianity*, Bloch both uncovers the way ruling class ideologies have been imposed on the text and examines the patterns of subversive slave talk."[89] He identifies the "murmurings" in the wilderness as a form of this "subversive slave talk." But in terms of our discussion, Bloch is interesting since he is one of the few Marxist theorists who explicitly endorses Korah's revolt and is sensitive to its specific class dynamics.

Bloch highlights Numbers 16 as one of the most important moments of the Torah. It is here "and almost nowhere else" in the Bible that the political murmurings of the Israelite nation are described in detail. These murmurings go even beyond Korah since they represent a broader popular movement. Unfortunately, the Bible mentions only the leaders of the revolt, and it looks as if these leaders are merely involved in an intra-Levite power grab. But looks might be deceiving, and even though Bloch admits that this might be a palace guard revolution, the real upshot of the revolt is that it is directed against the priestly upper class. The ruling-class god YHWH acts accordingly: "Priest-God, the God of priests and ruling classes, shows his reflexes in the face of a practical revolt by more than the mere suppression of red legends." Under the pens of Ezra and Nehemiah, this god is no longer a mere god of war, but – in reference to modern counter-revolutionaries – a god of "white-guard terror."[90]

There is a cover-up here according to Bloch, with priestly fingerprints all over it. Korah and his followers are maligned as selfish and power-hungry, while the masses they represent are hidden in the shadows of the text. As Bloch speculates, this "despotic cult-God of the priestly caste was, in ever increasing reinforcements and interpolations, set the task of denigrating [the revolt]."[91] This is a god that stands for pure obedience (not unlike the zoo-like obedience demanded of Adam in Edenic "paradise"), and Bloch contrasts it to the god of universal liberation who "promises to lead the people out of Egypt, the land of slavery, and through the desert into the land of freedom."[92] Instead, the god of Numbers 16 is a deity of an institutionalized bureaucracy. This isn't a god immanent to its people, but a god of a transcendence "so intense that it can only be approached via priests and cult: one where punishment consists in the high-and-mighty displeasure of a Transcendence which can only be treated with the most submissive attitude of repentance and atonement."[93]

Unfortunately, Bloch himself was committed to a similar bureaucratization of revolution in his own lifetime, specifically as a one-time adherent of Stalin. While Bloch became more critical of Stalinism after his experiences as a Marxist professor in East Germany, he never saw the same struggle of Korah and the Israelites against an unjust bureaucracy as anticipating Trotsky's own struggle against the Soviet bureaucracy. Quite the opposite: in the 1930s, Bloch supported the Moscow show trials and accepted the amalgamated frame-up of Trotsky, Zinoviev, and Bukharin, much in the same way Numbers amalgamates Korah, Dathan, and Abirham – Levites and Reubenites – into one subversive horde to be violently suppressed. If Bloch wanted to rehabilitate Korah, there was no attempt from Bloch or the Soviet bureaucracy in its last days to rehabilitate Korah's "late descendant" Trotsky.[94]

Conclusion: Reading Korah against the Grain

In rehabilitating Korah's revolt, we are not arguing that this revolt happened in time and space, just as we cannot be 100 per cent sure that Moses existed. It is beyond the scope of what Machiavelli calls "judicious readings" (i.e., secular understandings) to treat any of these characters or events as certainly real. Judicious readings from Machiavelli to Marx apply to the Bible itself as a human document, which can function as a collection of stories, laws, practices, and philosophical ideas, all of which must be independently evaluated as either good or bad. These events in Numbers do illustrate actual historical and sociological conditions, but in mythic form.

Beyond issues of sociology, however, a political philosophy cannot be grounded in any mere text; it must be based on independent arguments and demonstrations. One can always ask how you know that you have the right book; and if you want to be convincing, you cannot merely harp on that book's supposedly revealed status. A textually immanent approach to the Bible itself will also fail to ground what we should believe and how we should act. Exegesis, no matter how sophisticated, is no substitute for philosophy. As various commentators from Spinoza to Paine have argued, the Bible is not a consistent document; any attempt to erect an orthodox position upon it, free of incoherence, is doomed to failure. One cannot maintain orthodoxy for texts that contradict themselves. And once we start judging things allegorically or in terms of multiple layers of meaning, then we truly treat these stories as precisely that: stories illustrating broader philosophical concepts and political ideas.

In returning to Korah, one cannot say the Bible, the Talmud, or the Midrash was right in terms of Korah's purpose or legacy. Korah's revolt can be evaluated only depending on the world view in question. As we saw above, depending on context, Korah's role can be rewritten to mean something completely different. For instance, was Korah an egalitarian freedom fighter, as only Ernst Bloch seems to accept (and not without reservations)? Or was he a pseudo-populist in the style of Cataline, as Josephus insists in his *Antiquities*? This seems to be equivalent to asking: Is a character from Shakespeare or a recent television show inherently good or bad, reactionary or progressive? Perhaps, in the same manner as the rabbinic sages, we can write fan fiction to recast Hamlet as the villain and Uncle Claudius as the hero. There is nothing stopping us from recycling such stories – biblical or otherwise – just as nothing stopped the ancient world from rewriting the Greek titan Prometheus as a humanitarian in Aeschylus's plays or as an elitist in Ovid's poems. However, there is a sharp line between a literary image (which as a mere image is itself neutral) and the idea that animates such images. Finding where that line is is a key task in any conceptual-textual analysis.[95]

For those committed to the cause of egalitarian political philosophy, Korah's revolt seems like a great illustration of it, even perhaps one of its first illustrations. Korah has been read over the centuries as a proto-congregationalist (if not the first Protestant), a Spinozistic democrat, a socialist rabble-rouser, and as the first Left Opposition to a regime that promised human emancipation. Korah's revolt can be used to illuminate other contexts, even centuries beyond the events narrated in Numbers 16. What he signifies is not reducible to what the rabbinic sages, Moses, Aaron – or even God – said. Korah may be imaginary, but the universalistic and progressive impulses he represents are real in relation to the human condition and world history. In that regard, we can also appreciate Korah as the first modern political philosopher. From a literary and historical perspective, modernity starts with Numbers 16 in Korah's call for universal and equal access to the divine.

Chapter Four

The Moses Story in the Hebrew Bible: Puzzles and Paradoxes

Many claim that the Jews of the Old Testament do not act as God's chosen people ought to act. They kill the innocent, they renounce and betray the Lord, and it's hard to understand what's so special about them.[1]

The legislators of Connecticut occupied themselves first with penal laws; and, to compose them, they conceived the strange idea of drawing from sacred texts: "If any man [after legal conviction] shall have or worship any other God but the Lord God," they begin to say, "he shall be put to death." There follow ten or twelve provisions of the same nature, borrowed from the texts of Deuteronomy, Exodus, and Leviticus. Blasphemy, sorcery, adultery, and rape are punished by death; insult done by a son to his parents is struck with the same penalty. In this way they carried the legislation of a rude and half-civilized people into the heart of a society whose spirit was enlightened and mores mild; so one never saw the death penalty laid down more profusely in the laws, or applied to fewer of the guilty.

– Alexis de Tocqueville[2]

What is secular reason to make of the surpassingly odd and often incomprehensible text of the Five Books of Moses, with their wild variety of stories and teachings? As goes without saying, there is (as is also true of other religious traditions) a long Jewish tradition of commentary and debate aimed at making the incomprehensible comprehensible, the inscrutable scrutable. We have no desire to slight this tradition, though it is outside our competence to engage with it in any detail. But we would contest any notion that intra-Judaic commentary has any special, let alone exclusive, claim on this text. The Hebrew Bible is sacred for Jews, which is why they recite from it every Sabbath in their synagogues. But qua work of world literature, which it also is, it belongs to a universal community of readers of other faiths (or no faith) willing to put themselves in dialogue with an epic work of cultural vision that has left a permanent mark on world history. And as a work that has been seized upon by a long theory tradition as a vitally significant intellectual resource immanent to that tradition, theorists qua theorists also have the right (and probably the obligation) to ponder what this strange text is trying to teach. Political philosophy has a stake in the Five Books of Moses because, even if the Hebrew Bible is the product of multiple hands, and even if we have no idea who those authors were or when they composed their various contributions, they collectively articulate a comprehensive conception of human existence, including an authoritative regulation of life in all its moral, social, and political dimensions, and hence assert normative claims, implicit or explicit. Those normative claims are of universal relevance, not just Jewish relevance, insofar as they assert, as they must, a binding normative vision of the right way to live. The notion that the Hebrew Bible's god is a god both for the Jews and for the whole of humanity is one of that book's most intractable paradoxes, and one that we may never resolve,[3] but it is sufficient to open the door to the essentially universalistic form of inquiry into the good for human beings as human beings that is political philosophy.

What follows is a deliberately naïve engagement with the text that brackets what might be made of it within the horizon of Jewish piety. We embrace what Machiavelli memorably called a "judicious reading" of the Hebrew Bible – meaning a reading according to political (= secular) imperatives rather than sacred or religious or theological imperatives. Secular reason is surely entitled to its own reading, and while the two authors of this book happen to be Jewish (at least by upbringing), we read this text through secular eyes, for which we make no apology. Read as such, the Hebrew Bible is full of deep and inscrutable puzzles and riddles. Here is a partial list of some of the most obvious ones related to the figure of Moses.[4]

The Hubris of Moses

How could Moses think that it's appropriate to get into debates (sometimes quite heated ones) with the supreme Lord of the universe? Recall Numbers 12:3's assertion that Moses is "more [humble] than any person on the face of the earth."[5] Would a person that humble have the chutzpah to attempt to out-argue God? And how is it that Moses sometimes *wins* those debates? Isn't that pretty weird? (There is precedence for this, of course, in Abraham's earlier attempts to negotiate with God, also sometimes successfully: notably his haggling with God, in Genesis

18:16–33, over how many innocent souls it would take to spare the sinners in Sodom.) As Spinoza provocatively puts the point in chapter 2 of the *Theological-Political Treatise*, Moses's willingness to get into debates with God proves that Moses fails to "completely comprehend that God is omniscient, and that all human actions are governed solely by God's decree."[6] That is, having an argument with God implies that God is fallible, and how could Moses (or Abraham, for that matter) think *that*? The same question or difficulty is formulated by Daniel Jeremy Silver as follows: "If God is just and dependable, what reason or right would anyone, even His holy man [namely Moses], have to ask Him to change His mind?"[7]

The Problem of Chosenness

If the Hebrew God is the one and only god, a universal god, a god of the whole universe, why does he choose a particular nation as his "chosen people"?[8] Martin Buber, for one, seems not to be bothered by the notion of a god who treats different nations differentially: "[YHWH] has always been a God who wandered with his own and showed them the way. But now he has been revealed to them afresh through the secret of his name, as the one who remains present with his own."[9] Yet isn't it both theologically and morally problematic for God to be presented as privileging one particular tribal nation as "his own," thereby implying that other peoples have a subordinate status? Michael Walzer has called the doctrine of chosenness an "embarrassment" for liberal and leftist Jews, which it surely is.[10]

And why this people in particular – who are characterized as "stiff-necked" (God's characterization of the Hebrews, Exodus 33:5, echoed by Moses, Exodus 34:9; Fox translates it as "hard-necked")[11] – a people constantly falling into sin or violation of God's law? Given divine omniscience, could it have been unexpected or a surprise to God that this people falls short of his covenant with them to the extent that it does? Why does this elicit his "wrath"? In fact, he keeps threatening to "consume" (i.e., exterminate) them en masse! Assuming he knew in advance that this would be the outcome of giving privileged status to the Hebrews, why didn't he simply choose another nation for this privileged status? Or even better: treat all nations as equal? Spinoza's statement of his position on the question of the Hebrew Bible's emphatic particularism, or at least its highly imperfect universalism, strikes me as unanswerable: "Surely [the Israelites] would have been no less blessed if God had called all men equally to salvation, nor would God have been less close to them for being equally close to others, nor would their laws have been less just or they themselves less wise if those laws had been ordained for all men."[12]

One may also ask: Wouldn't the Hebrews have been much better off (i.e., less vulnerable to God's fury) if there had been no covenant? Thomas Pangle and Timothy Burns, in their commentary on the Hebrew Bible in chapter 4 of *The Key Texts of Political Philosophy*, suggest that the Hebrews are forcibly set apart as "a single, exemplary, chosen people" in order to instruct humankind by means of "the terrible tests to which this chosen people is put."[13] The exemplariness of the Hebrews, as Pangle and Burns formulate it, consists in undergoing "a long and painful process of humiliating and purifying education" in order to be properly humbled, thus gaining genuine awareness of humanity's utter subordination to God. If so, chosenness can indeed appear as curse rather than blessing. Consider Max Weber's judgment: "It is a stupendous paradox that a god does not only fail to protect his chosen people against its enemies but allows them to fall, *or pushes them himself*, into ignominy and enslavement, yet is worshipped only the more ardently."[14] John Bright, in his *A History of Israel*, makes a kindred observation: during the Babylonian exile, "it must have occurred to many of [the Hebrew exiles] to wonder whether Yahweh, patron God of a petty state which he seemed powerless to protect, was really the supreme and only God after all."[15] Arguably, the chosenness of the Hebrews entails many disadvantages and few advantages. In the apt words of Walzer: "All that we were chosen for was trouble."[16] YHWH, throughout the Hebrew Bible, is very vocal in voicing his complaints about the chosen people failing to fulfil their side of the covenant. But what about the other side of the equation – namely the possibility of a legitimate grievance on the part of the chosen people toward YHWH? It bears remarking here that the Promised Land pledged to the seed of Abraham, as traced out in various biblical texts (Genesis 15:18; Numbers 34:1–12; Ezekiel 47:15–22), is never delivered by YHWH to the Israelites in its entirety *at any time*, let alone in perpetuity.[17]

Rousseau, in *The Social Contract*, book 4, chapter 8, distinguishes between national gods (= polytheistic gods) and the singular god of monotheistic religions. But as Rousseau rightly suggests, the Hebrew God is *both* a monotheistic god *and* a national god.[18] This is a paradox – in fact, a paradox of monumental proportions. Perhaps the biggest question raised by the Hebrew Bible is: How can Judaism expect to have it both ways? Repeatedly, in the negotiations between Moses and Aaron on the one side and Pharaoh on the other, God is referred to as "YHWH, the God of the Hebrews" (Exodus 7:16, 9:1, 10: 3). In Exodus 6:7, God says: "I will take you for me as a people ... And you shall know that I am YHWH *your* God." That is, he announces himself as a *national* god: one god among other national gods – the singular God of the Hebrews over against the multiple gods of the Egyptians (and of other nations). Or consider Moses's statement in Exodus 33:13: "This nation is indeed your people!" And what is primarily at stake in the narrative is: *Whose god is stronger?* One gets the same implication in other such texts: for instance, Exodus 15:16: "Who is like you among the gods, O YHWH!" and Exodus 18:11: "YHWH is greater than all the gods." The clear suggestion is that there is a *plurality* of gods, among whom the Hebrew God is the most powerful and most fearsome. Judaism is *supposed* to represent the birth of monotheism.[19] But paradoxically, this monotheistic god inhabits a relentlessly polytheistic neighbourhood. If the universe were genuinely monotheistic, there would be no rival gods to triumph over.

Moses as Criminal

Moses, early in the story, commits an extrajudicial murder and flees into exile to escape punishment for this murder. Odd choice for the elected instrument of God's mission for the Hebrews?[20] Consider Robert A. Paul's astonishing suggestion in his brilliant book *Moses and Civilization* that "looked at from the post-Sinaitic viewpoint the primal rebellion of Moses [against Pharaoh as father/god/king] *has violated almost every one of the Ten Commandments*." According to Paul's Freudian interpretation, "the son rose against his father, god, and king to take for himself what the father had (abusively) held for himself; he thus denied the deity of his father, took his name in vain, failed to honor his father and mother, murdered, committed adultery by conspiring to take the father's wives, stole, and coveted his father's possessions."[21] "Moses also lied, in claiming that he wished, not to take the Israelites permanently out of Egypt, but to retire to the wilderness to perform a religious ritual."[22]

Idolatry as the Cardinal Sin

The signal act of Mosaic rulership is Moses's decision to order the Levite (priestly) tribe[23] to carry out an execution of three thousand members of the other eleven tribes as punishment for the supposed sin of idolatry.[24] Idolatry is a sin according to the inviolable laws laid out in the Ten Commandments. It is, it appears, a much bigger sin in the Hebrew Bible than murdering people by way of punishment for idolatry. Why? (It's worth noting that on the list of ten commandments, the ban on idolatry is number one and number two, whereas the prohibition of murder is number five.)

The Culpability of Aaron and His Exemption from Punishment

The golden calf was Aaron's idea. So why doesn't this disqualify him from becoming high priest? For that matter, why isn't he executed, given that thousands of Israelites who were implicated in the episode of the golden calf *are* executed to punish them for idolatry? Deuteronomy 9:20 informs us that Aaron is a particular target of God's wrath: "With Aaron, YHWH was exceedingly incensed, (enough) to destroy him, but I interceded also on behalf of Aaron at that time."[25] This is a clear recognition of Aaron's culpability in probably the main or most serious episode of Israelite insubordination. God gives in to Moses's pleas on Aaron's behalf for his brother to be spared. Fair enough. But of course, Aaron doesn't just get let off the hook for a crime for which others suffer capital punishment; he gets elevated to a position of supreme religious authority within the Mosaic religion! Why is idolatry a sin anyway, apart from the vanity and jealousy of the Hebrews' god? Even God himself describes himself as jealous! (See Exodus 34:14 and Numbers 25:11, for instance.) Isn't jealousy a vice?[26]

In Exodus 32:35, the golden calf is referred to as "the calf that Aaron made"![27] Why isn't he the first to suffer for the idolatry? To make matters worse, Aaron directly lies about it to Moses: Exodus 32:24: "I threw it into the fire, and out came this calf." But in Exodus 32:4, we are told that Aaron "fashioned it with a graving-tool" (i.e., it was cast in a mould).[28] So its taking the shape of a calf wasn't generated spontaneously out of the fire. Worse still, Exodus 32:25 suggests that the mutiny against Moses, the putting down of which Hobbes says requires the execution of three thousand Israelites, is instigated, or at least encouraged, by Aaron.[29] The guy is a traitor as well as an idolator! It is hard to disagree with Joep Dubbink's judgment: "The most problematic aspect [of the golden calf story] is the role of Aaron [who] goes on later to be the High Priest as if nothing had happened."[30]

Of course, somewhat similar considerations apply to Moses's other sibling, Miriam. She, no less than Aaron, participates in the revolt against Moses narrated in Numbers chapter 12, and she too gets off fairly lightly, at least relative to Korah, Datan, and Aviram in Numbers chapter 16, as well as the harsh fate meted out to Nadab and Abihu (Leviticus 10:1–2; Numbers 26:61). What is Miriam's punishment? She is cursed with leprosy,[31] along with banishment from the camp for seven days (Numbers 12:10, 12:14–15). But this relatively light punishment is not as jarring as the non-punishment of Aaron, for at least two reasons: First, Miriam is not directly complicit in the episode of the golden calf, as Aaron certainly is (or at least the Hebrew Bible gives us no indication of her complicity); and secondly, she doesn't hold the supremely high office occupied by Aaron within the Mosaic regime. "The anger of the Lord was kindled against them [= against both Aaron and Miriam]" (Numbers 12:9), yet Miriam gets stricken with leprosy (at least temporarily), whereas Aaron talks his way out of any punishment whatsoever, as he typically does.[32] Steffens's interpretation is an interesting one, even if it doesn't really resolve the puzzles one encounters in this story: "Miriam is called 'the sister of Aaron,' not of Moses, and she was a partisan, if not the prompter of the high priest's timid conspiracies. Evidently the Lord blamed her, since He punished her, not Aaron, for their treason … she was loyal, not to God and cause, but to a man: a brother, and, of course, not the strong brother, Moses, but the weak one, for whom her strength was ambitious."[33]

The Problem of Ex-slaves Retaining the Institution of Slavery

The Hebrews are liberated from slavery in Egypt by God and Moses. Yet they retain their own slaves. (See Exodus 21:2–10, 21:20–1, 21:26–7, and 21:32 as well as Deuteronomy 15:12.) Why would a people who themselves suffered under Pharaohic slavery not abolish that oppressive institution within their own community?[34] Walzer refers to "the reiterated argument that the experience of slavery in Egypt requires social justice in Israel."[35] Yet "social justice in Israel" obviously doesn't require the repudiation of slavery.[36] Defenders of slavery in the American South didn't fail to notice the conspicuous failure of the Hebrew Bible to declare a moral ban on the institution that they were defending. One prominent figure among them, George Fitzhugh, wrote, "We find slavery repeatedly instituted by God, or by men acting under his immediate care and direction, as in the instances of Moses and Joshua. Nowhere in the Old or New Testament do we find the institution condemned, but frequently recognized and enforced."[37] One wishes that Fitzhugh were wrong about this.

The Anthropomorphic Vices of the Hebrew God

Reading the book of Exodus easily conveys the sense of the Hebrew God as a big Donald Trump in the sky: vain, capricious, bullying, thin-skinned, a volcanic temper on a short fuse. That is, YHWH as the Hebrew Bible presents him has a recognizable "personality," although there are large inconsistencies in how this personality conducts himself (e.g., in relation to the chosen nation to which he sometimes offers providential care but that he sometimes threatens to wipe from the earth).

But this human-all-too-human inconstancy of the divine psyche is itself a very definite aspect of YHWH's personality as we come to encounter it in the pages of the Mosaic narrative. Why does God have (or why is he presented as having) all these anthropomorphic character flaws?[38]

Magic

It's fairly shocking (to me at least) just how large magic looms in the politics of the Hebrew Bible, very much including the politics of the Mosaic regime. God is a magician, forever pulling rabbits out of hats. And Moses is a magician, performing conjuring tricks enabled by God. Fox writes, "Magic as such was forbidden ... all over the Bible, as an attempt to manipulate God's world behind his back, as it were."[39] However, this abstracts, implausibly, from all the magic performed by God himself as well as all the magic performed at his instigation. In Exodus 34:10, God avows, "I will do wonders."[40] Why doesn't this count as magic? Consider Silver's suggestion that "in the Talmudic world miracle and magic are two sides of a single coin," and that according to Rabbinic Judaism's conception of *Moshe Rabbeinu* (Moses our rabbi), Moses, as "the agent of God's power," is "a magician."[41] Pharaoh, understandably, treats Moses's sorcery/miracles as on a par with the sorcery of his own priests, and it then becomes a contest between rival magicians, to see who has the more powerful magical tricks![42] Hence Pierre Bayle's account of the encounter between Moses and Pharaoh: "God has Moses perform astonishing miracles that are superior to the marvels of Pharaoh's magicians, and reduces this prince to the necessity of confessing that indeed the God of the Hebrews is the true God."[43] But the marvels don't cease when Pharaoh releases the enslaved Hebrews. Every time that the people doubt the wisdom of the political leadership that they're receiving, Moses gets God to pull another rabbit out of a hat. And whenever these magic tricks don't suffice, God metes out barbaric punishments, such as the collective stoning of someone deemed to have sinned against the divine law.

Ashley Walsh, in his book *Civil Religion and the Enlightenment in England, 1707–1800*, points out that Lord Bolingbroke, in common with Shaftesbury, saw Mosaic religion as simply a continuation of Egyptian superstition/priestcraft[44] – a view that on the face of it has more plausibility than many or most commentators on the Hebrew Bible seem willing to concede. But there are many scholars of the Hebrew Bible who seem determined to drive a firm wedge between the religion founded by Moses and the reliance upon magic associated with other types of religion in the ancient Middle East. Martin Buber is one notable example.

According to Buber, authentic experience of the divine name brings about "a demagisation of existence," and he claims that in contrast to Egypt, where "religion was in practice little more than regulated magic," "in the revelation at the Burning Bush religion is demagicized."[45] "Unlike the usual magician," according to Buber, Moses serves as foreteller of God's plagues upon the Egyptians "without any magical conjurations." Moses, he tells us, is "the man who experienced the futility of magic."[46]

Irving Zeitlin begins his book *Ancient Judaism* by citing Weber's theory according to which the ancient Israelites' rejection of magic marked a pivotal transition point in the direction of Western rationalism[47] – a theory that Zeitlin himself strongly endorses.[48] The "feats [of Pharaoh's magicians] were witchcraft and sorcery, the product of magical lore, techniques and secret arts. The wonders of Moses and Aaron, in contrast, were made possible by Yahweh and Yahweh alone."[49] Zeitlin later elaborates further: "The rod is not Moses' idea, for he is no mere magician as are his Egyptian counterparts. Why, then, does he resort at first to the appearance of performing magical tricks? The answer is that this is the beginning of a long process of education. One starts by speaking to the Egyptians in a language they readily understand – magic. One then proceeds from there to the really impressive acts of Yahweh."[50] Contrary to Zeitlin's efforts to distinguish Moses's tricks from those of Pharaoh's sorcerers, I am inclined to say more simply: magic is magic. Moreover, Zeitlin claims that the showdown between Moses and the Pharaoh's wizards was "not a contest between Yahweh and the Egyptian gods."[51] This claim too seems very questionable. Mary Douglas's discussion in chapter 1 of *Purity and Danger* is perhaps of some relevance here. Douglas suggests that there has been a long history within anthropology and sociology of valorizing the religion of the Hebrew Bible as the moment when human societies made the leap from magic (primitive) to ethics (civilized). For instance, she writes that for anthropologists in the tradition of William Robertson Smith, "magic was to the Hebrews what Catholicism was to the Protestants, mumbo-jumbo, meaningless ritual, irrationally held to be sufficient in itself to produce results without an interior experience of God."[52] Douglas's explicit purpose as an anthropological student of ancient Hebrew culture is to debunk this tradition.[53]

God's Visibility/Invisibility

Fox, in his commentary, offers a distinction between "visible gods/ magic and an invisible God,"[54] with the implication that the two issues (magic or the rejection of magic, the visibility or invisibility of God) are related or intertwined. But God is hardly invisible in many parts of the biblical narrative. Consider Exodus 33:23 as one example: "Then I will remove my hand; you shall see my back, but my face shall not be seen."[55] This is not invisibility! In Exodus 24:10–11, God is "seen" not only by Moses but also by Aaron, by two of Aaron's sons, Nadab and Abihu, and by seventy of the elders of Israel (KJV: "They saw the God of Israel").[56] And in the very last verse of Exodus (40:38), God appears "before the eyes of all the House of Israel" as by turns cloud and fire.[57] This too is not invisibility. Again, Fox is surely distinguishing more sharply between the pagan cults and the Hebrew cult than the text warrants. Martin Buber writes that the Hebrew God "is invisible and 'lets Himself be seen.'"[58] This is a good encapsulation of the basic contradiction, though Buber apparently doesn't see it as a contradiction.[59]

Eli Zaretsky, in the *Moses and Monotheism* chapter of *Political Freud*, makes an important observation related to this theme of visibility/invisibility. He points out that precisely in the context of punishing the Hebrews for wanting a god (the golden calf) that they could "see, touch, and feel," *Moses himself* asked to look at God – a request that naturally was refused.[60] The relevant text is Exodus 33:18: "Then [Moses] said: Pray let me see your Glory," eliciting the following response in Exodus 33:20: "But [God] said: You cannot see my face, for no human can see me and live!"[61] This actually contradicts Exodus 33:11: "And YHWH would speak to Moses face to face, as a man speaks to his neighbor."[62] That is, Moses himself was exposed to the very same temptation to have a god available to sensory perception for which he (severely!) punished the adherents of the Mosaic religion. Similarly, Spinoza, in chapter 2 of the *Theological-Political Treatise*, points out that Moses's expression of a desire to behold God proves that he "believed that God was visible, that is, visibility was not in contradiction with the divine nature."[63] If *Moses* could believe this, surely it undermines the presumption that the Hebrew God is distinguished by his unique unavailability to sensory perception! And it's particularly hard to see how the invisibility of God could be central to Judaism if Moses, the pre-eminent Hebrew prophet, believed otherwise (as he evidently did, according to the biblical text).

The question of the visibility/invisibility of the Hebrew God, of whether he is accessible to sensory apprehension, is also a big issue for Spinoza in chapter 1 of the *Theological-Political Treatise*.[64] Spinoza insists that Moses communed with God in a body-to-body (= corporeal) fashion, as opposed to God's relationship to Christ, which is mind to mind (= incorporeal).[65] Admittedly, he acknowledges, "Here lies some mystery."[66] Still, this seems a quite odd argument for Spinoza to make, given his own emphatically intellectual conception of God. It would seem that this is Spinoza's way of asserting the philosophical superiority of the New Testament to the Old Testament. I think one can probably state the point more forcefully than that: we are more or less obliged to interpret the text as Spinoza's way of impugning the primitiveness of the Hebrew conception of God (relative to Christianity), even if this conception looks like a decided improvement relative to the pagan cults, with their directly sensory gods. Spinoza lays this out pretty explicitly when he suggests that the Christian revelation is rational or intellectual in a way that the Hebraic revelation isn't, because the Christian revelation is conveyed "through the mind of Christ," whereas the Mosaic revelation is conveyed "through an *audible* voice."[67] That is, Hebrew prophecy, *even in its highest instance* – namely the prophecy of Moses – is merely "imaginative," not rational or intellectual, according to the crucial distinction that it's the purpose of chapter 1 of the *Theological-Political Treatise* to formulate. This account in Spinoza is diametrically opposed to Freud's account of the Mosaic religion, as presented in Zaretsky's chapter on *Moses and Monotheism*.[68] Freud sees Mosaic monotheism as uniquely "intellectual" or "spiritual" (i.e., rigorously oriented toward "conceptual thought"), on account of its prohibition on images (*Bilderverbot*).[69] Again, I am inclined to side with Spinoza against Freud: The Hebrew God really doesn't seem to exemplify the purity of strict invisibility that the ban on images would ostensibly imply. He is *seen* and *heard*, at least to some degree and on some occasions, even if it's always an attenuated visibility or perceptibility. In any case, this obviously remains a very important issue (or set of issues) for any serious reading of the Five Books of Moses.

The Theocratic Character of the Mosaic Regime

Probably the key question with respect to the Mosaic regime is to what extent it counts as a theocracy. Tellingly, the laws are more oriented to "sins" than to "crimes." What matters morally and politically is not observing fidelity to fellow citizens as partners in political community but observing fidelity to the covenant with God that defines the Hebrew nation as the Hebrew nation. Moses is hardly ever presented as taking political actions or making political decisions without consulting God, negotiating with God, or having God looking over his shoulder. God never seems to turn his attention in other directions, taking a break from preoccupation with the deeds or misdeeds of the Israelites. It's as if the performance of this particular people in upholding the covenant absorbs his "every waking moment," so to speak. The question of the prerogatives of the priestly class, and of Aaron as supremely privileged priest in particular, is often central to conflicts over Mosaic authority. If God withdrew his patronage of Moses (or had never granted this patronage in the first place), Moses's political authority would dissolve immediately.[70] This is not what secular political rulership looks like! Why would any theorist not thoroughly committed to a theocratic vision of politics see anything exemplary in Mosaic politics or the Mosaic regime? But as we've already seen in earlier chapters, a large number of anti-theocratic thinkers in the theory canon clearly do. We need really to ponder the profound paradox of a tradition of anti-theocratic theorizing, from Machiavelli to Harrington to Rousseau, that nonetheless places Moses in a pantheon of founder-heroes, as the modern republican tradition does.

There is one huge cleavage between theocratic politics and secularist politics that I will explicate as follows. (It is possible to consider it a variation on Locke's argument for a principled secularist politics in his *Letter Concerning Toleration*.) If we are trying to decide whether to build expressways or public transit, or to decide whether to give high priority or low priority to policies aimed at addressing climate change, or to decide whether to pursue a multilateral foreign policy or a unilateralist one, there are in principle tangible worldly outcomes that will eventually tend to vindicate one side or the other. The quality of these outcomes will always be contested by people with opposing political convictions, but there is at least something in the world to which one can appeal in pursuing these debates.[71] The case is quite otherwise, it seems to me, when we attempt to guide political life according to appeals to the realm of divinity (appeals to *God's* preferences, in effect). When Moses, in chapter 31 of Numbers, invokes divine authority in launching genocidal warfare against the Midianites, there is obviously no independent way of testing whether Moses's god, or any god, really wants this. We have seen something similar in our own time: ISIS – the most horrifying version of theocratic politics imaginable, claiming divine sanction for crimes no less brutal than those in Numbers chapter 31. When Barack Obama decided in favour of military intervention against the then-caliphate in Iraq and Syria, he gave a TV address on 10 September 2014 in which he stated quite confidently that the Islamic State "is not 'Islamic' … and [it] is certainly not a state."[72] Unfortunately, there was a problem with this pronouncement. One has to ask: How was Obama equipped to settle the *theological* question of which is more authentically Islamic – the Islam of contemporary liberal Muslims or the Islam of the conquering caliphs of early Islamic history? God or Allah doesn't speak to any of us, so it is an intrinsically open question whether he prefers the liberal Muslims of today or the illiberal Muslims of the seventh century. There's no way of independently adjudicating this. This, to be sure, is an extreme example of why it is problematic to base political claims on theological claims, but in fact it applies to *all* attempts to found a politics on a theology. Christian pacifists who assert that God demands that we desist from all wars face exactly the same problem: appealing to what God requires of us is politically problematic because it's epistemologically problematic, basing its politics on something that is intrinsically unknowable. It's unknowable *both* because we can't know if there is a god *and* because if there *is* a god, we can't know – apart from the dogmatic claims of non-universal religious traditions – what that god actually wants. God may be a warmonger, as Moses and Joshua seemed to believe and as the late Abu Bakr Al-Baghdadi also believed; or he may be a pacifist, as Christ believed and as Stanley Hauerwas believes. We just don't know. This gives us good reason to found our politics on desirable worldly outcomes that are available to public or intersubjective inspection rather than on invisible or inscrutable divine predilections. Bringing religion into politics requires us to do something that we are in principle incapable of doing: adjudicating among, in Salman Rushdie's vivid phrase, "fictional sky gods."[73] This is, I think, part of the reason why the great thinkers of the Enlightenment, starting with Spinoza in the *Theological-Political Treatise* and Locke in the *Letter Concerning Toleration*, committed themselves to a secularist political vision.

Montaigne, in his essay "Of Glory," suggests that all states, certainly all those encountered in the ancient world, are theocratic states and that the Mosaic theocracy was normatively privileged over those set up in the name of gods other than Moses's: "Every polity has a god at its head; falsely so the others, truly so the one that Moses set up for the people of Judea just out of Egypt."[74] Even Spinoza, proto-liberal that he is, acknowledges that there were ways in which Hebrew piety was helpful in significant measure in cultivating patriotism among the Israelites, and this acknowledgment obviously becomes an even more positive affirmation among other thinkers within the Western canon. Yet it's clearly the hope of anyone committed to a secularist vision of politics that it's possible to have a form of political community that engages civic allegiance and builds civic virtue without requiring that we put "a god at its head."[75]

The Theocratic Orientation toward Human Sinfulness

From a secular perspective, the politics of the Hebrew Bible is problematic simply by virtue of the heavy weight put on the category of sin by the biblical world view. But what constitutes sin? From an intra-biblical perspective, whatever the God of the Hebrews deems to be sinful (as presented in the Mosaic narrative) of course definitively counts as sin. There is no higher court of appeal to which one might resort. Moses has the status of a kind of super prophet; yet even his judgments of what counts as appropriate behaviour often get overruled, and he himself on multiple occasions gets convicted of "sin" by God. If God considered him fully virtuous – if he fully met the divine standard of virtue – then there would obviously be no reason to exclude him from the Promised Land as a kind of spiteful punishment on God's part.

There is a slew of problems from an extra-biblical perspective. First, consider a modest example: circumcision. Moses gets in big trouble with God because he is slow to circumcise his son, or so it seems, though the narrative is *extremely* compressed (Exodus 4:24–6).[76] Eventually the crisis gets resolved by Moses's wife taking it upon herself to circumcise the son. Still, Moses counts as having exhibited "sinful" behaviour, to the point where God is prepared to kill him (or again, so it seems). Why? Is circumcision morally required? The covenantal response would be yes. But morally required *for whom*? The answer is obviously: the Hebrews, as a nation and not as individuals.[77] Does the Hebrew God respect conscientious freedom of religious belief? No. The religion of the Israelites is a collective religion; hence membership in the religious community is *mandatory*. There is no "opt-out" clause.

Idolatry is another interesting example. Aaron Wildavsky quotes a scholar named Yehezhel Kaufmann as follows: "By making Israel enter a covenant with the one God, he made it a monotheistic people that alone among men was punishable for the sin of idolatry." "Before, idolatry was nowhere interdicted and punished."[78] According to Kaufmann's claim, God didn't threaten genocide against other nations of the ancient Near East (or elsewhere) for committing idolatry; but he does threaten this against the nation of Israel, as a privileged covenantal community.[79] That is: there are sins that do not apply (universally) to human beings as human beings but *do* apply to Israelites as Israelites. One could say (at least with respect to certain biblical texts) that other nations enjoy religious freedom that the Hebrews don't enjoy. In fact, there's a remarkable text in Deuteronomy (4:19) referring to the full panoply of pagan gods or pagan idols "whom YHWH has apportioned for all the (other) peoples beneath all the heavens"[80] (KJV: "which the Lord thy God hath divided unto all nations"). This suggests, astonishingly, that the Hebrew God is actually responsible for worship of non-Hebrew gods by non-Hebrews! One may also compare Deuteronomy 29:25, where the text also refers to YHWH's "apportioning" of the various gods[81] (KJV: "gods ... whom he had not given unto [the Hebrews]"), again as if the distribution of gods to the different nations is itself the work of the Hebrew God. And there seems to be a similar suggestion in Deuteronomy 32:8, at least as rendered by Fox and Alter (but translated differently in the KJV).[82] How are these texts consistent with Deuteronomy 32:39's assertion that "there is no god beside me"?[83] Why would YHWH be in the business of apportioning different gods to different peoples if he is the sole god?

This raises again a question broached earlier: Did God do the Hebrews a favour by making them his chosen people? Or is being the chosen people a kind of curse, a disadvantage in relation to other nations? The people of Israel get land, but to obtain this land, they have to forfeit a liberty of religion enjoyed by other nations, or at least *some* other nations. (Talking about "liberty of religion" is surely overstating the point: in Numbers 33:52, God orders the Hebrew army to "destroy" and "annihilate" all cultic representations of Canaanite religion.[84] So saying that he respects freedom of religion for non-Hebrews is in such texts strongly cast into doubt. In some cases YHWH is a tolerationist god; in other cases he emphatically isn't – corresponding roughly to Rousseau's helpful distinction between YHWH the national god and YHWH the jealous god. Further discussion is offered below under the rubric of "Are Non-Hebrew Religions Tolerated?")

Let's look at a more directly political example. God wants the Hebrews to invade Canaan (Numbers chapters 13–14).[85] They send out scouts to do reconnaissance. The scouts are not keen. From God's point of view, this counts as sinful. Meaning: if God wants the Hebrews to commit imperial conquest against nations that have done nothing to injure them, reluctance to do so counts as sin. Walzer, in *Exodus and Revolution*, puts overwhelming emphasis on the emancipatory dimension of the Mosaic exodus: the liberation of the Israelite slaves from oppression in Egypt as an archetype of revolutionary justice (which no doubt it is).[86] But of course this is only half the story of Mosaic politics. Consider this passage from Assmann's *The Invention of Religion*, a text that provides a good and important counterweight to Walzer's privileging of the emancipatory, justice-oriented aspect of the story:

> Liberation and invasion, revolution and colonization belong together as two sides of the same story. Just as the Israelites' exodus from Egypt forms the primal scene of revolutionary freedom movements, so too their conquest of Canaan, with the permission and indeed duty to drive out and destroy the original inhabitants, forms the primal scene of colonialism. Emigrant Puritans and Boers who saw themselves as God's chosen people identified Native Americans and Africans, respectively, with the

> Canaanites, as did the Spanish conquistadors upon encountering the Incas. Charles V "eased his royal conscience" by having chapter 20 of Deuteronomy read to him.[87]

Wildavsky, in *Moses as Political Leader*, consistently assumes that what the Bible declares to be sin is sin. But try explaining to someone who does not already subscribe to the Hebrew Bible as divine revelation why refusal to invade someone else's legitimately held territory counts as sinful.

Confiscation of Gentile Land

The texts are very clear that YHWH is responsible for "dispossessing" nations who occupy land in the Promised Land before the Hebrews arrive, and that what is dispossessed by God gets handed to his chosen people as an essential aspect of the covenant.[88] Consider the following three passages from the book of Joshua: "I [Caleb] will dispossess them, as YHWH promised" (14:12); "YHWH your God, he will push them out before you and will dispossess them from before you, so that you will possess their land, as YHWH your God promised you" (23:5); "YHWH your God has dispossessed before you nations great and numerous" (23:9).[89] The Hebrew Bible falls well short of an account that properly explains why land held by non-Hebrew peoples at the time of the Exodus in fact belongs to the Hebrews, apart from the fact that God chose to promise this land to his chosen people – although there are some unconvincing attempts at an explanation, discussed below.[90] And does it not seem sort of odd that the basis of the covenantal relationship between God and the Israelites is so directly territorial? Why does it matter to God whether a particular parcel of land belongs to one nation rather than another? The New Testament God offers individual salvation in an afterlife. The Old Testament God offers real estate. Same God? Donald Harman Akenson interestingly points out that covenantal cultures "strongly influenced by the Hebrew [conceptual] grid will be profoundly attached to specific pieces of land. This will not be mere land hunger, but land will be seen as sacralised, as holy, and as a Promised Land."[91]

Presumably, what God wants is automatically just. But why? Are the other nations unjust holders of territory in the Promised Land because they are sinners? But the Hebrews are sinners too! – as both God and Moses insist again and again. Why do dispossession and imperial conquest count as just simply because they correspond to the whims of a capricious god who happens to favour one particular nation over all other nations in that part of the world? What would we say about a contemporary society that invaded and dominated its neighbours by appealing to divine favour or a divinely ordained mission? Didn't ISIS do precisely that in its bid for conquest of Iraq and Syria?

We read in Deuteronomy 9:5 that "because of the wickedness of these nations is YHWH your God dispossessing them from before you."[92] This, I guess, is a rationale. Except that, again, the Hebrews, from both a divine perspective and a Mosaic perspective, are *also* guilty of wickedness. The context here (Deuteronomy 9:3–7) makes perfectly clear (in fact explicitly *emphasizes*) that the to-be-enriched land-acquiring Hebrews are *not* more virtuous than the to-be-dispossessed non-Hebrews. Lands held by the sinful are snatched away from them and ... donated to the sinful! Another relevant text is Deuteronomy 18:12: "Because of these abominations [namely magical pagan practices] YHWH your God is dispossessing them [the Canaanites] before you!"[93] That suggests that the basis of God's wrath against the Canaanites is not generic sin but their reliance on magic in particular – which raises the question of whether the religion of Moses is as innocent of magic as the Hebrew Bible suggests, a question that I've already attempted to wrestle with.

Deuteronomy 5:17 enjoins, "You are not to steal!"[94] Yet Deuteronomy 6:10–12 makes explicit that Israel is to enjoy the fruits for which others invested their labour: "Now it shall be when YHWH your God brings you to the land that he swore to your fathers, to Abraham, to Isaac, to Jacob, to give you, towns great and good that you did not build, houses full of every good thing that you did not fill, cisterns hewn out that you did not hew, vineyards and olive groves that you did not plant, and you eat and you are satisfied, take you care lest you forget YHWH who brought you out of the land of Egypt."[95] Contradiction? Or is Deuteronomy saying that it's okay for *God* to steal and hence okay for the Hebrews to receive the stolen goods donated to them by God? (God as "fence"?)

Moses or God as Source of the Hebrew Laws?

The privileged image of Moses within the civic-republican tradition is of course the image of Moses as *lawgiver*.[96] But relative to a faithfully biblical perspective, this view of Moses is blasphemous, since the "Mosaic" law, seen from an intra-biblical perspective, is *God's* law, not *Moses's* law. God is the lawgiver, not Moses, though Moses may be the vehicle by which God delivers his laws to the Hebrews. Hence it would seem that the civic-republican view of Moses and the biblical view of Moses are in necessary contradiction, as highlighted, for instance, in Walzer's claim that Moses as prophet and teacher "is how Moses is remembered in the Jewish interpretive tradition – not as a prince or a judge or even a 'founder' (though in first-century Alexandria Philo describes him as 'the best of all lawgivers in all countries, better in fact than any that have ever arisen among either the Greeks or the barbarians,' and Machiavelli and Rousseau arrive at a roughly similar estimate)."[97]

Interestingly, Hobbes, right near the end of *Leviathan*, states a very strong position on this issue, and indeed one that surely conforms to the intra-biblical view (as opposed to, say, Machiavelli's "judicious reading" and to all the civil-religionist successors to Machiavelli). He says: "In this [Hebraic] Kingdome Moses was Gods Lieutenant on Earth; and that it was he that told them what Laws God appointed them to be ruled by."[98] That is: the laws are *God's* laws, and Moses is simply the medium or spokesperson for transmission of those laws to the people.[99] Yet I confess that I'm pretty sceptical that Hobbes is here stating what he really thinks, since he lets us know with ample clarity in chapter 12 of *Leviathan* of his awareness of the old trick of statecraft whereby founders of new religions presented their precepts as proceeding not "from their own device, but from the dictates of some God … that their Lawes might the more easily be received."[100] Why would it be Hobbes's view that it would be any different in the case of the Mosaic law? This two-sided rhetoric is similar to Rousseau's in *The Social Contract*, book 2, chapter 7, when he affirms that "the Jewish law, which is still in existence," evidences a power and a grandeur that bespeak authenticity rather than imposture while having indicated to the reader in virtually the same breath that "any man can engrave stone tablets."[101]

Intermarriage

Exodus 33:16 asks, "Is it not (precisely) in that you go with us, and that *we are distinct*, I and your people, *from every people that is on the face of the soil*?"[102] What happens to this "distinctness" of the Hebrews when they intermarry with non-Hebrews and have children that, ethnically or tribally speaking, are partly Hebrew and partly non-Hebrew? (According to religious law, of course, the children are either one or the other, which helps to reinscribe the distinctness.) Does it follow from Exodus 33:16's appeal to distinctness that intermarriage between nations or peoples is normatively prohibited? Exodus 34:16 explicitly condemns intermarriage. So does Deuteronomy 7:3: "And you are not to marry (with) them!"[103] That sounds pretty categorical (though it's limited to the nations that Israel will be conquering, as distinct from nations that God doesn't command the Hebrews to conquer). Indeed, in Numbers 36:6–7 the Mosaic law strongly discourages intertribal marriage *among Hebrews*, let alone between Hebrews and non-Hebrews. But remember: *Moses himself* married a non-Hebrew, Zipporah, who, the Bible tells us, was a Midianite. Moreover, Numbers 12:1 refers quite clearly to Moses's having taken "a Cushite wife" (KJV refers to her as "an Ethiopian woman"), seemingly suggesting not just that he had two wives, *neither* of whom was Israelite, but that this second marriage was an *interracial* one.[104]

What do we make of all this? Relevant here is John Toland's highlighting of the "strong propensity [on the part of the ancient Hebrews] to mix or marry with the women of other nations, contrary to their fundamental Laws."[105] Walzer writes that "the biblical texts ... suggest a peculiar fear of alien women, the carriers of religious pollution."[106] Rousseau seems to endorse a similar policy, namely a ban on intermarriage, in chapter 3 of *The Government of Poland*: "les empêchera [les Polonais] de s'allier avec [les autres peuples]." Willmoore Kendall gives this a literal translation as "allying themselves" with other peoples,[107] but Rousseau likely has in mind the notion of "pairing up" with partners from other nations. Later in the same chapter, Rousseau urges cultivation of "an instinctive distaste for mingling with the peoples of other countries."[108] The French reads: "une répugnance naturelle à se mêler avec l'étranger." One of course can't rule out that he conceived these ideas about strictly enforced Polish nationality at least partly on the basis of what he found admirable about the regime of the ancient Hebrews, whose segregationist "customs and practices" are explicitly praised in the immediately preceding chapter.[109]

Numbers 12:1 warrants a bit more comment. The context is a revolt against Moses's authority on the part of his two siblings, Miriam and Aaron. It seems that their primary complaint against him is his partiality for non-Hebrew spouses. (Or perhaps they merely seize upon it as a handy wedge issue in their scheme to subvert his authority.) Yet God sides with Moses – and punishes Miriam, though, oddly, Aaron again escapes any real punishment. But the question is: Given the texts we have cited above (Exodus 33:16 and 34:16), why *isn't* this a legitimate complaint? Why does God apparently grant Moses an exemption to Moses's own laws? There is a genuine puzzle here. Isn't God's indifference to the complaint issued by Miriam and Aaron inconsistent with the law laid down in Exodus 34:16?

There's a larger issue as well, highlighted by an observation by Fox. Referring to the story of Balaam's ass (Numbers chapters 22–4), Fox writes, "The Torah uses [Balaam] (as the Bible may have used Job and other such personalities) for its own purposes, picking up a theme it has utilized earlier: the acknowledgment of God's power and Israel's glory by a wise or inspired pagan."[110] Fox then cites the figure of Jethro in Exodus chapter 18, as well as a few other examples later in the Hebrew Bible. Fox refers to Balaam as a "pagan prophet."[111] That tells us that there is such a thing as non-Hebrew prophets, which seems a little odd. In fact, Numbers chapter 22 records direct conversations between Balaam and YHWH. Even more jarringly, in Numbers 22:18, Balaam refers to "YHWH my God," as if he were in effect a kind of honorary Hebrew. (Incidentally, notwithstanding Balaam's status as a bona fide non-Hebrew prophet, he is eventually executed by the Hebrew army, as reported in Numbers 31:8 – more or less with the blessing of God, so it would seem.)

The larger issue here, it seems to me, is why the Hebrews, so single-mindedly focused on their own tribal identity and their own collective destiny, would incorporate in their sacred text significant stories relating to non-Hebrews. The puzzle is that the actual text of the Hebrew Bible seems a fair bit more *inter*-tribal, or more *pluri*-national, than the biblical normative vision or normative horizon "officially" is (if I can put it that way). Why aren't the stories exclusively intra-national? This, again, strikes me as a broader way of formulating the puzzle posed by the fact that there are transnational dimensions to Moses's own family. This, even apart from the fact of his Egyptian upbringing – to say nothing of Freud's speculations about Moses being himself non-Hebrew.[112]

I'd like to pursue this important theme just a bit further. This concerns the involvement of Moses's (multinational) family in the Mosaic regime. As flagged in a previous chapter, Harrington puts a lot of emphasis on the fact that Moses's senate of seventy elders was the brainchild of his father-in-law, Jethro (at least according to one of the two biblical narratives devoted to this issue: Exodus 18:14–27). Fox's phrase, "a wise or inspired pagan," nicely captures Harrington's view of Jethro. Harrington's disciple, John Toland, in *Hodegus*, his secularizing commentary on the Exodus story, offers an interesting and somewhat plausible theory according to which Jethro's son and Moses's brother-in-law, Hobab (rendered by Fox as Hovav), was in fact the one who guided the Israelites through the wilderness during their wanderings in the desert (obviously basing this interpretation on Numbers 10:29–36).[113] Let me note two relevant points here: First, the Mosaic regime, like the 2017–2021 regime of Donald Trump, was prominently staffed by members of Moses's own family, Aaron being the most visible but not the only example. But secondly, as regards the two other family members who seem to loom large in the Mosaic narrative, namely Jethro and

Hobab, they are emphatically identified in the narrative as *Midianites*.[114] Not to get too carried away with the Moses-Trump analogy, but this casts Jethro and Hobab in a role something like that of Ivanka Trump and Jared Kushner. Just to spell out what I have in mind (though again one should not get too carried away with it): In the Trump case you had a political leader whose defining signature was nativist rhetoric and not-so-subtle pandering to white nationalists; yet the two most powerful members of his family, who occupied advisory posts within his administration, were Jewish. In Moses's case, we have a political leader embodying a fundamentally tribal/national vision of life, yet prominent family-based figures within his circle were Midianite (i.e., non-Hebrew). My gloss, for what it's worth: Even in a world that seems rigorously divided up into warring nations (seemingly with God's blessing), life is a lot more multinationally or multi-tribally complex than one would expect.

Are Non-Hebrew Religions Tolerated?

Despite seeming tensions or contradictions sketched in the earlier section devoted to the theme of theocracy, it seems that in the end the God of the Hebrews (qua "jealous god") doesn't believe in religious toleration. This is powerfully expressed in Exodus 34:13: "Their slaughter-sites you are to pull down, their standing-pillars you are to smash, their tree-poles you are to cut down." "Standing-pillars" and "tree-poles" refer to the accompaniments of religious practices of other nations and are to be destroyed.[115] Other religions are therefore not to be tolerated, at least in the case of nations that Israel is instructed to expel or subjugate. It's exactly the same story in Deuteronomy 7:5 and 12:2–3 as well as Judges 6:25. What do we think of a god who rejects the principles of Locke's *Letter Concerning Toleration*?

The Seeming Arbitrariness of Divine Justice

Another big issue (maybe the biggest) is the arbitrariness of divine justice. Exodus 33:19: "I [God] show-favor to whom I show-favor [KJV: to whom I will be gracious] … I show-mercy to whom I show-mercy."[116] Put more colloquially: Don't tell me upon whom I should bestow justice! My will is subject to no higher authority! Can we speak of a just god if "justice" is determined by pure caprice on the part of a wilful deity? In one episode, God kills two of Aaron's four sons (nephews of Moses) on account of a minor slip-up in ritual performance (Leviticus 10:1–2 and Numbers 26:61). In another key episode, Moses and Aaron are denied entry to the Promised Land not because of a sin but because of what Fox refers to as an "indiscretion,"[117] though even when regarded as an indiscretion, it's fairly difficult to see exactly what they did wrong.[118] It almost seems as if God pulls these kinds of stunts just to prove that he is God, meaning that he can do whatever the hell he wants.[119]

Some Concluding Thoughts: The Hebrew Bible and Political Philosophy

In this book, we have surveyed a substantial variety of appropriations of the Hebrew Bible, encompassing political visions of very different hues. This certainly suggests a tremendous elasticity in the text, which has served as a pliable or Procrustean resource drawn upon by later thinkers to lend authority to political philosophies spanning a wide spectrum. Still, it is not a hopeless task to ask, prior to or in abstraction from all these appropriations, what the original text in its own voice seeks to contribute to the never-ending dialogue about the human good. It is not necessary to attribute a single authorship to the text (which would be wildly implausible) in order to see it as comprising an organic unity, more or less, in how it views the human condition in its normative dimensions. From a methodological point of view, I don't see a problem in principle with reading the Five Books of Moses just as I read Machiavelli's *The Prince* or Hobbes's *Leviathan* or Rousseau's *On the Social Contract*. In its own way, it's as strange and perplexing as those other defining texts of the Western canon.[120] And as with those other books, one tries to puzzle through its oddities and quirks and if possible exploit its more inscrutable, riddlesome aspects as a hermeneutical window into the vision of life that it articulates.

It is possible to deny that there is a political philosophy in the Hebrew Bible on the grounds that the vision of life that it articulates is insufficiently political. Clifford Orwin is a political theorist who has made precisely an argument of this sort. The argument is developed in an interesting and provocative response to Walzer's *In God's Shadow*.[121] Politics is about the self-rule of citizens and hence "necessarily tends towards the freedom of human beings from divine tutelage"; yet this is a freedom that the children of Israel never enjoyed. Politics was a Greek invention, and hence the life of the biblical Israelites was pre-political. "Politics in the strict sense is entirely alien to the Bible." This is an extremely strong claim, and it's difficult to see how it can be sustained. Plato and Aristotle privilege the polis, and Orwin does too. If commitment to the polis is what defines the standard for "politics in the strict sense," then millennia of political experience would have to be discounted. While Walzer himself recognizes the subordinateness of politics within the biblical horizon, as the title of his book makes clear, Orwin's denial of the politicalness of the Hebrew Bible is decidedly more radical than Walzer's.[122] Yet what we have in the stories of the Hebrew Bible manifestly speaks to an experience of rulership, of law, of collective deliberation, of battles for power and contests over supreme authority, and not least, of a striving for social justice.[123] As we know, Moshe Halbertal and Stephen Holmes go so far as to identify the book of Samuel as "the beginning of politics." And of course, if it were true that politics appears as entirely alien relative to the Hebrew Bible's vision of life, it would be hard to grasp why so many thinkers in the later theory canon see much in the Hebrew text that is regarded as exemplary within their own political philosophies and hence as having something important to teach the societies addressed by those later political philosophies.[124] Contrary to Orwin's view that the Mosaic way of life was in some basic sense pre-political, it seems hard to disagree with Buber's judgment that the historical Moses "does not differentiate between the spheres of religion and politics; and in him they are not separated."[125]

Is there a "political philosophy" in the Hebrew Bible? I would have to say yes.[126] An alternative view would be that the political-philosophic relevance of the Hebrew Bible is reducible to the sum of its appropriations in the subsequent (much later) theory tradition. But in principle it should be possible to judge an appropriation in relation to what has been appropriated. If one can appropriate the Hebrew Bible for political-philosophic purposes, it is likely to contain a political-philosophic vision of things in advance of any particular appropriation. In any case, if one sees a political philosophy expressed in the Five Books of Moses, the voice of this political philosophy is not Moses, who is presented as merely the servant or executor of God's intentions. The voice of that political philosophy is God. What is that political philosophy? The world of the Hebrew Bible is a world of warring tribes. God is not normatively neutral in the midst of these warring tribes. He takes sides. They fight over territory, and God both incites war on the part of one of these nations against other nations and intervenes to favour his chosen people (i.e., the nation he wants to win). YHWH as the Hebrew Bible presents him is a blatant warmonger (see, e.g., Deuteronomy 2:24). Couldn't a universal god urge peace among these warring nations? Couldn't his covenant involve "global governance"? But immediately upon release from slavery in Egypt, the Israelites are already an army ("went up armed": Exodus 13:18).[127] Exodus 15:3 tells us, "YHWH is a man of war."[128] Indeed he is! God tells us in Exodus 34:24, "I will dispossess nations before you, and widen your territory."[129] And the Israelites are told in Deuteronomy 3:22: "YHWH your God, he is the one who wages-war for you!"[130] Halbertal and Holmes point out that in 1 Samuel chapter 15, God withdraws support for the hereditary monarchy of Saul because Saul has failed to carry out with sufficient rigour the *herem* (genocidal holy war) that God had declared against the Amalekites.[131] Arguably, Deuteronomy 20:16–17 offers the clearest case of divine sanction for uninhibited genocide: "Of the cities of the peoples that the LORD thy God giveth thee for an inheritance, thou shalt save alive nothing that breatheth. But thou shalt utterly destroy them; namely, the Hittites, and the Amorites, the Canaanites, and the Perizzites, the Hivites, and the Jebusites; as the LORD thy God hath commanded thee."[132] We received a shocking reminder of the horror of genocide with the report in April of 2023 that the late Yevgeny Prigozhin, then head of the Wagner Group, had ordered his soldiers to murder Ukrainian children as well as their parents.[133] How can we not be shocked when we read in the pages of Deuteronomy that YHWH sometimes issues commands to the Israelites that are as brutal and heartless as those issued by Prigozhin to the Wagner Group?

Tribalism per se is problematic, and it's especially problematic in the context of normatively unchecked or unbounded warfare over contested territory. The Israelites of the Hebrew Bible are clearly tribalists in a very basic sense, and their god very strongly encourages and enforces that tribalism. They are committed to a view of the world as premised on the division of the world into essentialist tribes fundamentally in conflict with each other – and their god is as well! Lord Bolingbroke put the point very sharply when he wrote that the "whole tenor of the Jewish laws, took them out of all moral obligations to the rest of mankind."[134] I don't see how one can avoid acknowledging that that is a problem of large proportions for normative theory. The problem of the politics of the Hebrew Bible, I would say, is essentially the problem of tribalism (in the most literal sense, obviously) as a normative vision. The problem is powerfully highlighted by Akenson in *God's Peoples* when he points out that "covenantal societies" that model themselves on the ancient Israelites as a chosen people "are likely to set great store by the concept of group purity, either religious or racial or both. They will be given to quotations of the scriptural prohibitions on the mixing of their pure seed with the impure seed of lesser peoples."[135] However, even apart from the Hebrew Bible's distasteful emphasis on the theme of ethnic purity versus inter-ethnic contamination, it seems already questionable enough to have articulated a conception of divinity capable of favouring one particular people, to which it assigns special duties and privileges. The voice of piety will of course say that if this is how revealed scripture presents God, it is illegitimate for reason-guided political philosophy to claim to overrule this conception. Yet the whole enterprise of independent normative reflection, as embodied in the tradition of Western political philosophy from Socrates onwards, would be fatally impugned if it allowed itself to be subordinated to the supposedly higher authority of theology.

Let me say straight-up that, from my perspective, Spinoza, among the most important canonical thinkers, is especially exemplary in offering a normatively appropriate response to the Hebrew Bible. (My suspicion is that Spinoza's reactions to much of what he reads in the Hebrew Bible are akin to those we quoted from Thomas Paine in chapter 1. But Spinoza finds ways of intimating that critical stance without stating it explicitly in the way that Paine does.) To be sure, Spinoza has many positive things to say about the Mosaic regime.[136] Still, he fundamentally repudiates the tribalist horizons of the Hebrew Bible, namely the presentation of a set of images of God as a warrior god who sets off one particular nation as privileged over against other less privileged nations, and he decisively opts philosophically for the universalistic moral horizons of the New Testament over the particularist moral horizons of the Hebrew Bible.

Nietzsche famously sided with the Old Testament over the New Testament:

> I do not like the "New Testament," that should be plain; I find it almost disturbing that my taste in regard to this most highly esteemed and overestimated work should be so singular (I have the taste of two millennia against me): but there it is! "Here I stand, I can do no otherwise" – I have the courage of my bad taste. The *Old* Testament – that is something else again: all honor to the Old Testament! I find in it great human beings, a heroic landscape, and something of the very rarest quality in the world, the incomparable naïveté of the *strong heart*; what is more, I find a people. In the New one, on the other hand, I find nothing but petty sectarianism, mere rococo of the soul, mere involutions, nooks, queer things, the air of the conventicle, not to forget an occasional whiff of bucolic mawkishness that belongs to the epoch (*and* to the Roman province) and is not so much Jewish as Hellenistic.[137]

Many or most readers of Nietzsche have always quoted such a text as a vindication of Nietzsche, because they see it as establishing his credentials as an "anti-anti-Semite." I don't really read the text that way. It's Nietzsche's way of asserting a warrior philosophy in opposition to a pacifist and morally universalist creed. Nietzsche is supposed to be anti-nationalist (and in relation to garden-variety German nationalism, he certainly is). Yet he celebrates the peoplehood of the Hebrews: "I find a people." He reasserts the same judgments in *The Antichrist*: the cosmopolitanism of the Christians is to their discredit; the rooted nationhood of the people of ancient Israel is to their credit. Why would a principled anti-nationalist arrive at these judgments?[138] It's clearly Nietzsche's view that one has, at least in those parts of the Hebrew Bible that he likes, a particular political philosophy (i.e., a comprehensive articulation of the ends of human life) and that one has in the Christian half of the Bible an opposing political philosophy, and he confidently sides with one against the other. Think back to what we said in chapter 1 about Paine's shock and indignation about what he read in the pages of the Mosaic narrative. That, I think, gives one an apt measuring rod for weighing Nietzsche's diametrically opposed judgment.[139] What appeals to Nietzsche in the Hebrew epic is its robust and often brutal particularism, which offers a powerful encapsulation of what is most fundamentally at issue in political-philosophic reflection on the Hebrew Bible. What is at stake here is well captured in the fact that Nietzsche celebrates the Hebrew Bible for precisely the reason that Spinoza does the opposite.[140]

~

Finally, let us return to the contention between reason and revelation with which we started this chapter.[141] According to the defining Socratic mission of political philosophy as we've known it since Plato, we start from the fact that as human beings we naturally encounter claims to overarching normative authority from within our own cultural horizon (our "cave"), and it is the duty of one who participates in the philosophical tradition to submit these claims to authority to disciplined rational scrutiny. The natural tendency of any deeply rooted culture is to exalt the normative superiority of its own way of life, especially if that way of life is held to enjoy divine sanction. But how well do these claims stand up to disinterested examination? In the Jewish case, pretty clearly, an important part of what defines the tradition is a claim about the exemplariness of Moses as the ultimate founder-prophet, just as Christian civilization in an important measure rests its claim to moral authority on the exemplariness of Jesus and Islamic civilization in important measure rests its claim to moral authority on the exemplariness of Mohammed. Yet when one goes to Judaism's founding text, what one encounters is something less than the story of inspiring displays of civic virtue and unblemished justice that one might hope for; rather, what one encounters is a fairly bizarre and enigmatic account of Moses, and how he relates to his people, and how that people relates to the God of the Hebrews.

This is not meant to be a comfortable exercise, and it can provoke strong reactions. But living in a liberal society as we do empowers us to interrogate our culture (or subcultures within that culture) in a way impossible in pre-liberal societies, and we should fully avail ourselves of this "freedom to philosophise," as Spinoza called it.[142] Kant beautifully encapsulated the Enlightenment view of how reason relates to revelation when he wrote that in an age of *Kritik*, everything, including religion, must submit itself to rational scrutiny. It may seek to exempt itself by appeal to its sanctity, but then it awakens "just suspicion, and cannot claim the sincere respect which reason accords only to that which has been able to sustain the test of free and open examination."[143] It's in this spirit of the properly superior authority of human reason, running in common between Socrates and Kant, that we have put a series of basic questions to the Mosaic narrative, whereas biblical faith, by contrast, is likely perfectly content to tolerate the enduring paradoxicality or unanswerability of such questions.

Of course, there's an easy response to many of the challenges that we've raised, although I'd urge readers not to be too quick to embrace such a solution. It consists in saying: This was a tribal society that existed perhaps fifteen or sixteen centuries before the birth of Christ (hence far more than three thousand years before us). It's folly to expect the morality of that time to jive with contemporary moral standards. Take the Mosaic law about collective stoning of adulterers. That strikes us as utterly barbaric – and no less so when we have seen fundamentalist extremists like the Islamic State re-institute punitive practices of similar barbarity. Why should the Hebrew Bible be condemned by norms that were a product of its historical moment? As I say, that's a response that easily suggests itself, and it will be happily embraced by many who reflect on what's in the Bible. Why do I say that we should not be too quick to go that route? The Hebrew Bible presents its Mosaic law-code as of permanent validity – binding for at least as long as there is a Hebrew nation. Those who read those laws as emanating not from *Moses* (a human being) but from God – and countless people will read the text as actual revelation! – will be obliged to treat it as something far beyond a historically conditioned artefact of a particular human culture.[144] Let me say here that I lean strongly in the direction of Freud's view, as expressed at the beginning of chapter 2 of *Civilization and Its Discontents*, that efforts to offer rationalized and liberalized versions of religion will always ring hollow or fail to touch what at the deepest level truly motivates people to be religious; hence there will always be people for whom the words of revealed scripture – however bizarre and shocking they may be, which they often are – issue straight from the mouth of God.[145]

If we take seriously the claims that the Bible makes on its own behalf, it would be wrong to let it off the hook so easily with respect to its claim to permanently binding validity. After all, the god of the Hebrew Bible says again and again that the laws that define his covenant are valid "throughout your generations" (to quote Exodus 31:13).[146] If there continues to be a people of Israel, the content of Mosaic legislation is not limited in its validity to the generation of Moses or any finite number of generations following Moses; it applies in perpetuity. Either the Hebrew Bible is or isn't the revealed word of the true God. From an intra-biblical perspective, it clearly is. If so, surely its laws are binding on the Hebrew nation until such a nation ceases to exist (when presumably the covenant lapses). How on earth would mere mortals have the authority to decide that the illiberal aspects of the Mosaic regime are too harsh and are in need of being liberalized? (That is to say: no more stoning of adulterers; no more death for those who violate the Sabbath; and so on.) So the real question is: How well does the morality of the Hebrew Bible meet the standard it itself presents as the relevant standard (namely, validity for all times if not for all places)? And there's another essential point here. The aspects of the Moses story that are most abhorrent *are still with us*. This kind of politics unfortunately *isn't* absent from the contemporary landscape, as we saw to our horror during the Islamic State's conquest of large chunks of Iraq and Syria. We can't dismiss the horrifying dimensions of Mosaic politics as irrelevant to us, because we can't assume that they *are* irrelevant. (The drawing of any association between Mosaic politics and what we witnessed with the Islamic State may seem extreme, and perhaps it is. But consider Graeme Wood's startling revelation that associates of Abu Musab al-Zarqawi "remembered him as a Moses-like figure [who was] granted a chance to see his promised land but not to set foot in it.")[147]

In the reading sketched above, is there an aspect of siding with a fundamentalist reading of the Hebrew Bible over against a centuries-long tradition of liberalizing Jewish commentary? I don't think so (or at least that's certainly not the intention). Yet liberal piety, in its continuing recognition of the sacredness of a highly illiberal text, seems to be saying that God wanted our ferociously illiberal ancestors to stone adulterers but that the same God also welcomes centuries of liberal interpretation in order to release us from those rather barbaric normative horizons. Liberal piety in this respect would seem to comprise something of a have-your-cake-and-eat-it stance: Mosaic law has lost nothing of its primal sacredness, it suggests, yet its specific injunctions can be relaxed to accord with evolving moral horizons. As Akenson rightly observes, "the Bible is sulphurous in spots, not nice," and we have to be aware of the intellectual costs in permitting liberal theology or a liberalizing hermeneutics to sanitize the Hebrew scriptures.[148] In the words of Akenson, it is only natural for modern piety to seek to "theologize" what is often harsh and amoral in YHWH's dealings with the Israelites, "to gentle it, to smooth away the hard edges," but it would be wrong to allow such massaging of the narrative to get in the way of "our reading of what the text actually says."[149] One obviously feels immense gratitude for the patient work of liberalization, unfolded within Jewish interpretive traditions over centuries, just as one does in the parallel case of liberalizing Islamic commentary – although it has to be said: in neither the Jewish nor the Islamic case have these liberalizing traditions succeeded in eliminating Jewish and Islamic fundamentalisms, with all their considerable political perils. Notwithstanding that gratitude, from the standpoint of secularist reason one feels compelled to ask: Why put such heroic hermeneutical (i.e., apologetical) efforts into liberalizing the original text when it would be so much simpler just to deny its binding normative authority?

It's impossible to think that liberal piety doesn't exist. It surely does – in contemporary Judaism and in other world religions. But it's perfectly possible to think, as Freud clearly did, that liberal versions of religiosity will tend to lose out in any contest with illiberal versions. Casting an eye over the broader landscape of contemporary religion, it's hard not to notice that illiberal religions, religions that refuse to bow to the superior authority of secular reason, are generally quite a bit more robust than the liberal (rationalistic) ones. The former grow, the latter shrink. One may, for instance, compare the state of Anglicanism in Africa with that of the Anglican Church in England. How is liberal Islam faring compared with illiberal Islam? Why are the rates of conversion to, for instance, Mormonism and Pentecostalism so much stronger than those for conversion to liberal forms of Protestantism? And so on. One important reason why liberalized versions of religion tend to be disadvantaged in relation to illiberal versions of religion is that the former will appeal to the ultimate authority of human reason, whereas the latter will appeal to *God's* authority. Which side is likely to prevail in an asymmetrical contest like that? Moreover, it seems fair to ask: Would a liberalized version of Judaism have been able to keep the law of Moses in business for three millennia? David Hume was impressively clear-sighted when he wrote that although "it will probably become difficult to persuade [nations in a future age] that any human, two-legged creature could ever embrace [principles as absurd as the Catholic doctrine of transubstantiation], it is a thousand to one, but these nations themselves shall have something full as absurd in their own creed."[150] Alas, most of what we see in the world today in regard to liberal and illiberal forms of religion has the effect of vindicating Humean pessimism and Freudian pessimism alike.

The issues at play here bear a substantial relation to the argument I try to make in *Civil Religion*. At the risk of oversimplifying the alternatives, let me end by proposing what I admit is a fairly crude fourfold typology. Religious liberals believe that what is properly divine in ancient scriptures is far more liberal than what those scriptures seem to suggest, and hence their aim is to bend the scriptures in the desired direction. Religious anti-liberals believe that one can't liberalize the holy texts without doing violence to them and hence doing violence to what God intends for the community of the faithful. Civil religionists believe that the scriptures are a serviceable resource useful for a range of political purposes independent of religion, and one should appropriate them in ways that realize this utility and that simultaneously domesticate religion vis-à-vis politics. Full-on secularists don't necessarily lack sympathy for what religious liberals and civil religionists are endeavouring to accomplish with respect to the Hebrew scriptures (or other scriptures). But they believe that the projects of liberalization and domestication pursued by religious liberals and civil religionists, respectively, are unlikely to attain their ends, and that it is safer or more prudent fully to face up to what in the texts resists such liberalizing efforts. In that sense, our challenges to the Hebrew Bible in this chapter are intended to support secularism among the four alternatives that we have just sketched.

With respect to the ultimate question of how to live, philosophy and piety (Athens and Jerusalem) represent rival claimants, although attempts to harmonize them are obviously not absent within the Western philosophical tradition. That is, political philosophy, simply by virtue of its existence as an intellectual discipline, promises (or at least aspires to) a comprehensive and authoritative adjudication of this ultimate question strictly within the bounds of human reason, just as piety claims to make available a comprehensive and authoritative adjudication of the same question on a basis that supposedly surpasses human reason. The legacy of Moses, like everything else in life, is subject to the perennial tug of war between these contending claims to normative authority, which is why the figure of Moses cannot be the exclusive property of a particular religious tradition and also why it has generated within the theory tradition the fascinatingly diverse appropriations surveyed in this book.[151]

Notes

Introduction

1 Throughout this chapter, I generally cite the Everett Fox translation in the first instance, but I often follow this with citations from the Robert Alter translation and/or the King James Version (KJV) where they are interestingly different so as to avoid dependence on a single rendering. The Fox translation is Everett Fox, trans., *The Five Books of Moses: Genesis, Exodus, Leviticus, Numbers, and Deuteronomy*, Schocken Bible, vol. 1 (New York: Schocken Books, 1997). Fox typically uses names that are closer to the original Hebrew, and in order to minimize confusion, I generally switch them to the versions more commonly used in English (e.g., Moses rather than Moshe; Aaron rather than Aharon). The Alter translation is Robert Alter, trans., *The Hebrew Bible: A Translation with Commentary*, vol. 1 (New York: W.W. Norton, 2019).

It should be noted that biblical quotations in chapter 3 below refer to "the LORD," whereas biblical quotations elsewhere in the book refer to "YHWH." This is a consequence of my relying in the first instance on the Fox translation (though I consult the other translations), whereas Harrison Fluss relies primarily on the Alter translation. For an extremely helpful discussion of the relevant issues, see Alter, *The Hebrew Bible*, xxxix–xl.

2 Are they actually slaves? The answer is not nearly as straightforward as the traditional narrative of national emancipation may suggest to us. Irving M. Zeitlin tends to speak not of Israelite slavery in Egypt but rather of the Israelites being subject to a corvée imposed by Pharaoh: see, e.g., Zeitlin, *Ancient Judaism* (Cambridge: Polity Press, 1984), 93. One encounters similar claims in Max Weber, *Ancient Judaism*, trans. Hans H. Gerth and Don Martindale (New York: Free Press, 1952), 8; Jan Assmann, *The Invention of Religion* (Princeton: Princeton University Press, 2018), 103; and Richard A. Gabriel, *God's Generals: The Military Lives of Moses,*

Buddha, and Muhammad (New York: Skyhorse Publishing, 2017), 11–12, 21, 25, 27–30, 67–68. Gabriel, *God's Generals*, 28, makes the persuasive point that "Exodus 13:19 states clearly that the Israelites were armed when they departed [Egypt]," and it is hard to fathom how emancipated slaves would come to be armed. It should also be noted that the Fox translation sometimes refers to the Israelites under Pharaohic domination as "serfs." See, e.g., Fox, *The Five Books of Moses*, 325: "YHWH brought us out of Egypt, out of a house of serfs" (Exodus 13:14). However, Alter, *The Hebrew Bible*, 267, translates this text as "the house of slaves"; and KJV translates it as "the house of bondage."

One important question here is whether YHWH intends for the Israelites to be "free." Or does he intend for Pharaoh's servants to become *his* servants? There are texts that suggest the latter. Martin Buber, for instance, quotes Exodus 4:22–23: "Let my son go that he may serve me" (KJV); Buber, *Moses* (Oxford: East and West Library, 1946), 65. Cf. Buber, *Moses*, 34: "The God of Israel has liberated his people from the 'servitude' of Egypt in order to take them into his own 'service.' 'Go, serve,' cries Pharaoh for instance to his Hebrew overseers"; 167: discussing YHWH's wish that Israel become "a royal retinue of kohanim [priests]" as "bondsmen of their Melek [king]"; and 177: "The children of Israel have left the service of Egypt for the service of YHWH." See also Martin Buber, *Kingship of God*, trans. Richard Scheimann (New York: Harper & Row, 1967), 138, referring to the divine Liberator "who broke the bands of [the people's] yoke" yet imposed upon them "the yoke of the kingship of heaven"; as well as Joel S. Baden, *The Book of Exodus: A Biography* (Princeton: Princeton University Press, 2019), 38, citing Leviticus 25:55, and 159–61, citing Leviticus 25:42 and 25:55. Similarly, Hegel, in his highly critical interpretation of Exodus, emphasizes that the Hebrews were entirely passive in the business of their supposed emancipation, hence continuing to bear "the most slavelike demeanor," and that Moses, their putative liberator, in freeing his nation from one yoke, "had laid on it another"; see G.W.F. Hegel, *Early Theological Writings*, trans. T.M. Knox (Philadelphia: University of Pennsylvania Press, 1971), 190–1.

3 "Some years later" is from Fox, *The Five Books of Moses*, 264. The KJV translation is more literal: "in those days."

4 Is Moses's killing of the Egyptian taskmaster an "eye-for-an-eye" retribution for the murder of the Hebrew slave? KJV uses the verb "smite" for what was suffered by the slave, and both Fox, *The Five Books of Moses*, 264, and Alter, *The Hebrew Bible*, 217, employ the verb "strike," appearing to suggest that the slave was assaulted but not murdered. However, Fox, *The Five Books of Moses*, 264, note for chapter 2, verse 12, points out that the Hebrew verb used in verse 11, *hakkeh*, is the same as that applied to

the murder of the taskmaster in verse 12 (translated as "slew" in KJV and translated as "struck down" by both Fox and Alter). Hence Fox accepts that the assault in verse 11 involved a "fatal beating."

5 Fox, *The Five Books of Moses*, 265; Alter, *The Hebrew Bible*, 219.

6 There are ambiguities in the biblical text that suggest Hobab (or for Fox, Hovav) as a third name. When one reads Numbers 10:29, whether in Fox, Alter, or KJV, it certainly sounds as if Hobab is Moses's brother-in-law rather than his father-in-law. However, according to Fox, *The Five Books of Moses*, 269, note to Exodus 3:1, and Alter, *The Hebrew Bible*, 511, note to Numbers 10:29, Hobab is not the son of Jethro/Reuel (and hence brother of Zipporah) but rather Jethro himself, son of another Reuel (or in KJV, Raguel, presumably Zipporah's grandfather). I assume that there's something in the Hebrew (or at least in the exegetical tradition) that prompts Fox and Alter to read Hobab as another name for Jethro, and other scholars do so as well. Moreover, Judges 4:11 very clearly refers to Hobab as Moses's father-in-law. As regards the latter text, see Everett Fox, trans., *The Early Prophets: Joshua, Judges, Samuel, and Kings*, Schocken Bible, vol. 2 (New York: Schocken Books, 2014), 159, note to Judges 4:11. Both Fox, *The Five Books of Moses*, 706, and Alter, *The Hebrew Bible*, 511, in their respective editorial notes for Numbers 10:29, acknowledge that the pervasive confusion concerning Jethro, Reuel, and Hobab is far from easy to disentangle. Of course, if the canonical version of the Pentateuch is patched together from distinct and incomplete source documents (as claimed by the so-called documentary hypothesis), such inconsistencies are hardly surprising. For a good discussion, see Baden, *The Book of Exodus: A Biography*, chap. 1.

7 Fox, *The Five Books of Moses*, 271; Alter, *The Hebrew Bible*, 221; same in KJV.

8 Fox, *The Five Books of Moses*, 277. KJV: "I am not eloquent … I am slow of speech, and of a slow tongue."

9 Fox, *The Five Books of Moses*, 291; Alter, *The Hebrew Bible*, 238; same in KJV.

10 See Daniel Jeremy Silver, *Images of Moses* (New York: Basic Books, 1982), 20: "The Torah reports only the names of Moses' sons, Gershon and Eleazar, and the fact that Moses delayed the youngest's circumcision, for reasons not given. Beyond this they are not in view, except for a single mention in an archaic fragment embedded in the Book of Judges, which seems to indicate that descendants of Gershon, 'son of Moses,' were officiating as minor priests at a local shrine in the territory of Dan (Judg. 18:30)." (KJV refers to Menasseh rather than Moses, but as Fox explains in a note in *The Early Prophets*, 241, a scribe had changed Moses to Menasseh in order to avoid associating descendants of Moses with idolaters.) For a highly patriarchal culture, it seems very strange indeed that the two sons of Moses don't figure at all in the Mosaic narrative, apart from the story of the belated circumcision.

11 Silver, in the previous note, informs us that Eliezer was the uncircumcised son. But the text doesn't tell us that.

12 Simon Goldhill writes that Freud's "deeply strained relation with his Judaism" is proven by the fact that "he did not have his own sons circumcised." *Freud's Couch, Scott's Buttocks, Brontë's Grave* (Chicago: University of Chicago Press, 2011), 113. But by the strangest of ironies, the same was actually true of Moses!

13 Fox, *The Five Books of Moses*, 279; Alter, *The Hebrew Bible*, 228. Alter, in his note devoted to this baffling incident, writes, "This elliptic story is the most enigmatic episode in all of Exodus. It seems unlikely that we will ever resolve the enigmas it poses."

14 Alter, *The Hebrew Bible*, 263. Fox, *The Five Books of Moses*, 321: "They strip Egypt." KJV: "They borrowed [!] of the Egyptians jewels of silver, and jewels of gold, and raiment … The Egyptians … lent unto them such things as they required. And they spoiled the Egyptians." John H. Geerken calls it "the plundering of Egypt." "Machiavelli's Moses and Renaissance Politics," *Journal of the History of Ideas* 60, no. 4 (October 1999): 580.

15 Fox, *The Five Books of Moses*, 327; Alter, *The Hebrew Bible*, 268. KJV: "went up harnessed."

16 Fox, *The Five Books of Moses*, 321; same in KJV. Alter, *The Hebrew Bible*, 263, calls it "a motley throng." Zeitlin, *Ancient Judaism*, 97, describes it as "a heterogeneous agglomeration of tribal and other groups"; cf. 93.

17 Fox, *The Five Books of Moses*, 331.

18 In I Samuel 8:8, God complains that the people's demand that divine kingship be jettisoned in favour of conventional monarchy is "just like all the deeds that they have done *from the day I brought them up from Egypt* until this day: they have abandoned me and served other gods!" Fox, *The Early Prophets*, 313; my italics. Alter, in his note on this text, interprets it as a Deuteronomistic interpolation: see Robert Alter, trans., *The Hebrew Bible: A Translation with Commentary*, vol. 2 (New York: W.W. Norton, 2019), 203. In other words, the chronicle of the Hebrew people, right from the get-go, is a story of never-ceasing faithlessness and revolt. Zeitlin, *Ancient Judaism*, 254, interestingly points out that "Ezekiel employs [the legends of rebellion in the wilderness era] to accuse the nation of rebellion from the start," in contrast to earlier prophets who "look upon [the wilderness era] as a golden age in which Israel enjoyed God's grace." Clearly, God's own view of Israel corresponds to Ezekiel's view, certainly not the "golden age" view!

19 Fox, *The Five Books of Moses*, 345; Alter, *The Hebrew Bible*, 278. KJV: "The people murmured."

20 Fox, *The Five Books of Moses*, 346. As Alter observes in a note on p. 279, "fleshpots," deriving from the KJV, refers to a cauldron for the cooking of meat.

21 Fox, *The Five Books of Moses*, 347.

22 Fox, *The Five Books of Moses*, 348; Alter, *The Hebrew Bible*, 281.

23 Fox, *The Five Books of Moses*, 349, 351; Alter, *The Hebrew Bible*, 282.

24 Fox, *The Five Books of Moses*, 351, 353.

25 Fox, *The Five Books of Moses*, 353; Alter, *The Hebrew Bible*, 283. As we'll see later in the narrative, this worry on Moses's part becomes a more active threat in Numbers 14:10.

26 Fox, *The Five Books of Moses*, 759; Alter, *The Hebrew Bible*, 549 (Numbers 20:24): God states that both Moses and Aaron "rebelled against my orders at the Waters of Meribah." It is fairly difficult to see what Moses actually did wrong, or at least certainly not obvious, since Numbers 20:11 tells us that Moses did indeed strike the boulder with his staff (Fox, *The Five Books of Moses*, 756), just as God commanded in the Exodus version of the story. The version in Numbers speaks of "speaking to the rock" rather than striking it, so that may have been Moses's sin. For commentary, see Alter, *The Hebrew Bible*, 547, note to Numbers 20:10.

27 Fox, *The Five Books of Moses*, 353, 355.

28 Ibid., 357–8; Alter, *The Hebrew Bible*, 290. KJV: "able men."

29 Fox, *The Five Books of Moses*, 365; Alter, *The Hebrew Bible*, 291. Same in KJV.

30 Fox, *The Five Books of Moses*, 366; Alter, *The Hebrew Bible*, 292.

31 Fox, *The Five Books of Moses*, 366–7, 369. In Exodus 20:18, the storm cloud representing God is described as "fog" (Fox, *The Five Books of Moses*, 373). Alter, *The Hebrew Bible*, 298: "the thick cloud." KJV: "the thick darkness." Fox's numbering of the verses is a bit different from that in Alter and KJV.

32 Fox, *The Five Books of Moses*, 389. Although they were warned in Exodus 24:1 not to get too close, in 24:10–11 they seem to get close enough to "see" the God of Israel (Fox, *The Five Books of Moses*, 391; Alter, *The Hebrew Bible*, 315). Fox, *The Five Books of Moses*, 392: "They beheld Godhood." Alter: "They beheld God." KJV: "They saw God."

33 KJV here calls Joshua Moses's "minister." Fox, *The Five Books of Moses*, 392, and Alter, *The Hebrew Bible*, 315, call him Moses's "attendant"; cf. Exodus 33:11. When Moses begins re-descending the mountain in Exodus 32:15–17, his first re-encounter is with Joshua. Presumably, Joshua had stayed at the spot on the mountain where Moses had left him.

34 Alter generally opts for "Tabernacle." So does KJV.

35 Fox, *The Five Books of Moses*, 436; more or less the same in KJV. Alter, *The Hebrew Bible*, 338: "two tablets of the Covenant."

36 Fox, *The Five Books of Moses*, 441.

37 Ibid., 443.

38 KJV, Exodus 32:9. Fox, *The Five Books of Moses*, 443, translates it as "hard-necked people." Cf. Exodus 33:3 and 33:5. In a speech to God at Exodus 34:9, Moses himself adopts God's characterization of Israel as a stiff-

necked/hard-necked people. He does the same in Deuteronomy 9:6, this time addressing the people themselves.

39 Fox, *The Five Books of Moses*, 444: "YHWH let himself be sorry." Alter, *The Hebrew Bible*, 341: "The LORD relented." KJV: "The LORD repented."

40 See Aaron Tugendhaft, *The Idols of ISIS* (Chicago: University of Chicago Press, 2020), 7–8, for an intriguing attempt at retelling the story of the golden calf in a way that is somewhat more favourable to Aaron and less favourable to Moses; cf. the book's epigraph by Muhyi al-Din Ibn ʿArabi, which sides with Aaron against Moses. There's a long and dubious history of the politics of iconoclasm in the very literal sense of the smashing of idols. Tugendhaft's Islamic sources treat Ibrahim/Abraham as the one who inaugurated this tradition; but it's clear that Moses, in his role as destroyer of the golden calf, was also an important figure in the same tradition. Yet if, as Tugendhaft suggests, idols are simply shared images that are inescapably constitutive of political life, then the politics of iconoclasm is both futile and anti-political, and Moses was perhaps wrong to have destroyed what Aaron wrought on the people's behalf.

41 See Michael Walzer, "Exodus 32 and the Theory of Holy War: The History of a Citation," *Harvard Theological Review* 61, no. 1 (January 1968): 1–14, for an interesting discussion of how this text (Exodus 32:26–8) was drawn upon in various contexts in the Christian era in order to justify persecution of the unholy. Walzer focuses on Augustine, Aquinas, and Calvin in sketching this Christian "holy war" tradition.

42 KJV, Exodus 32:27. Fox, *The Five Books of Moses*, 447: "Thus says YHWH, the God of Israel."

43 Geerken, "Machiavelli's Moses and Renaissance Politics," 582–3. Similarly, Ronna Burger, in an interesting account of this story of Mosaic statecraft in its harshest manifestation, calls this attempted attribution to God of responsibility for the order to the Levites a "noble lie" on the part of Moses qua Machiavellian founder. She also notes the puzzling conclusion of Exodus chapter 32 – "And YHWH plagued the people because they made the calf that Aaron made" (Fox, *The Five Books of Moses*, 448) – and suggests that it may have been an effort on the part of biblical redactors to shift responsibility for the slaughter from Moses to God. The lecture in which Burger offers this interpretation is entitled "In the Wilderness at Sinai: Moses as Lawgiver and Founder" and can be accessed on YouTube: https://www.youtube.com/watch?v=qQ6978844mM&t=1831s.

44 Jean-Jacques Rousseau, *On the Social Contract*, ed. Roger D. Masters, trans. Judith R. Masters (New York: St. Martin's, 1978), 69 (book 2, chap. 7); Thomas Hobbes, *Leviathan*, ed. Richard Tuck, rev. student ed. (Cambridge: Cambridge University Press, 1996), 82 (chap. 12).

45 Moses's offer in Exodus 32:32 to be blotted out of God's book (KJV) constitutes for Jean Bodin proof of Moses's true greatness as a "prince." Bodin writes, "Best of all examples is that of Moses, whom Philo calls the wise legislator, just king, and great prophet. He prayed God the rather to blot out his name from the book of life than that the people should go unpardoned, preferring rather his own damnation than that the people should perish. Here indeed is the likeness of the true prince and the father of his people." *Six Books of the Commonwealth*, trans. M.J. Tooley (Oxford: Basil Blackwell, 1955), 62 (bk. 2, chap. 4). I owe this reference to Zachariah Black.

46 Fox, *The Five Books of Moses*, 448.

47 Ibid., 449. Alter, *The Hebrew Bible*, 345, calls it "the Tent of Meeting." Perhaps Moses moves the tabernacle outside of the camp so that God can continue conversing with Moses, as he does in Exodus 33:9–11, without God needing to be in the "midst" of this stiff-necked people. On this occasion, God appears as a "column of cloud" (Fox, *The Five Books of Moses*, 449; Alter, *The Hebrew Bible*, 345: "pillar of cloud"; KJV: "cloudy pillar"), and we are informed that Moses is addressed by YHWH "face to face, as a man speaks to his neighbor" (Fox, *The Five Books of Moses*, 451; Alter, *The Hebrew Bible*, 346: "to his fellow"; KJV: "unto his friend"). Cf. Numbers 11:8, Fox, *The Five Books of Moses*, 719: "Mouth to mouth I speak with him, in-plain-sight, not in riddles, and the form of YHWH (is what) he beholds"; and Deuteronomy 34:10, Fox, *The Five Books of Moses*, 1014: "Moses, whom YHWH knew face to face."

48 Fox, *The Five Books of Moses*, 452. It is extremely puzzling that Moses is told so emphatically that seeing God's face means immediate death so soon after a Moses-YHWH rendezvous is described as "face to face" (Exodus 33:11). After all, these two contradictory texts are in the same chapter of Exodus!

49 Fox, *The Five Books of Moses*, 456.

50 Ibid., 459. Alter, *The Hebrew Bible*, 351: "The skin of his face glowed." KJV: "The skin of his face shone." It was a famous mistranslation of this text as "sprouted horns" that gave rise to traditional depictions of Moses as horned. For discussion, see Alter's note on pp. 351–2.

51 Fox, *The Five Books of Moses*, 459–60.

52 Ibid., 489–90.

53 Ibid., 706. See note 6 above for our discussion of riddles about Hobab's identity and his relation to Moses. He is either Jethro in another guise or Jethro's son, hence Moses's brother-in-law.

54 Fox, *The Five Books of Moses*, 706.

55 The same complaints recur in Numbers 21:5, and on this occasion YHWH punishes the people with "vipers" (Fox, *The Five Books of Moses*, 760). KJV: "fiery serpents."

56 Fox, *The Five Books of Moses*, 715.

57 Alter, *The Hebrew Bible*, 517. KJV: "The LORD smote the people with a very great plague."

58 As I've pointed out previously, one can well ask how Moses, raised within the Egyptian royal family, could even know who his Israelite brother and sister were. The Hebrew Bible tells us little on this score. Numbers 26:59 spells out more clearly than anywhere else that Aaron, Moses, and Miriam were the three children of Amram and Jochebed.

59 Fox, *The Five Books of Moses*, 718; Alter, *The Hebrew Bible*, 518. KJV (Numbers 12:1) refers to the mystery wife as "the Ethiopian woman."

60 Alter, *The Hebrew Bible*, 518.

61 Fox, *The Five Books of Moses*, 719; Alter, *The Hebrew Bible*, 518–19.

62 Alter, *The Hebrew Bible*, 520. KJV: "Miriam became leprous." Fox doesn't attempt to translate the name of the skin disease.

63 Aaron always seems to evade punishment, but two of his sons are not so lucky. Leviticus 10:1–2 narrates how Nadab and Abihu, Moses's nephews, were consumed by fire (KJV: "devoured" by fire) on account of some obscure ritual misdeed.

64 The story of the scouts or spies is re-narrated by Moses in Deuteronomy 1:23–38.

65 Fox, *The Five Books of Moses*, 726: "The entire community of Israel thought to pelt them with stones," although it's not quite clear from any of the translations whether "them" refers to Moses and Aaron or Joshua and Caleb. See also the speech by Moses in Josephus, *Jewish Antiquities*, bks. 4–6, trans. H. St. J. Thackeray and Ralph Marcus (Cambridge, MA: Harvard University Press, 1998), 91 and 93 (bk. 4): "Never display towards [Eleazar and Joshua] the like of that wrath which ye have oft-times dared to vent on me, for ye know that my life has more often been imperiled by you than by the enemy."

Central to the Mosaic drama as narrated – or more likely mythicized – by Freud is the idea that Moses was at some point murdered by the Israelites and that this murder was repressed within subsequent Jewish tradition, though not repressed without the possibility of a psychoanalytic excavation of the traumatic deed (which Freud all too briefly sketches in his Moses book) by hunting for elusive traces of it in the "Jewish collective unconscious," as it were, spread over millennia. Yosef Hayim Yerushalmi, in his powerful book on Freud, poses formidable challenges to this Freudian thesis. But as Yerushalmi, in his commentary on Freud's book, concedes, and as Jacques Derrida, in his commentary on Yerushalmi's book, emphasizes, the Bible itself, at least in this hazy text, seems to disclose a willingness on the part of the Israelites to murder Moses (and Aaron too). Derrida makes the important point that as far as the Freudian unconscious is concerned, the intent to murder Moses is as salient as the performance of this intent. See Yosef Hayim Yerushalmi, *Freud's Moses: Judaism Terminable and Interminable* (New Haven: Yale University Press, 1991), 85; Jacques Derrida, *Archive Fever: A Freudian Impression* (Chicago: University of Chicago Press, 1996), 65–6. For Freud's discussion, see *The Standard Edition of the Complete Psychological Works of Sigmund Freud*, vol. 23, ed. James Strachey (London: Vintage, 2001), 88–90; the *Moses and Monotheism* translation is by Strachey. Freud doesn't cite any primary texts but instead relies on the authority of Ernst Sellin, who, Freud tells us, was able to locate "traces of [the killing of Moses] in tradition," without relaying what those traces were. It should be noted that rather than quoting Numbers 14:10, Yerushalmi on p. 85 quotes a Midrashic commentary on Numbers 14:10, since the biblical text is fairly vague ("the congregation bade stone them with stones," in the words of the KJV), whereas the Midrash explicitly spells out the assault on the life of Moses and God's intervention to save him. Let me mention, finally, that Freud's conception of Christ as a "resurrected Moses" (p. 90) seems quite bizarre, since it would appear that the only thing in common between Moses and Christ is Freud's image of them as both murder victims at the hands of a Jewish mob. We offer a fuller commentary on Freud's Moses in the last section of chapter 1.

66 Fox, *The Five Books of Moses*, 726.

67 Ibid., 737.

68 Ibid., 737–8. KJV: "Seemeth it but a small thing unto you, that the God of Israel hath separated you from the congregation of Israel, to bring you near to himself to do the service of the tabernacle of the LORD, and to stand before the congregation to minister unto them?" Numbers 18:2–7 spells out the role of the Levites as "attendants," stationed "in front of the Tent of the Testimony" (Fox, *The Five Books of Moses*, 746). Cf. Numbers 18:21 and 18:23: "the serving-tasks" of the Levites (Fox, *The Five Books of Moses*, 750); Alter, *The Hebrew Bible*, 542–3, merely speaks of "their work that they perform." Fox, *The Five Books of Moses*, in his commentaries on pp. 740 and 744, interprets this delimited function as following from the Korah rebellion; but Moses's speech emphasizing the status of the Levites as less than full priests surely suggests that their subaltern status preceded, and likely caused, the rebellion. Numbers 17:5 reinforces the point that Korah and the others have sinned primarily by trying to usurp religious functions that properly belong only to those "of the seed of Aaron" (Fox, *The Five Books of Moses*, 742; Alter, *The Hebrew Bible*, 537). The same emphasis on the privileged priestly status of Aaron's sons relative to the general run of Levites is to be found in Numbers 18:6–7 (Fox, *The Five Books of Moses*, 747).

69 Alter, *The Hebrew Bible*, 534–5. Fox's translation is "play-the-prince over us" (p. 738). KJV: "Make thyself altogether a prince over us."

70 Fox, *The Five Books of Moses*, 739. The same threat to annihilate the whole of Israel is repeated in Numbers 17:9–10 (Fox, *The Five Books of Moses*, 743); a similar threat is issued in Numbers 25:11 (Fox, *The Five Books of Moses*, 784–5). As Fox highlights on p. 748, it appears that the effort by Moses and Aaron to get God to spare the broader community is only partially successful, since Numbers 17:12–14 informs us that the people suffered a plague costing 14,700 lives "aside from those that died in the matter of Korah" (Fox, *The Five Books of Moses*, 743). Was the timing of this plague coincidental, or was it a collateral effect of God's wrath against the rebels? One has to suspect the latter.

71 Fox, *The Five Books of Moses*, 741. Interestingly, Martin Buber sides decisively with Moses against Korah. See *Moses*, 189, where Buber proclaims that Korah represents "empty stubbornness," "willfulness," and "resistance ... to the coming of the Kingdom." Moses, he states, represents "the way of God," whereas Korah and his fellow rebels represent "the wrong paths of their own hearts." There is little in the biblical text to back up either Buber's harsh judgment about the rebels or his generous assumptions about Moses, who, he claims, "does not wish to use force, [and] does not wish to impose himself." Still, reluctant as Moses may have been on Buber's retelling of the story, "he must now doom the rebels to destruction, just as he once ordered Levites to fight against Levites." There is a tension here: Moses is said to be disinclined "to use force," yet it is Moses's own agency that "dooms the rebels to destruction." We might also note the oddness of Buber's suggestion that the episode of the golden calf was an intra-Levite fracas rather than a Levite massacre carried out against other tribes.

The question of whether the Korah rebels were wiped out by God or by Moses is also highlighted by Spinoza; see Baruch Spinoza, *Theological-Political Treatise*, 2nd ed., trans. Samuel Shirley (Indianapolis: Hackett, 2001), 202. Spinoza says that when the original revolt was extinguished, a second, larger revolt on the part of "the entire people" arose, sparked by the belief "that the [Korah rebels] had perished not by God's judgment but by the devising of Moses." Hobbes, too, weighs in on the question of whether God or Moses was the true agent of punishment when the imperatives of civil order were violated. In *On the Citizen*, Hobbes points out that the actual infliction of punishment typically "depended on private initiative," such as the multitude's inclination to stone the offenders. "This was why Moses did not condemn anyone to death on his own authority; but when anyone was to be put to death (whether it was one man or several men), he relied upon divine authority to rouse the crowd against him or them, saying, Thus saith the Lord." Thomas Hobbes, *On the Citizen*, ed. Richard Tuck and Michael Silverthorne (Cambridge: Cambridge University Press, 1998), 198; cf. Exodus 32:27. But pretty obviously, "rousing the crowd" in this way suggests not divine agency but rather Mosaic agency. Chapter 3 below seeks to offer a much fuller account of what renders the jarring story of Korah's revolt such a problematical episode within the Mosaic narrative.

72 Numbers 17:23 in Fox, *The Five Books of Moses*, 745, and Alter, *The Hebrew Bible*, 539. The same verse is 17:8 in KJV. For some reason, in KJV the first fifteen verses of chapter 17 are added to the end of chapter 16; hence chapter 17 has a total of thirteen verses in KJV, whereas it has a total of twenty-eight verses in both Fox and Alter.

73 Fox, *The Five Books of Moses*, 750; same in KJV. Alter, *The Hebrew Bible*, 543: "bear their guilt." Admittedly, they receive a regular tithe in lieu of the land that they are denied.

74 Alter, *The Hebrew Bible*, 546, note to Numbers 20:1.

75 Numbers 33:39 tells us that Aaron was 123 at the time of his death on Mount Hor. This is at the conclusion of forty years of wandering in the desert (Numbers 33:38). This is consistent with Exodus 7:7's assertion that Aaron was 83 before commencement of the trek in the wilderness. Deuteronomy 31:2 and 34:7 tell us that Moses was 120 when he died. This too is consistent with Exodus 7:7.

76 Fox, *The Five Books of Moses*, 759; Alter, *The Hebrew Bible*, 549. The same verdict is applied to Moses in Numbers 27:13–14: Fox, *The Five Books of Moses*, 798–9. Since Moses's days are numbered, the appointment of Joshua as his successor is announced in Numbers 27:15–23 (Fox, *The Five Books of Moses*, 799, 801). The appointment is officially activated in Deuteronomy 31:7, 31:14, 31:23, 34:9.

77 Fox, *The Five Books of Moses*, 754.

78 Fox, *The Five Books of Moses*, 756; Alter, *The Hebrew Bible*, 547. KJV: "Ye believed me not."

79 *The Diaries of Franz Kafka, 1914–1923*, ed. Max Brod (New York: Schocken, 1965), 196.

80 Fox, *The Five Books of Moses*, 759. Fox renders this as "devoting to destruction." Alter's rendering (p. 550) is "put its towns under the ban." KJV: "utterly destroy their cities." Cf. Deuteronomy 13:13–18 and 20:16–17 as well as Joshua 6:21: "And they devoted-to-destruction everyone who was in the city, from man to woman, from young lad to old man, to ox and sheep and donkey, with the mouth of the sword"; and Joshua 11:20: "For [the refusal on the part of the enemy kingdoms to conclude peace with Israel] was from YHWH, to make their heart strong-willed toward battle with Israel, in order to devote-them-to-destruction, without there being

any compassion toward them; indeed, it was to wipe them out, as YHWH had commanded Moses" (Fox, *The Early Prophets*, 37, 63). Chapters 10 and 11 of the book of Joshua give an account of the "devoting to destruction," in all its harshness, of the southern and northern city states of Canaan, respectively. The intended implication of devoting to destruction is that the razing of the cities is in effect a divine sacrifice, just as one would sacrifice rams or sheep. This concept of *herem* is a crucial one, and will receive further discussion elsewhere in this book.

81 Fox, *The Five Books of Moses*, 763.

82 Ibid., 785. KJV: "Vex the Midianites, and smite them."

83 Fox, *The Five Books of Moses*, 812; Alter, *The Hebrew Bible*, 587. The vengeance is for incidents narrated in chapters 22 and 25.

84 Fox, *The Five Books of Moses*, 813. Alter, *The Hebrew Bible*, 589, simply writes "let live," glossing over the implication of the taking of virgin sex slaves. KJV agrees with Fox in acknowledging that the virgins are to be kept "for yourselves." Rules for the unilateral taking of "wives" (i.e., sex slaves) in war are set out in Deuteronomy 20:10–14. It is painful to reflect that practices of this kind have existed as recently as the pinnacle of the Islamic State's power in 2014–17.

85 Fox, *The Five Books of Moses*, 812.

86 Ibid., 827; Alter, *The Hebrew Bible*, 597. Cf. Deuteronomy 12:1–3.

87 Fox, *The Five Books of Moses*, 827; Alter, *The Hebrew Bible*, 598.

88 Fox, *The Five Books of Moses*, 1013–14. The same in KJV. The "He" at the beginning of 34:6 on the face of it suggests that Moses was buried by YHWH himself, which is odd. Why no burial by family and followers? But Alter, in his note on this verse (p. 743), informs us that the passive verb ("he was buried") is a possible rendering and one that Alter believes is more credible. Both Fox and Alter point out that, as Alter puts it, "the occultation of the grave of Moses serves to prevent any possibility of a cult of Moses, with pilgrimages to his gravesite" (ibid.).

89 Robert A. Paul, *Moses and Civilization* (New Haven: Yale University Press, 1996), 78. Paul himself is determined not to make this mistake: "My analysis remains within the confines of the myth" (ibid.). See also Assmann, *The Invention of Religion*, 33: "Questions about historical reality [in regard to Moses and the Exodus story] end in a blind alley. The biblical stories contradict each other, while extrabiblical sources are in short supply. The 'historical Moses' has vanished into thin air." Martin Buber begins his book on Moses with a harsh attack on Freud: "That a scholar of so much importance in his own field as Sigmund Freud could permit himself to issue so unscientific a work, based on groundless hypotheses, as his 'Moses and Monotheism' (1939), is regrettable." Buber, *Moses*, 5n1. It seems highly questionable to appeal to "science" as the appropriate

standard when it is largely a question of sifting among legends. Cf. Silver's point that Buber's own conclusions "are impressionistic, not historical": *Images of Moses*, 298.

90 Silver, *Images of Moses*, 4.

91 Ibid., 5. Cf. Jan Assmann, *Moses the Egyptian* (Cambridge, MA: Harvard University Press, 1997), 1–2. Baden, in *The Book of Exodus: A Biography*, 4, points out the remarkable fact that despite ancient Egypt's impressive record-keeping, there is nothing in its archival records to support the events narrated in Exodus; nor has modern archeology been able to uncover "a single material trace of Israel's presence" either in Egypt or in the Sinai wilderness.

1. Images of Moses in the Modern Western Theory Canon

1 Lincoln Steffens, *Moses in Red* (Pittsburgh: Dorrance, 1926), 44. Cf. Jan Assmann, *The Invention of Religion* (Princeton: Princeton University Press, 2018), 78: "When, by whom, and to what end the story is retold can be clearly understood with reference to [a particular] historical context. For example, in the case of Arnold Schoenberg, Sigmund Freud, and Thomas Mann, all three were émigrés; all three turned to the Bible under the shock of Nazi barbarism and anti-Semitic persecution; and all three sought to bring the symbolic figure of memory known as 'Moses' to the attention of their time as a source of judgment and solace."

2 Leo Strauss, "Reason and Revelation," in Heinrich Meier, *Leo Strauss and the Theological-Political Problem* (Cambridge: Cambridge University Press, 2006), 148.

3 For helpful commentaries on the frontispiece, see Justin Champion, *Republican Learning: John Toland and the Crisis of Christian Culture, 1696–1722* (Manchester: Manchester University Press, 2003), 105–7; Justin Champion, "*Mosaica Respublica*: Harrington, Toland and Moses," in *Perspectives on English Revolutionary Republicanism*, ed. Gaby Mahlberg and Dirk Wiemann (Farnham: Ashgate, 2014), 166–8; and D.N. DeLuna, "Topical Satire Read Back into Pocock's Neo-Harringtonian Moment," in *The Political Imagination in History: Essays Concerning J.G.A. Pocock*, ed. DeLuna (Baltimore: Owlworks, 2006), 154.

4 Niccolò Machiavelli, *The Prince*, trans. Harvey C. Mansfield, Jr. (Chicago: University of Chicago Press, 1985), 21–5.

5 Ibid., 22.

6 There are hardly any references to Moses in the oeuvre of Nietzsche. But one of these references bears remarking. In a notebook, Nietzsche writes that "in that which moved Zarathustra, Moses, Muhammed, Jesus, Plato, Brutus, Spinoza, Mirabeau – I live too." Clearly, Nietzsche classed himself

among the founders of *civilizational dispensations*, along with Moses and the others. The fragment is quoted by Kaufmann in Friedrich Nietzsche, *The Gay Science*, trans. Walter Kaufmann (New York: Vintage Books, 1974), 151n42.

7 Machiavelli, *The Prince*, 22.

8 Everett Fox, trans., *The Five Books of Moses: Genesis, Exodus, Leviticus, Numbers, and Deuteronomy*, Schocken Bible, vol. 1 (New York: Schocken Books, 1997), 851, note to Deuteronomy 1:22; my italics.

9 Machiavelli, *The Prince*, 23.

10 For the full interpretation, see Ronald Beiner, *Civil Religion* (New York: Cambridge University Press, 2011), chaps. 2–4. There are suggestions in Machiavelli (e.g., in Niccolò Machiavelli, *Discourses on Livy*, trans. Harvey C. Mansfield and Nathan Tarcov [Chicago: University of Chicago Press, 1996], bk. 1, chap. 11) that the real founder of Rome was Numa, not Romulus, because Numa was responsible for the Roman religion (and see Beiner, *Civil Religion*, 18–19n7, where I cite a parallel judgment by Rousseau). Graham Hammill offers an interesting formulation when he refers to Machiavelli's Moses as "a synthesis of Romulus and Numa," because he both "founds a state and develops a religion that ensures obedience to it." *The Mosaic Constitution* (Chicago: University of Chicago Press, 2012), 217. Although Machiavelli notably fluctuates in his relative ranking of Romulus and Numa, it is Numa, not Romulus, who is presented as an equal of Moses in the iconic frontispiece of Toland's 1700 edition of Harrington.

11 Machiavelli, *The Prince*, 24. John H. Geerken, "Machiavelli's Moses and Renaissance Politics," *Journal of the History of Ideas* 60, no. 4 (October 1999): 591–2, argues that one important polemical purpose of raising up the biblical Moses as an icon of the armed prophet is to expose Savonarola, qua unarmed prophet, as a false Moses, or even an "anti-Moses." In contrast to Savonarola, who presented himself as a spiritualized Moses, Machiavelli wanted an Italian Moses who would embody "the tough, muscular, territorial Hebraism of the Torah." Geerken, "Machiavelli's Moses and Renaissance Politics," 595, quoting Werner Gundersheimer.

12 Daniel Jeremy Silver judges Mohammed to be more of an armed prophet in the full sense than Moses was: "Unlike Moses, Mohammed prepares his troops for battle and sets out the strategy that they are to follow." *Images of Moses* (New York: Basic Books, 1982), 231. That is: Mohammed is Moses and Joshua rolled into one.

13 Machiavelli, *The Prince*, 102.

14 Ibid., 103.

15 Machiavelli, *Discourses on Livy*, 30.

16 Ibid., 280. Mansfield and Tarcov's rendering, "infinite men," seems overly literal, so I've changed this to "countless men." Reading the Bible

"judiciously" is the Mansfield-Tarcov translation for *sensatamente*. Leslie J. Walker, SJ, translates it as "with discernment"; Allan Gilbert translates it as "He who reads the Bible intelligently." For the Walker translation, see Machiavelli, *The Discourses*, ed. Bernard Crick (Harmondsworth: Penguin, 1970), 486; for the Gilbert translation, see Machiavelli, *The Chief Works and Others*, vol. 1 (Durham: Duke University Press, 1965), 496. Spinoza also zeroes in on the theme of envy. See *Theological-Political Treatise*, 2nd ed., trans. Samuel Shirley (Indianapolis: Hackett, 2001), 202: "As soon as the [Israelites] found themselves with abundant leisure in the wilderness, many of them, of no mean standing, began to resent [the election of the Levites], and found in this a reason for believing that Moses was acting not by divine decree, but at his own pleasure, in that he had chosen his own tribe before all others and had bestowed on his own brother the office of high priest in perpetuity." However, as is pretty obvious, resentment of the Levites cannot explain the Korah rebellion, since it was itself a Levite uprising.

17 Machiavelli, *Discourses on Livy*, 280n4. Geerken, "Machiavelli's Moses and Renaissance Politics," 580, also assumes that Machiavelli is referring to Exodus 32:25–8.

18 Ronna Burger also observes that Machiavelli's theme here fits the Korah story better than it fits the golden calf story; see Burger's lecture, "In the Wilderness at Sinai: Moses as Lawgiver and Founder," which can be accessed on YouTube: https://www.youtube.com/watch?v=qQ6978844mM&t=1831s. It should be recalled that "countless men" are killed in the Korah episode as well; however, they perish by being slayed not by the Levites but by God, via a devastating plague. It's possible that Machiavelli runs together all three stories (the golden calf, the Korah revolt, and the revolt of Aaron and Miriam) – significantly, Aaron figures centrally in two of them – on the assumption that envy of the leadership is the primary driver behind all revolts.

19 Geerken, "Machiavelli's Moses and Renaissance Politics," 589.

20 We return to this Freudian narrative in the last section of this chapter.

21 Cf. the condemnation of Moses's conduct in the episode of the golden calf by Voltaire, who describes it as an "orgy of bloodletting" carried out by "bloodthirsty priests." *A Pocket Philosophical Dictionary*, trans. John Fletcher (Oxford: Oxford University Press, 2011), 209. Hobbes's view of the cruelty of Moses is presented as an illustration of his broader view of human cruelty in *Aubrey's Brief Lives*, ed. Oliver Lawson Dick (Harmondsworth, UK: Penguin Books, 1972), 317. This is less clear in the version of the same text in John Aubrey, *Brief Lives*, ed. John Buchanan-Brown (London: Penguin, 2000), 441. What does this tell us about Hobbes's attempt to present himself in his books as a man of

unadulterated piety? In *Leviathan*, he gives every impression of taking at face value the Bible's image of Moses as a holy vehicle of God's providence and justice. Hobbes's private views seem quite different. One gets a further indication of Hobbes's irreverent attitude vis-à-vis the Mosaic narrative in another story narrated by Aubrey. According to Aubrey, Hobbes was being tormented by "Divines" of various denominations during an illness in France. "Sayd he to them, 'Let me alone, or els I will detect all your Cheates, from Aaron to yourselves.'" *Brief Lives*, ed. John Buchanan-Brown, 441.

22 Thomas Hobbes, *Leviathan*, rev. student ed., ed. Richard Tuck (Cambridge: Cambridge University Press, 1996), 487–8.

23 This is Edwin Curley's version of what is rendered in Aubrey, *Brief Lives*, ed. Buchanan-Brown, 441, as "cut through him a barre's length." For discussion, see Beiner, *Civil Religion*, 87n1.

24 Machiavelli, *Discourses on Livy*, 8.

25 Ibid., 144; cf. 9.

26 *New York Review of Books*, 22 March 2018.

27 Machiavelli, *Discourses on Livy*, 145.

28 Michael Walzer, *In God's Shadow: Politics in the Hebrew Bible* (New Haven: Yale University Press, 2012), 169.

29 Jean-Jacques Rousseau, *On the Social Contract*, ed. Roger D. Masters, trans. Judith R. Masters (New York: St. Martin's, 1978), 127.

30 See Thomas Hobbes, *On the Citizen*, ed. Richard Tuck and Michael Silverthorne (Cambridge: Cambridge University Press, 1998), 195.

31 Walzer, *In God's Shadow*, xiv; cf. top of 177. I was once asked by Walzer in person what I made of the whole image of "neo-Hebraic republicanism" conjured up by the group of scholars assembled around the (unfortunately now-defunct) journal *Hebraic Political Studies*. I told him I found it intellectually exhilarating. Walzer chuckled and gave roughly the following response: "But it's all just made up. It's a fiction." Reading a "Hebraic republican" like Harrington helps clarify why Walzer said that, as we'll see in the next section.

32 Hobbes, *On the Citizen*, 198; Hobbes's italics.

33 Ibid., 198.

34 Ibid., 195.

35 Ibid., 195–6.

36 Ibid., 196.

37 Ibid.

38 Ibid.

39 Ibid.

40 Cf. Steffens, *Moses in Red*, 120: "The motive was probably ambition." I return to the puzzle about Aaron's non-punishment in chapter 4.

41 Hobbes, *On the Citizen*, 197; my italics. It's surely worthy of note that Hobbes goes so far as to call Eleazar a "king," which, if taken literally, means that strictly speaking, the Israelite monarchy did not commence with Saul.

42 Ibid.

43 Ibid.

44 Ibid., 199.

45 Ibid., 201; my italics.

46 Ibid.

47 Ibid.

48 Rousseau, *On the Social Contract*, 127.

49 Quoted in Jeffrey R. Collins, *The Allegiance of Thomas Hobbes* (Oxford: Oxford University Press, 2005), 267.

50 Alison McQueen, "Mosaic Leviathan," in *Hobbes on Politics and Religion*, ed. Laurens van Apeldoorn and Robin Douglass (Oxford: Oxford University Press, 2018), 116–34. My thanks to Zachariah Black for alerting me to this fine article.

51 Ibid., 117; cf. 125, 129.

52 Ibid., 118; cf. 131–2. A leading figure among these republican thinkers and polemicists is Harrington, who will be treated in the next section. Milton is obviously another such figure.

53 Ibid., 118.

54 Ibid., 126–7.

55 Hobbes, *Leviathan*, 324, 336. Cf. 282 (chap. 35): "The High Priest was to be (*after the death of Moses*) his sole Viceroy, or Lieutenant" (my italics). The implication of the parenthesis is surely that the office of God's "sole Viceroy or Lieutenant" is held by Moses, not Aaron.

56 McQueen, "Mosaic Leviathan," 129.

57 Walzer, *In God's Shadow*, 137.

58 Also pointing in the same direction is Leviticus 10:16–20, as was helpfully pointed out to me by one of the publisher's reviewers. In the words of this reviewer, "Aaron corrects Moses and Moses accedes." The text is difficult and admits of conflicting interpretations, which are summarized well by Robert Alter in a note on verse 19. But it appears that Aaron is letting Moses know that Moses's "fury" at Aaron's two surviving sons takes insufficient account of Aaron's legitimate mourning for his two other sons, who had been struck dead. See Robert Alter, trans., *The Hebrew Bible: A Translation with Commentary*, vol. 1 (New York: W.W. Norton, 2019), 400–1.

59 Hobbes, *Leviathan*, 386. The context here is the papacy's appeal to Deuteronomy 17:12 as a basis for rendering the priesthood the supreme authority, superior even to civil authority. Hence, Hobbes's collapsing of any distinction, under the Mosaic regime, between priestly authority and civil authority is intended to have the effect of negating that papal claim.

60 Highly relevant to this question are two texts cited by Cunaeus – Exodus 25:22 and Numbers 7:89 – that suggest that Moses was absolutely privileged in relation to Aaron with respect to encountering God in the Holy of Holies: see Petrus Cunaeus, *The Hebrew Republic*, trans. Peter Wyetzner (Jerusalem: Shalem Press, 2006), 92–3. Clearly, these two biblical texts are inconsistent with Exodus 40:35 (or certainly seem to be).

61 Hobbes, *On the Citizen*, 197.

62 Ibid., 196.

63 I'm grateful to Sarah B. Greenberg for sharing with me the Hobbes chapter in her recently completed Cornell University PhD thesis. This chapter, entitled "The Many Moses's of Hobbes's *Leviathan*: Covenant, Sovereignty, and Authority," offers a helpful and interesting discussion of the multiplicity of Hobbesian images of Moses. Greenberg distinguishes four distinct aspects of the Hobbesian Moses: "Moses personating the Israelites, Moses personating God, Moses as God the king's lieutenant, Moses as legitimate ruler by consent of the people." On her account, Hobbes seeks to elide rather than acknowledge the tensions among these different personae; and he deliberately excludes the trope privileged by the republican tradition, namely Moses as lawgiver. As Greenberg rightly points out, "it is hard to reconcile [Hobbes's] Moses-as-leviathan with … the Moses of the Hebrew Bible [who] is born in, shaped by, and dies due to disobedience and dissent."

64 For a broad account of such appropriations, see Eric Nelson's extremely helpful book, *The Hebrew Republic: Jewish Sources and the Transformation of European Political Thought* (Cambridge, MA: Harvard University Press, 2010). See also Rachel Hammersley, *James Harrington: An Intellectual Biography* (Oxford: Oxford University Press, 2019), 170–6. We will return to Cunaeus's work, *The Hebrew Republic*, in the next chapter.

65 Ronald Beiner, "James Harrington on the Hebrew Commonwealth," *Review of Politics* 76, no. 2 (Spring 2014): 169–93.

66 For relevant references in Harrington's work, see Beiner, "James Harrington on the Hebrew Commonwealth," 191–2n59.

67 *The Political Works of James Harrington*, ed. J.G.A. Pocock (Cambridge: Cambridge University Press, 1977), 374.

68 Cf. Thomas L. Pangle and Timothy W. Burns, *The Key Texts of Political Philosophy: An Introduction* (New York: Cambridge University Press, 2015), 132.

69 *The Political Works of James Harrington*, 519. Note that Harrington makes a distinction between "the priests" and "the Levites." This fits with the idea, discussed earlier, of the Levites as sub-priests. See Cunaeus, *The Hebrew Republic*, 106–7 for a good explanation of how the Levites related to the priests. Priests were descendants of Aaron's sons Eleazar and Ithamar and hence were privileged in relation to Levites who had not descended from Aaron. The priests, by virtue of their descent from Aaron, were

obviously also "sons of Levi," but they were not considered Levites on account of their superior status. Eric Voegelin hypothesizes that the split between priests and Levites arose from the centralization of the cult in Jerusalem, thus imperilling the livelihood of further-afield Levites. These provincial Levites migrated to Jerusalem with the expectation that they would share equally in priestly income, an expectation sharply rebuffed by the Jerusalem priests. See Voegelin, *Order and History*, vol. 1, *Israel and Revelation* (Baton Rouge: Louisiana State University Press, 1956), 370–1. Yet the story of the Levite revolt under the leadership of Korah tells us fairly unmistakably that the subordination of Levites to priests goes back to the Hebrews in the desert.

70 McQueen, "Mosaic Leviathan," 124. Kalman Neuman has pointed out that one of Harrington's Hebraist sources, Carlo Sigonio, "used the Roman model to fill in the blanks in the biblical text," hence assuming "that when the Bible describes assemblies of the people, it is referring to a formal institution subject to precise laws." "Political Hebraism and the Early Modern 'Respublica Hebraeorum,'" in *Political Hebraism: Judaic Sources in Early Modern Political Thought*, ed. Gordon Schochet, Fania Oz-Salzberger, and Meirav Jones (Jerusalem: Shalem Press, 2008), 63. Thus Harrington, following Sigonio, may have made the same dubious assumption.

71 Philo, *On the Special Laws*, bk. 4, Loeb Classical Library: Philo, vol. 8, trans. F.H. Colson (Cambridge, MA: Harvard University Press, 1939), 105, 107.

72 Contrary to this argument, Cunaeus points out aspects of Moses's regime that he claims rested upon *chirothesia* – for instance, the appointment of those elevated to the Sanhedrin and the appointment of Joshua as Moses's successor: see Cunaeus, *The Hebrew Republic*, 48; cf. 51, 54. It's not obvious on what basis one would adjudicate between Cunaeus and Harrington on this question, though I'm fairly strongly inclined to think that Cunaeus's view is more plausible. As regards Moses's "laying of hands upon" Joshua, see Numbers 27:18 and 27:23, which certainly make no reference to any popular election of Moses's successor.

73 As regards the theme of priestly corruption of the originally virtuous Mosaic republic, one can find narratives similar to this in book 1, chapters 15 and 16 and book 2, chapter 9 of Cunaeus's *The Hebrew Republic* and in chapter 18 of Spinoza's *Theological-Political Treatise*.

74 Fox, *The Five Books of Moses*, 850. Alter's translation (*The Hebrew Bible*, 618–19) is very similar to Fox's.

75 *The Political Works of James Harrington*, 520–1.

76 Ibid., 520.

77 Ibid., 522–3; cf. bottom of 530.

78 See, e.g., ibid., 177, 305, 617, 629, 652.

79 Beiner, "James Harrington on the Hebrew Commonwealth," 191–2.

80 *The Political Works of James Harrington*, 629.

81 Ibid., 652.

82 Ibid., 629. Harrington doesn't specify who were the "politicians" accused of being irreverent or atheistical for assimilating Israel to profane commonwealths and assimilating Moses to pagan founders of such commonwealths, but Pocock, in note 5, plausibly suggests Machiavelli. For a full referencing of relevant texts, see Beiner, "James Harrington on the Hebrew Commonwealth," 191–2n59.

83 *The Political Works of James Harrington*, 652; my italics.

84 Gary Remer, "James Harrington's Commonwealth of Israel," in *Political Hebraism*, ed. Schochet, Oz-Salzberger, and Jones, 222.

85 Walzer, *In God's Shadow*, 205. Irving Zeitlin, in *Ancient Judaism* (Cambridge: Polity Press, 1984), 101–3, offers a view more supportive of Harrington than Walzer's view. Zeitlin (following Robert Gordis) calls ancient Israel a "primitive democracy." He claims that the two Hebrew words for assembly – *edah* and *kahal* – used in conjunction with the word for people – *am* – "point to the existence of a public assembly of the male 'citizenry.' This assembly is the sovereign political and judicial authority" (p. 102).

86 Pangle and Burns, *The Key Texts of Political Philosophy*, 135. Donald Harmon Akenson calls Korah "a protocongregationalist." *God's Peoples* (Montreal: McGill-Queen's University Press, 1991), 17. It's possible to say that the championing of Korah offered by Harrison Fluss in chapter 3 is not only Spinozistic (as the chapter explicitly emphasizes) but also Harringtonian, in the sense that Korah represents the stirring of a more democratic potential within the Hebrew regime. But of course, what is actually unfolded in the story is the brutal crushing of this potential. We will return to all these difficult questions concerning the nature of the Hebraic regime, including the Harringtonian interpretation of it, in chapter 2.

87 See Noel Malcolm, *Aspects of Hobbes* (Oxford: Clarendon Press, 2002), chap. 12. Consider that Vico still assumes Genesis to have been written by Moses: *The New Science of Giambattista Vico*, trans. Thomas Goddard Bergin and Max Harold Fisch (Ithaca, NY: Cornell University Press, 1984), 211–12 (para. 585), 220 (para. 601).

88 Spinoza, *Theological-Political Treatise*, 51.

89 Ibid.

90 Ibid., 51–2.

91 Ibid., 60. Spinoza's suggestion that the Hebrew God promises his chosen people merely "worldly success" is echoed in Locke's statement that the kind of messianic fulfilment promised to the Hebrews was strictly oriented toward "the Grandeur of a Temporal Kingdom in this World, and the Protection and Prosperity they had promised themselves under it." John Locke, *The Reasonableness of Christianity as Delivered in the Scriptures*, ed. John C. Higgins-Biddle (Oxford: Clarendon Press, 1999), 62.

92 Hobbes, *On the Citizen*, 205.
93 Spinoza, *Theological-Political Treatise*, 41.
94 Ibid., 38; my italics.
95 Ibid., 39.
96 Ibid., 60.
97 Ibid.
98 Ibid., 31.
99 Here Spinoza cites Psalm 139:21–2: "Do not I hate them, O LORD, that hate thee? … I hate them with perfect hatred: I count them mine enemies."
100 Spinoza, *Theological-Political Treatise*, 197–8.
101 Ibid., 198n4. Feldman refers to Spinoza's text as "false allegations" driven by Spinoza's "political agenda."
102 See Beiner, *Civil Religion*, 125n20, 131–2n61.
103 Cf. ibid., 129: "Spinoza is far more sympathetic to Moses's achievements as a *legislator* than he is to the content of Mosaic *religion*."
104 Galatians 2:16, 2:19, 2:21; Romans 2:28–9. Cf. Pangle and Burns, *The Key Texts of Political Philosophy*, 148.
105 It's worth noting that Freud's view, in *Moses and Monotheism*, of the Judaism-Christianity relationship is the direct opposite of Spinoza's: "The Christian religion did not maintain [the lofty spiritual/intellectual heights] to which Judaism had soared. It was no longer strictly monotheist, it took over numerous symbolic rituals from surrounding peoples, it re-established the great mother-goddess and found room to introduce many of the divine figures of polytheism only lightly veiled … Above all, it did not, like the Aten religion and the Mosaic religion which followed it, exclude the entry of superstitious, magical and mystical elements." *The Standard Edition of the Complete Psychological Works of Sigmund Freud*, vol. 23 (London: Vintage, 2001), 88. That is, for Freud Christianity represents "a cultural regression" back to pagan materiality and sensuality from the purity, abstraction, and spirituality/intellectuality (*Geistigkeit*) of Jewish monotheism. It's possible that Freud's conception of Judaism as pre-eminently intellectual/spiritual was an appropriation of Tacitus's dictum (intended as criticism!) that "the Jews … have a purely spiritual conception" of their god. Tacitus, *The Histories*, ed. D.S. Levene, trans. W.H. Fyfe (Oxford: Oxford University Press, 1999), 236 (bk. 5). Jan Assmann offers a more literal translation: "The Jews conceive of [their god] with the mind only [*mente sola*]." *Moses the Egyptian* (Cambridge: Harvard University Press, 1997), 37. We'll discuss Freud's view further in chapter 4 under the rubric of "God's Visibility/Invisibility."
106 Rousseau, *On the Social Contract*, 125; Rousseau's biblical citation is the book of Judges 11:24.

107 Cf. Fox, *The Five Books of Moses*, 859, note to Deuteronomy 2:34; but see Walzer's point about the god of the Moabites discussed below, near the end of the Thomas Paine section.

108 "Doomed to destruction" is the translation in Jean-Jacques Rousseau, *The Social Contract and Other Later Political Writings*, ed. Victor Gourevitch (Cambridge: Cambridge University Press, 1997), 143.

109 Alter, *The Hebrew Bible*, 665, 686, translates these texts as "putting it under the ban"/"put them under the ban." As discussed elsewhere, the Hebrew concept is *herem*.

110 Fox, *The Five Books of Moses*, 941n17.

111 In an accompanying note, Rousseau complains that a French translation of the biblical text "weakens [the] recognition" of the rights of the Ammonite god, relative to the Latin translation in the Vulgate. For an interesting discussion of "holy war" and its mandating of genocide, as opposed to wars *not* commanded by one's god, which can abide by a "limited war doctrine," see Walzer, *In God's Shadow*, chap. 3.

112 Cf. Pangle and Burns, *The Key Texts of Political Philosophy*, 136: "God's unambiguous commandment of pitiless exterminating conquest." We'll return to these issues of paramount significance in chapter 4.

113 For a full elaboration of my reading of Rousseau on civil religion, see Beiner, *Civil Religion*, chaps. 1, 7, 8, as well as Ronald Beiner, "Rousseau's Place in the Civil-Religion Tradition," in *The Rousseauian Mind*, ed. Eve Grace and Christopher Kelly (Abingdon, UK: Routledge, 2019), 365–75. In those commentaries, I make clear why the civil religion chapter as a "brief for paganism" is not the full story concerning Rousseau's stance toward paganism in that chapter. On the contrary, Rousseau also offers powerful criticisms of the moral deficiencies of paganism, similar to those offered by Montesquieu, and rightly so. It's also Rousseau's view that in a post-Christian world, pagan horizons are utterly irrecoverable.

114 Jean-Jacques Rousseau, *The Government of Poland*, trans. Willmoore Kendall (Indianapolis: Hackett, 1985), 5–6. The Machiavelli section above offers some discussion of the significance of opting for Numa over Romulus as privileged Roman lawgiver.

115 Ibid., 8.

116 Ibid., 6. Rousseau's claim that the Hebrews fleeing Egypt "possessed no arms" is inconsistent with the biblical text, as is clear from texts we cited and discussed in the introduction.

117 Ibid. Gabriel Rom has brought to my attention a letter in which Rousseau confessed to Emmanuel de Croÿ-Solre that he "found more truth in Moses … than in anything else." Emmanuel Croÿ and Paul Cottin, *Journal inédit du duc de Croÿ, 1718-1784* (Paris: Flammarion, 1907), 15.

118 *The Collected Writings of Rousseau*, vol. 4, ed. Roger D. Masters and Christopher Kelly (Hanover, NH: University Press of New England, 1994), 33–4. The concluding paragraph initially suggests that "a unique marvel" like this must exhibit "the hand of God." But his subsequent reference to "divine *or human* causes" (my italics) reintroduces doubt about whether Providence or human design accounts for the exemplary staying power of the Jews ("none except [the Jewish nation] sustained all trials and always resisted"). And as I have highlighted, Rousseau's account in *The Government of Poland* gives *exclusive credit to Moses* for the Hebrew institutions praised by Rousseau.

119 Rousseau, *The Government of Poland*, 6. Cf. Everett Fox's commentary in Fox, *The Five Books of Moses*, 882. "On the Jews" begins with a criticism of the pervasive "transplanting," "intermingling," and "mixing" of peoples and races that cause human beings to be thoroughly alienated from their "autochthonous" homelands. *Collected Writings*, vol. 4, 33. Rousseau's story about the Jews is that for them uniquely, migration to other lands inhabited by other peoples did *not* obliterate their distinct identity as a people.

120 In political fragment 26 (*Collected Writings*, vol. 4, 34–5), Rousseau imagines a kind of "dialogue in Hades" between Moses on the one hand and Lycurgus, Solon, and Numa on the other so that Moses can "come to taste at last the sweetness of conversing with [his] fellows." The pagan founders express surprise that Moses, "who scorned us so," would seek out their company. Moses, in reply, insists that it is precisely in the midst of his fellow lawgivers that "I come among my own kind." That is, the community to which he genuinely belongs is not the merely ethnic-religious community of Hebrews but the philosophically higher community of epic founders of states that have left a lasting imprint on world history.

121 Freud offers an interesting suggestion in regard to the riddle of Israel's endurance: "The historians say that if Jerusalem had not been destroyed, we Jews would have perished like so many races before and after us. According to them the invisible edifice of Jerusalem became possible only after the collapse of the visible Temple"; quoted in Yosef Hayim Yerushalmi, *Freud's Moses: Judaism Terminable and Interminable* (New Haven: Yale University Press, 1991), 67. But surely other civilizations have had their visible temples destroyed. Why should that in itself contribute to solving the riddle?

122 *The Collected Writings of Rousseau*, vol. 9, ed. Christopher Kelly and Eve Grace (Hanover, NH: University Press of New England, 2001), 54. Vico similarly refers to "the hostility with which … the Jews have always regarded the gentiles." *The New Science*, 125 (para. 396).

123 Jean-Jacques Rousseau, *Emile*, trans. Allan Bloom (New York: Basic Books, 1979), 308. This is one among many Spinozistic gestures in the "Profession of Faith of a Savoyard Vicar" (*Emile*, 266–313). Rousseau seems to replicate the tension-ridden attitude that we noted in our discussion of Spinoza: strong admiration for Moses qua civil-religionist paired with severe unhappiness with the religion that Moses originated.

124 John Toland, *Nazarenus*, ed. Justin Champion (Oxford: Voltaire Foundation, 1999), 237. *Nazarenus* was originally published in 1718 – that is, fifty-four years before Rousseau completed *The Government of Poland* (1772). Miriam Bodian has unearthed a very similar suggestion in a seventeenth-century Dutch work, *The Triumph of Popular Government*, by Daniel Levi de Barrios: "While the Chaldeans, Phoenicians, Egyptians, Persians, Medeans, Greeks, and Romans had all perished along with their monarchies and laws, 'the Law of Moses persists among the people who observe it.'" "The Biblical 'Jewish Republic' and the Dutch New Israel in Seventeenth-Century Dutch Thought," in *Political Hebraism*, ed. Schochet, Oz-Salzberger, and Jones, 160.

125 Toland, *Nazarenus*, 239.

126 Ibid., 235. Toland's reference to "the Atlantis of Plato" is presumably a reference to Plato's dialogues *Timaeus* and *Critias*.

127 Toland, *Nazarenus*, 236. Cf. Nietzsche's reference in *Beyond Good and Evil*, § 251, to "the Jewish type" as *aere perennius* (more enduring than bronze), by comparison with which modern European nations appear as "evolving, young, and easily changed." *Basic Writings of Nietzsche*, ed. Walter Kaufmann (New York: Modern Library, 1968), 378. Of course, this assumes that whatever it is that renders the Jews Jewish is monolithic across the centuries, which is, to say the least, a highly dubious assumption.

128 Toland, *Nazarenus*, 239. Henry Neville is another significant figure in the Harringtonian orbit who similarly appropriates Moses for republican purposes. See Neville's "Plato Redivivus," in *Two English Republican Tracts*, ed. Caroline Robbins (Cambridge: Cambridge University Press, 1969), 86, 94, 102–3. However, there is a strangely opposing side to Toland's relationship to Moses. Bronisław Baczko, "Moïse, législateur ...," in *Reappraisals of Rousseau*, ed. S. Harvey et al. (Manchester: Manchester University Press, 1980), 113–14, places Toland within a tradition of deist and free-thinking *critics* of Moses; on p. 113, Baczko refers to Toland's "denunciation" of Moses and the Mosaic law. (My thanks to Emma Planinc for bringing this useful article to my attention.) There's a similar account in Assmann, *Moses the Egyptian*, 91–6. Assmann's book is a terrifically ambitious survey of such anti-biblical intellectual traditions, whose resumption he sees in Freud's account of Moses. Both Baczko and Assmann focus on Toland's *Origines Judaicae* (1709). All of this certainly

suggests that, like Rousseau a half-century later, Toland celebrates Moses as the founder of a civilizational polity without approving of Mosaic religion. As Baczko notes (p. 122), to treat Moses as a great legislator, no matter how exalted, is to posit "un Moïse laïcisé, personage profane" (a secularized, profane Moses). For an interesting discussion of *Origines Judaicae*, which was Toland's attempt to weaponize Strabo in his war against priestcraft, see Sundar Henny, "Caught in the Crossfire of Early Modern Controversy: Strabo on Moses and His Corrupt Successors," *Intellectual History Review* 28, no. 1 (2018): 35–59. On pp. 49–51, Henny gives an extremely helpful account of how Toland manages to balance the positive and negative aspects of his highly tension-ridden stance toward Moses. The most comprehensive treatment of this labyrinthine topic can be found in the work of Justin Champion, notably: "Toland and the Traité des trois imposteurs c1709–1718," *International Archives of the History of Ideas* 148 (1990): 333–56; *Republican Learning*, chap. 7; and "*Mosaica Respublica*: Harrington, Toland and Moses."

129 Thomas Paine, *The Age of Reason*, ed. Moncure Daniel Conway (Mineola, NY: Dover, 2004), 34–5.

130 Ibid., 90.

131 Ibid., 102.

132 Ibid.

133 Ibid., 103.

134 Ibid.

135 Ibid., 106.

136 See, e.g., Davor Džalto, "Nationalism, Statism, and Orthodoxy," *St. Vladimir's Theological Quarterly* 57 (2013): 503–23; M.D. Suslov, "'Holy Rus': The Geopolitical Imagination in the Contemporary Russian Orthodox Church," *Russian Politics and Law* 52 (2014): 67–86.

137 Paine, *The Age of Reason*, 96. As is clear from Baczko, "Moïse, législateur …," 115–17, there's little in Paine's indictment of Moses that can't already be found in Voltaire and Diderot.

138 Beiner, *Civil Religion*, 75n5.

139 Walzer, *In God's Shadow*, 35. Exactly the same point is made by Robert A. Yelle on p. 6 of an unpublished article entitled "A Return to or an Exit from Sacred Kingship? Thomas Hobbes contra Jan Assmann on the Meaning of the Exodus and the Relation between Religion and Politics" (2020), available at the following link: https://www.academia.edu/42097385/_A_Return_to_or_an_Exit_from_Sacred_Kingship_Thomas_Hobbes_contra_Jan_Assmann_on_the_Meaning_of_the_Exodus_and_the_Relation_between_Religion_and_Politics_

See also Assmann, *The Invention of Religion*, 87; Everett Fox, trans., *The Early Prophets: Joshua, Judges, Samuel, and Kings*, Schocken Bible, vol. 2

(New York: Schocken Books, 2014), 9; Zeitlin, *Ancient Judaism*, 147. Zeitlin comments, "The annihilation of one's enemies was not uncommon in the ancient world … The non-Israelites in the region also practised the *herem* [= wholesale destruction of one's enemy]."

140 Zeitlin, *Ancient Judaism*, 147, quotes the inscription on the Moabite stone, which, in the translation he cites, uses exactly the same phrase, "devoted to destruction," that is sometimes used to translate the Hebrew *herem*. In this case, the *herem* is on behalf of the Moabite god, and the victims are the Israelites of Nebo.

141 Paine, *The Age of Reason*, 115: "such monsters and imposters as Moses and Aaron, Joshua, Samuel, and David"; 139: "impostors and liars"; and 151.

142 Ibid., 153.

143 For a contemporary edition and elaborate commentary, see Abraham Anderson, *The Treatise of the Three Impostors and the Problem of Enlightenment* (Lanham, MD: Rowman & Littlefield, 1997). See also Jonathan Israel, *Radical Enlightenment* (Oxford: Oxford University Press, 2001), 694–700.

144 Rousseau, *On the Social Contract*, 70.

145 For my full commentary on Maistrean theocracy, see Beiner, *Civil Religion*, chaps. 25–7.

146 Joseph de Maistre, *On God and Society*, ed. Elisha Greifer (Chicago: Henry Regnery, 1959), 40; Maistre's italics.

147 Ibid., 41; cf. 42: "a magnificent exception."

148 Ibid., 41. By contrast to this claim of the law's timeless perfection "even to the smallest details," Montesquieu states that "divine wisdom" claims only relative goodness, not absolute goodness, on behalf of the Mosaic laws with their many "difficulties." *The Spirit of the Laws*, ed. Anne Cohler, Basia Miller, and Harold Stone (Cambridge: Cambridge University Press, 1989), 322 (bk. 19, chap. 21). Maistre's reference to "fifteen hundred years" is puzzling. Does he mean that the Mosaic dispensation lapses with the start of the Christian dispensation? But if so, in what sense can one speak of it having "withstood time"?

149 Maistre, *On God and Society*, 41–2. The sentence continues with an attack on William Warburton's *The Divine Legation of Moses*. Maistre doesn't spell out what he calls the book's "miserable fallacy," though it is fairly clearly Warburton's attempt to vindicate the divinity of Mosaic law by turning deist arguments against themselves. Cf. Baczko, "Moïse, législateur …," 118.

150 Maistre, *On God and Society*, 43n24.

151 Ibid., 42. The "general law" is: no written constitutions. But the Author of this general law is simultaneously the Author of the written Mosaic constitution that constitutes a supposed exception to this general law – a veritable paradox!

152 Ibid.; my italics.

153 Ibid., 42n23: "*No institution whatsoever may endure if it be not founded on religion*"; Maistre's italics.

154 Even more paradoxical are the echoes, in Maistre's conception of the Mosaic regime as a kind of eternal constitution, of Toland's conception, quoted in an earlier section, of the Mosaic polity as the unique model of an immortal commonwealth. Rousseau and Toland are both ardent republicans, a vision of politics obviously despised by Maistre.

155 Fox, *The Five Books of Moses*, 736.

156 John Locke, *A Letter Concerning Toleration and Other Writings*, ed. Mark Goldie (Indianapolis: Liberty Fund, 2010), 41; Locke's italics.

157 Ibid., 42.

158 Ibid.; Locke's italics.

159 Ibid. On the same page, Locke issues the following challenge: "Now if any one can shew me where there is a Commonwealth, at this time, constituted upon that Foundation, I will acknowledg that the Ecclesiastical Laws do there unavoidably become a part of the Civil; and that the Subjects of that Government both may, and ought to be kept in strict conformity with that Church, by the Civil Power" – i.e., acknowledge that it is normatively legitimate to suspend his own liberal-secularist principles. But as I point out in *Civil Religion*, 155, it would have sufficed for Locke to have considered the Calvinist theocracy in Geneva (a theocratic regime that Locke himself attacks merely a few pages earlier!) in order to have the "Commonwealth constituted upon that Foundation" that he suggests is nowhere to be found "at this time." For the repudiation of Genevan theocracy, see Locke, *A Letter Concerning Toleration and Other Writings*, 38–9. Goldie (p. 39n92) refers to "Calvin's burning of Michael Servetus for heresy in 1553" as the kind of thing that Lockean principles categorically prohibit but that apparently are permitted in the context of ancient Israel. For a helpful sketch of Calvin's intention to model his Genevan theocracy on the ancient Hebrew archetype, see Akenson, *God's Peoples*, 111–12.

160 Locke, *A Letter Concerning Toleration and Other Writings*, 43; Locke's italics. Hobbes, of course, had his own version of this conception, and one can't rule out that Locke partly borrowed it from him, as he seems to have borrowed so much else. (See Beiner, *Civil Religion*, 161n33.) At the start of chapter 35 of *Leviathan*, Hobbes offers a discussion of the Hebrews as "peculiar Subjects" of God, which explains how God can legislate civil laws relevant only to them, hence securing his status as their "King"; see *Leviathan*, 280–2. Cf. McQueen ("Mosaic Leviathan," 132), who calls this the "exceptionalism" of the Hebrews in relation to God.

161 Locke, *A Letter Concerning Toleration and Other Writings*, 43.

162 Ibid., 40.

163 Ibid., 42. We return in chapter 4 to the question of what to make of a god who apparently doesn't subscribe to Lockean principles of religious toleration.

164 See Richard J. Bernstein, *Freud and the Legacy of Moses* (Cambridge: Cambridge University Press, 1998), 118. Some have resorted to biographical explanations for Freud's Moses obsession, focusing, for instance, on Freud's father's intriguing Hebrew inscription in an edition of the Bible presented to Sigmund on his thirty-fifth birthday. For a powerful account, see Yerushalmi, *Freud's Moses*, chap. 4.

165 Quoted in Bluma Goldstein, *Reinscribing Moses: Heine, Kafka, Freud, and Schoenberg in a European Wilderness* (Cambridge, MA: Harvard University Press, 1992), 96; it's from a letter to Zweig dated 16 December 1934. It would seem that ancient Egypt pursued Freud even more incessantly than Moses did. Simon Goldhill rightly notes the irony of Freud composing *Moses and Monotheism* at 20 Maresfield Gardens on a desk adorned with statues of "pagan, polytheistic gods." *Freud's Couch, Scott's Buttocks, Brontë's Grave* (Chicago: University of Chicago Press, 2011), 116.

166 According to Richard Wolin ("Biblical Blame Shift," *Chronicle of Higher Education*, 19 April 2013), Freud erected his Moses interpretation "on the basis of some rather threadbare textual and historical evidence." There is of course no lack of critics for Freud's work in general, but the Moses book seems to have attracted especially intense critical judgment. As Anthony Storr puts it, "*Moses and Monotheism* has been rejected by most critics as one of the least convincing of Freud's writings." *Freud: A Very Short Introduction* (Oxford: Oxford University Press, 1989), 110. Goldhill calls *Moses and Monotheism* Freud's "last and most wacky work." *Freud's Couch, Scott's Buttocks, Brontë's Grave*, 110. Silver (*Images of Moses*, 142) calls the book Freud's "hapless detour into Biblical history." Harold Bloom, on the other hand, includes Freud's "late fiction" among "the best modern literary interpretations of Exodus": see Bloom, ed., *Exodus* (New York: Chelsea House, 1987), vii. Goldstein (*Reinscribing Moses*, 94–5, 103) points to Freud's own doubts about his theories concerning Moses. Freud is explicit about those doubts in *Standard Edition*, 17, 27n2, 41 ("I know myself that my structure has its weak spots"), and 58 (the book "appears like a dancer balancing on the tip of one toe").

167 It's with good reason that theorists have recruited Freud into the canon of political philosophy, whether or not Freud himself would have welcomed this. I have offered my own attempt at making the case for Freud's status as a political philosopher in Ronald Beiner, *Political Philosophy: What It Is and Why It Matters* (New York: Cambridge University Press, 2014), xxx–xliii.

168 Goldstein, *Reinscribing Moses*, 122.

169 Ibid., 134–5. As regards Goldstein's claim that "it was current attacks on Jews that once again aroused his interest in Moses," see Freud, *Standard Edition*, 105, referring to "problems ... which recent events have forced upon our observation anew," which certainly seems to imply that it was the rise of fascism that drew Freud back to reflection on the "special character-traits" of the Jews, much of which derives, according to Freud, from the sense of chosenness conferred on the Jews by Moses.

170 Freud, *Standard Edition*, 7.

171 Ibid., 15. On p. 38, he calls him "a great lord."

172 See note 128 above. Freud puts a fair amount of weight on the fact that Moses was in all probability an Egyptian name, the suggestion in Exodus 2:10 to the contrary notwithstanding: see ibid., 7–10. Cf. Voegelin, *Israel and Revelation*, 393–4, which presents the biblical interpretation of the name as a matter of "putting a Hebrew veneer on the Egyptianized Moses." Voegelin goes on to point out that "since the element [in Egyptian names such as Thutmosis or Ahmosis] means 'son,' ... the conjecture is plausible that the missing father was an Egyptian god. In that case the name would have been shortened to Moses (perhaps by himself?) because the theophorous name did not sit too well on the bearer who was in revolt against the Egyptian Son of God [namely Pharaoh]."

173 Freud, *Standard Edition*, 21, 34. On p. 50, Freud calls the volcano god "a coarse, narrow-minded local god, violent and bloodthirsty" – by sharp contrast with the "pacifism" of Aten (p. 63). The suggestion here (which Freud pretty much spells out) is that the Midianite YHWH adopted by Israel was a merely national god among other national gods (to employ Rousseau's conception) and hence didn't rise to the exalted monotheism of the god that Moses inherited from Akhenaten. "It is not even certain that [YHWH's] religion was a genuine monotheism" (p. 50). See also p. 69: YHWH "differed little from the Baalim [local gods] of the neighbouring peoples."

174 Ibid., 41.

175 Ibid., 28.

176 Ibid., 41.

177 Ibid., 40–1. On p. 44, Freud attributes the founding of the religion to a *singular* "priest of Yahweh." Cf. 48: "the other man," meaning the Midianite priest who actually accomplished the founding of the religion subsequently credited to Moses.

178 Ibid., 40. Was there a second Midianite Moses? Sometimes Freud seems to suggest that there was. But I think his main theory is that the story of the Egyptian Moses is embellished in such a way that it subsumes deeds accomplished by some unknown Midianite figure (the "priest

of Yahweh" cited in the last note). Another related inconsistency is that sometimes the founding of the religion is presented as a product of collective deliberation on the part of the tribes, at other times as the brainchild of a particular individual.

179 Ibid., 60–1; cf. 36: "In 1922, Ernst Sellin made a discovery which affected our problem decisively." There are other places in the text where we see slippage from treating Sellin's murder scenario as an interpretation or a theory to treating it as a "fact." See, e.g., p. 69: "Facts and ideas which were intentionally disavowed by what may be called official historians were in fact never lost," and Freud intimates that the "tradition about the end of Moses" discovered by Sellin falls in this category. In the letter to Lou Andreas-Salomé cited in note 164 above, Freud states that Sellin "*has shown that* [my italics] Moses was probably killed a few decades later in a popular uprising."

180 Sellin's "hypothesis": Freud, *Standard Edition*, 37, 47. On p. 58, Freud calls it "Sellin's *suspicion* about the end of Moses" (my italics).

181 Ibid., 37. Freud further speculates (p. 38) that this amalgamation of one segment of the Hebrew people that had experienced bondage in Egypt and another (larger) segment that didn't led in time to the re-segmentation of Israel into a northern kingdom and a southern kingdom.

182 Thomas Mann, *The Tables of the Law*, trans. Marion Faber and Stephen Lehmann (London: Haus Publishing, 2012), 50; cf. 44: "a grumbling reproach [against Moses] that was never very far from the thought of a stoning." Mann's novella had been commissioned for a volume meant to respond to Hitler's Nietzsche-like rejection of the Judeo-Christian moral code (as reported by Hermann Rauschning). But as Michael Wood in his afterword interestingly suggests, contrary to what the project of reaffirming Mosaic morality might have led us to expect, Mann presents Moses as "something of a fanatic, not a gentle humanist we can easily set up against Hitler," at least in part because "Mann had read his Nietzsche too – and had read a lot more Freud than Hitler had." *The Tables of the Law*, 111, 108.

183 Freud, *Standard Edition*, 38–9. This account of the Levites is in tension with the Bible's story of the Korah revolt (a Levite rebellion). But as we observe in note 186 below, Freud didn't feel himself constrained by what the Bible reports about Moses.

184 Ibid., 47.

185 Ibid., 51.

186 Ibid., 33; cf. 41–2. Elsewhere (p. 27n2), he brashly asserts his right to appropriate biblical tradition "arbitrarily," "bringing it up to confirm my views when it suits me and unhesitatingly rejecting it when it contradicts

me." It is rather cheeky for Freud to describe the efforts of biblical redactors as imaginative fiction, since he almost certainly knows that the same is true of his own depiction of Moses, in all likelihood also for tendentious purposes. Hence the subtitle given by Freud to the original version of the book: "An Historical Novel."

187 Ibid., 47.

188 Ibid. Clearly, what Freud means by Moses and Akhenaten sharing "the same fate" is that in both cases, the religious revolutions that they initiated suffered reactionary overthrow.

189 Ibid., 48.

190 Ibid., 50. On pp. 51, 64, and 111, Freud suggests that there is a moral purity in the Mosaic teaching that much later finds full expression in the preaching of the Hebrew prophets. On p. 68, Freud spells out that "contempt for ceremonial" and "great emphasis on ethics" are essential to "the monotheist idea." It is easy to identify parallels here with Max Weber's interpretation of ancient Judaism.

191 Ibid., 50–51. Cf. the suggestion on p. 52 and p. 68 that the Aten religion was "repressed" by the YHWH religion, but nevertheless later emerged victorious over the latter. On p. 63 he formulates the outcome as follows: "In the course of time the god Yahweh lost his own characteristics and grew more and more to resemble the old god of Moses, the Aten."

192 Ibid., 89.

193 As Freud summarizes the theory in the letter to Andreas-Salomé dated 6 January 1935: "Religions owe their compulsive power to the *return of the repressed*" in the sense that "they are reawakened memories of very ancient, forgotten, highly emotional episodes of human history"; Freud's italics. In the same letter, Freud also points out that the basic theory is rooted in the analysis that he had set out in *Totem and Taboo*, and he claims that it was "in the course of six to eight centuries" that the "half-extinguished tradition" of the Mosaic god once again gained the upper hand over the volcano god by which it had been usurped. Bernstein, *Freud and the Legacy of Moses*, 118.

194 Freud, *Standard Edition*, 89.

195 Ibid., 93; cf. 124.

196 Ibid., 94.

197 Ibid., 86.

198 Ibid., 93.

199 Ibid., 90; cf. 135–6.

200 Ibid., 88.

201 Ibid., 91; cf. 106 ("the jealousy of one's brothers and sisters" toward "the declared favourite of the dreaded father").

202 Ibid., 43.

203 Robert A. Paul, *Moses and Civilization* (New Haven: Yale University Press, 1996), 72. Cf. 219: "Throughout his career, [Freud] held to the view that neurosis could be cured by helping the patient remember a forgotten trauma from childhood. And, since people in fact rarely do remember such things, he regarded it as necessary for the analyst to reconstruct the trauma from the clues offered by the symptoms and to present that trauma to the patient. Treating Western civilization as his 'patient,' Freud constructed the supposed historical event of the rebellion of the brothers against the jealous sire of the primal horde" and then extended this template to the interpretation of the Moses story. The weaknesses of this theory "are only too visible. It mistakenly treats a civilization as if it were a person; it appears to assume a transgenerational collective unconscious containing repressed memories on the part of that civilization; and it proposes as real historical traumas a deed and a replay of it in the murder of Moses that have no basis in fact and have never been corroborated with any independent evidence." The murder of Moses constitutes a "replay" in the sense that it re-enacts the primal drama depicted in *Totem and Taboo*. "Fate had brought the great deed and misdeed of primaeval days, the killing of the father, closer to the Jewish people by causing them to repeat it on the person of Moses, an outstanding father-figure" (Freud, *Standard Edition*, 88–9; cf. 101, 129). It seems to have been Freud's somewhat bizarre idea that the original archetype of monotheism was precisely the tyrannical rule of the all-powerful father within the primal horde, and all subsequent versions of monotheism, including Moses's, merely reinstate this archetypal monotheism. That's more or less what he claims on pp. 129–30 and 133–4.

204 Freud, *Standard Edition*, 80: "The reader … is invited to take the step of supposing that something occurred in the life of the human species similar to what occurs in the life of individuals." This supposition, it goes without saying, involves an enormous intellectual leap. On pp. 98–101, Freud attempts to "bridge the gulf between individual and group psychology" by invoking hazy notions of "memory-traces" that derive from "an archaic heritage" having "a phylogenetic origin." On this basis, Freud pronounces himself fully confident in asserting "that men have always known … that they once possessed a primal father and killed him" (p. 101). But all of this is conceptually murky and highly dubious. As Alasdair MacIntyre rightly points out, the notion that "every individual's development recapitulates the history of the race … is a doctrine which it is difficult to make sense of except as an elaborate and fanciful metaphor." *Herbert Marcuse: An Exposition and a Polemic* (New York: Viking, 1970), 54.

205 Freud, *Standard Edition*, 90; cf. 136.

206 Assmann, *Moses the Egyptian*, 167.

207 Freud, *Standard Edition*, 91–2.

208 Ibid., 108.
209 Ibid., 107.
210 Ibid., 109.
211 Ibid., 109–10. And if the great man is a tyrant, he fashions his god in the same image, which is why the God of the Hebrew Bible so often comes across as a capricious bully and autocrat (p. 110). On p. 122, Freud suggests that even the practice of circumcision is a symbolic submission to tyranny since it harks back to "the castration which the primal father once inflicted upon his sons." Here perhaps is the explanation for why Freud refused to circumcise his sons (see the introduction, note 12).
212 I'm grateful to my co-author, Harrison Fluss, for very interesting exchanges about possibly anti-democratic currents in Freud's thinking.
213 I should make clear that I don't go along with Goldhill's judgment that the Moses book is "wacky" or Martin Buber's judgment that it was a terrible mistake for Freud to tread on ground where he was lacking all scholarly competence. Goldhill, *Freud's Couch, Scott's Buttocks, Brontë's Grave*, 110; Buber, *Moses* (Oxford: East and West Library, 1946), 5n1. On the contrary, my view is that the book – whether one finds its overall thesis convincing or not – is genuinely thought-provoking and contains an abundance of ingenious insights.
214 See Yerushalmi, *Freud's Moses*, 58–60.
215 Frederick Crews, *Freud: The Making of an Illusion* (New York: Metropolitan Books, 2017), 22.
216 *The Freud/Jung Letters*, ed. William McGuire (Princeton: Princeton University Press, 1974), 196–7. As was entirely to be expected, Freud before long came to see Jung as a patricidal renegade rather than an anointed successor.

2. The Question of a Mosaic Regime: A Perennial Debate

1 Aristotle, *The Politics*, trans. Carnes Lord (Chicago: University of Chicago Press, 1984), 94 (bk. 3, chap. 6); italics in the Lord translation. Cf. p. 119 (bk. 4, chap. 1). Other translations, such as those by Benjamin Jowett and Ernest Barker, translate *politeia* as "constitution."
2 It would be reasonable to say that even Hobbes held this belief, because Hobbes and Harrington *share* the view that Hebrew monarchy, starting with Saul, was established on a foundation of popular will. Indeed, it can be plausibly argued that Harrington followed Hobbes's lead concerning the interpretation of 1 Samuel 8. For further discussion, see Ronald Beiner, "James Harrington on the Hebrew Commonwealth," *Review of Politics* 76, no. 2 (Spring 2014): 185–7, including the summary of relevant commentaries on Harrington's debt to Hobbes on p. 186n45.

3 The regime question is also salient in some of the intellectual history sketched by Fabrizio Lelli in "Moses as Legislator in Fifteenth-Century Italian Jewish and Christian Authors," *Intellectual History Review* 29, no. 1 (2019): 35–52. The thinkers discussed by Lelli all draw upon Platonic and Aristotelian philosophical frameworks in analysing Mosaic law-giving, thereby generating an interesting variety of perspectives with respect to a suitable doctrine of regime. The Platonically oriented tradition often appeals to Moses as a kind of "philosopher-king." But Lelli surveys other noteworthy aspects. For instance, he records Yohanan Alemanno's suggestion that in moving from Pharaoh's Egypt to Jethro's Midian, it became possible for Moses to be schooled in republican virtues (p. 39). Lelli also interestingly juxtaposes Abraham ibn Ezra's criticism of Moses for letting Jethro persuade him to attenuate his monarchy by giving power to "feudal lords" with Isaac Abravanel's praise of Moses for instituting a Venice-like mixed constitution (pp. 43–4). Lelli points out that Abravanel, even though he regarded monarchy as "a sinful institution," acknowledged Moses as "the first king who reigned over Israel" (p. 43).

4 *The Political Works of James Harrington*, ed. J.G.A. Pocock (Cambridge: Cambridge University Press, 1977), 161. Cf. Graham Hammill, *The Mosaic Constitution: Political Theology and Imagination from Machiavelli to Milton* (Chicago: University of Chicago Press, 2012), 219–20 as well as p. 211: one of the "scriptural models" on which Harrington founds his own conception of popular prerogative is "Moses's constitution of Israel as a representative government," with Harrington citing Deuteronomy 1:13 as the relevant text. ("Take you wise men, and understanding, and known among your tribes, and I will make them rulers over you.") See also p. 233: "By the 1650s, Israel had become a central figure among English republicans by which to portray a vision of government grounded in popular sovereignty. So, for example, … Marchamont Nedham turns to the Mosaic constitution in order to argue that "the first and most eminent evidence of the institution of Popular Government in Scripture doth notoriously demonstrate that its origin is *in* or *from the People*""; Nedham's italics. Hammill cites an April 1652 *Mercurius Politicus* editorial by Nedham, which was reprinted in book form in 1656: see Marchamont Nedham, *The Excellencie of a Free-State*, ed. Blair Worden (Indianapolis: Liberty Fund, 2011), 73. For a broader survey of antecedents of Harrington's vision of an original Mosaic commonwealth, Hammill aptly cites Eric Nelson, *The Hebrew Republic* (Cambridge, MA: Harvard University Press, 2010), 20–2, 117–22.

5 *The Political Works of James Harrington*, 205; quoted by Hammill in *The Mosaic Constitution*, 230. Hammill (pp. 231–2) also quotes Harrington's important line that "as the kingdom of God the Father was a

commonwealth, so shall be the kingdom of God the Son" (*Political Works*, 332), projecting forward to a future democratic republicanism that Cromwell's regime, in Harrington's view, failed to deliver. Finally, on p. 234 Hammill highlights the interesting text (*Political Works*, 178) where Harrington notes that Hobbes blamed Greek and Latin authors for "seditions and civil wars" by stoking up an enthusiasm for republican virtue, and then adds that Hobbes might have included Hebrew authors as well.

6 Baruch Spinoza, *Theological-Political Treatise*, 2nd ed., trans. Samuel Shirley (Indianapolis: Hackett, 2001), 189. Cf. Hammill, *The Mosaic Constitution*, 95.

7 Spinoza, *Theological-Political Treatise*, 190.

8 Ibid.

9 Ibid.; my italics. As is generally the case, the confusing division of authority between Moses and Aaron complicates the question of the nature of the regime. Because Aaron was designated "supreme interpreter of God's laws, … his position would have been that of an absolute monarch" *if* "he had held the right of issuing commands" (ibid., 191). But since Moses arguably trumped Aaron with respect to being supreme interpreter of God's laws (notwithstanding Aaron's notional "supreme" authority), and since Moses pretty clearly *did* have a right of issuing commands, we are left with the question of why we should not consider Moses to have been "an absolute monarch."

10 There is one reference to Cunaeus in *Oceana* (*The Political Works of James Harrington*, 280). Harrington also refers to him in *Pian Piano* (*Political Works*, 383), implying strongly that Cunaeus was, along with Selden, Grotius, and a few others, one of the important sources for Harrington's understanding of the Hebrew republic.

11 The normative basis for the institution of Israelite kingship is an important issue in the history of political thought, an authoritative account of which is offered in chapter 1 of Nelson, *The Hebrew Republic*. Various commentators have suggested that it was, in the words of Irving Zeitlin, "the Philistine expansion and their domination of the land that impressed upon Israel the need for the greater organizational unity which a monarchy would bring about." *Ancient Judaism* (Cambridge, UK: Polity Press, 1984), 68; cf. 142, 149. See also Martin Buber, *Kingship of God*, trans. Richard Scheimann (New York: Harper & Row, 1967), 162; Everett Fox, trans., *The Early Prophets: Joshua, Judges, Samuel, and Kings*, Schocken Bible, vol. 2 (New York: Schocken Books, 2014), 128. One gets the same suggestion in Moshe Halbertal and Stephen Holmes, *The Beginning of Politics* (Princeton, NJ: Princeton University Press, 2017), 8: namely, that monarchy "arose under emergency conditions, from the worldly needs of a rickety confederation of tribes that, at this particular moment, were

seeking protection from the better-armed and better-trained Philistines – a new and threatening enemy nation." According to Alison McQueen, this was also Sir Robert Filmer's view: "Filmer was quick to claim that the request [for a king] had been borne of short-term prudential concerns, rather than a considered decision in favour of regime change: 'The people ... hoped for a certainer and speedier deliverance from danger in time of war.'" "Mosaic Leviathan," in *Hobbes on Politics and Religion*, ed. Laurens van Apeldoorn and Robin Douglass (Oxford: Oxford University Press, 2018), 133.

12 Petrus Cunaeus, *The Hebrew Republic*, trans. Peter Wyetzner (Jerusalem: Shalem Press, 2006), 46. Kalman Neuman, "Political Hebraism and the Early Modern 'Respublica Hebraeorum,'" in *Political Hebraism*, ed. Gordon Schochet, Fania Oz-Salzberger, and Meirav Jones (Jerusalem: Shalem Press, 2008), 57–71, helps to situate Cunaeus within a broader intellectual tradition of early-modern political Hebraism. Neuman dubs this "the 'Mosaic moment' in political thought" (p. 60).

13 Cunaeus, *The Hebrew Republic*, 55.

14 Ibid., 3; cf. p. 6: "I ask you ... to study over and again the Hebrew Republic – the holiest and best of all."

15 Ibid., 144. Josephus, in *Against Apion*, goes so far as to claim, not only that "our legislator is the most ancient of all legislators in the records of the whole world" (2.154), but that "Plato followed the example of our legislator" (2.257) and that the Greek philosophers ("our earliest imitators") "were Moses' disciples" (2.281). *The Life/Against Apion*, trans. H. St. J. Thackeray (Cambridge, MA: Harvard University Press, 1926), 353, 397, 405.

16 Cunaeus, *The Hebrew Republic*, 12. For the actual text in Josephus, see *The Life/Against Apion*, 359: "Some peoples have entrusted the supreme political power to monarchies, others to oligarchies, yet others to the masses. Our lawgiver, however, was attracted by none of these forms of polity, but gave to his constitution the form of what – if a forced expression be permitted – may be termed a 'theocracy,' placing all sovereignty and authority in the hands of God" (*Against Apion* 2.16). Cf. Edward W. Said, "Michael Walzer's 'Exodus and Revolution': A Canaanite Reading," *Grand Street* 5, no. 2 (Winter 1986): 93: "Auguste Comte unsurprisingly accorded Moses the dubious privilege of having founded the first theocracy."

17 Cunaeus, *The Hebrew Republic*, 38.

18 Ibid., 3.

19 Ibid., 11.

20 Ibid., 12.

21 Ibid., 11. Cf. 207: "Moses, the wisest of all legislators." How is the exemplary virtue of Moses consistent with the "complete lack of faith"

(p. 218, citing Numbers 20:12) that caused Moses to be excluded from Canaan? Cunaeus doesn't tell us.

22 Ibid., 34.

23 Ibid., 156. Spinoza makes a similar claim: "In [the Hebrew state] civil law and religion ... were one and the same thing; the tenets of religion were not just teachings but laws and commands ... In short, there was considered to be no difference whatsoever between civil law and religion." *Theological-Political Treatise*, 189.

24 Cunaeus, *The Hebrew Republic*, 12–13; my italics.

25 At one place (ibid., 147), Cunaeus refers to *God* as "the greatest of all lawgivers." Elsewhere (pp. 11 and 207, for instance), *Moses* is referred to in this way. It surely matters whether the laws were authored by Moses or by God. If God were the real lawgiver, it would presumably detract from Moses's claimed legal-political genius. If Moses were the real lawgiver, it would presumably detract from the divine authority of the laws. But arguably, the Hebrew Bible itself muddies this issue.

26 Ibid., 13. In chapter 1, we encountered the same idea in Maistre.

27 It's clear throughout Cunaeus's treatise that the Hebrew Republic didn't cease being a republic when it opted for kingship. Cunaeus gives an account of Israel's adoption of monarchy in book 1, chapter 14 (*The Hebrew Republic*, 56–8). He states that God, in Deuteronomy 17:14–20, accepted that Israel would eventually embrace kingship because God realized that "very few of [the people who live in that part of the world] desire freedom; most want only to have just rulers" (p. 56). What this tells us is that Cunaeus didn't require republican liberty as a necessary condition of calling a state a "republic" (as most genuine republican thinkers would). Presumably, the Hebrew republic, on Cunaeus's view, retained its status as a republic even when its kings were *unjust* rulers. It should be noted that the 1653 translation of book 1 by Clement Barksdale was entitled *Of the Common-wealth of the Hebrews*, and Barksdale consistently translated *republica* as "Common-wealth."

28 Cunaeus, *The Hebrew Republic*, 3.

29 Ibid., 13.

30 Ibid., 14–19. For a full discussion, see Nelson, *The Hebrew Republic*, chap. 2. Michael Walzer, in *The Struggle for a Decent Politics* (New Haven: Yale University Press, 2023), 36, suggests that the egalitarianism of the Israelite Jubilee, despite being enshrined in the Mosaic law-code, was "almost certainly" never actually put into practice, hence basically a fiction.

31 Cunaeus, *The Hebrew Republic*, 18; and Niccolò Machiavelli, *Discourses on Livy*, trans. Harvey C. Mansfield and Nathan Tarcov (Chicago: University of Chicago Press, 1996), 8. To be sure, though both Cunaeus and Machiavelli emphasize the paramount theme of republican virtue, their

treatments are different. Machiavelli prefers that cities are built where the soil is sterile so that men "are constrained to be industrious and less seized by idleness," whereas Cunaeus argues that even with fertile land like that seized by the Hebrews in Palestine, well-designed agrarian laws, by preventing social inequality, can keep the citizens virtuous in a sense quite close to Machiavelli's.

32 Aristotle, *The Politics*, bk. 4, chap. 6, quoted in Cunaeus, *The Hebrew Republic*, 21–2. Aristotle argues that being kept busy rather than falling into idleness is a key republican virtue because the citizens "put the law in charge and assemble only for necessary assemblies." But significantly, he makes this argument only for farmer-citizens, not for "craftsmen," and Cunaeus does so as well.

33 Cunaeus, *The Hebrew Republic*, 35.

34 Ibid.; my italics.

35 Ibid., 39.

36 Ibid., 38, 40.

37 Ibid., 41. Cunaeus is here referring to Rome (including imperial Rome); but he clearly implies that the same principle characterizes the Mosaic polity qua republic (p. 38).

38 Ibid., 40. Cunaeus appeals to the authority of Cicero, Livy, and Seneca in articulating this doctrine of popular sovereignty. In chapter 1 we quoted Alison McQueen's comment that "in Harrington's hands, the Mosaic polity became a Roman commonwealth"; and clearly something quite similar applies to Cunaeus.

39 Cunaeus, *The Hebrew Republic*, 48: "These men were not, Heaven forbid, chosen from the common people [*de plebe*]; they were all of the noblest descent." Cf. p. 240n119 (Wyetzner's note), pointing out Cunaeus's debt to "the classical idea that the best form of government is aristocracy."

40 Ibid., 50–1: "The mob [*plebs*], which lacks intelligence and training, is not qualified" to hold offices and magistracies. Cunaeus goes on to endorse Aristotle's view in *Politics*, bk. 3, chap. 11, that by deliberating collectively in an assembly, a multitude can pool their judgments, hence acquiring a "discernment and understanding" that they lack as individuals (p. 51). See also p. 62, where Cunaeus refers to popular freedom as an "empty slogan" manipulated by Jeroboam.

41 Ibid., 50–1. These "highest matters of state" are in addition to the judicial functions of the Sanhedrin, briefly sketched by Cunaeus on p. 50.

42 Michael Walzer, in "Exodus 32 and the Theory of Holy War," *Harvard Theological Review* 61, no. 1 (January 1968): 10, calls it "a careful analysis of the Mosaic polity," which seems a bit more generous than is warranted.

43 *Basic Writings of Saint Thomas Aquinas*, ed. Anton C. Pegis, vol. 2 (New York: Random House, 1945), 919–48.

44 Hammill, *The Mosaic Constitution*, 17. On p. 18, Hammill goes on to discuss the interesting fact that Moses was invoked on both sides of the later Catholic debates between defenders of conciliarism and apologists for unlimited papal authority.

45 Douglas Kries, "Thomas Aquinas and the Politics of Moses," *Review of Politics* 52, no. 1 (Winter 1990): 84–104, at p. 85.

46 Ibid., 85: "Thomas's first task … is to show subtly that although the coming of the New Law abrogates the Old, it does not necessarily forever exile the judicial precepts from Christian political theory." See Hebrews 7:18 (cited by Aquinas in *Basic Writings of Saint Thomas Aquinas*, p. 922): "There is verily a disannulling of the commandments going before for the weakness and unprofitableness thereof."

47 Kries, "Thomas Aquinas and the Politics of Moses," 87. In question 104, article 3, Aquinas states very clearly that "the judicial precepts are no longer in force" (*Basic Writings of Saint Thomas Aquinas*, 922) – obviously because Saint Paul, in Hebrews 7:12 and 7:18, had declared their abrogation. So if Kries is right that Aquinas offers a rational account of the exemplariness of the Mosaic legislation in order to preserve the possibility of "retrieving" the Mosaic laws for Christian politics, it must be a matter of reactivating the validity of laws that for centuries have been in abeyance (and as we will shortly discuss, reactivating them on a completely different basis). Put like this, it seems a very odd project. Kries is fully faithful to the argument as Aquinas presents it. However, Kries doesn't attempt to explain why a legislator of the thirteenth century, or of some later century, would be tempted to restore or retrieve laws that had been designed for a tribal society two and a half millennia before the age in which Aquinas wrote.

48 Hammill, *The Mosaic Constitution*, 17–18.

49 Kries, "Thomas Aquinas and the Politics of Moses," 88. On p. 89, Kries attributes this rationalizing impulse to the influence of Maimonides.

50 Ibid., 88.

51 Ibid., 98.

52 Ibid., 89.

53 *Basic Writings of Saint Thomas Aquinas*, 920. On p. 925, Aquinas informs us that it's also the case with ceremonial precepts that they possess a "binding force, derived, not from natural reason, but from their institution alone."

54 Ibid., 922.

55 Ibid.

56 Ibid., 923.

57 Ibid.

58 Ibid. One must also observe that if the core purpose of the Mosaic laws was to facilitate the reception of Christ by the Jews, it singularly failed in that defining purpose!

59 Ibid., 927. Cf. 924: "Law is the art, as it were, of directing or ordering the life of man."

60 Ibid., 926.

61 Ibid. Aquinas cites Deuteronomy 17:14–15, which projects forward to the events of 1 Samuel 8, whereby *the people* take responsibility for choosing the regime.

62 Aquinas rightly responds (ibid., p. 929) that the harsh depiction of kingship in 1 Samuel 8:11–18 was a prediction of what kingship would become, not a divine authorization of tyranny. But it's curious that kingship's seemingly natural slide into tyranny (fully acknowledged by Aquinas) doesn't raise a much more severe impediment to any talk of monarchy being "the best form of government."

63 Cf. Neuman, "Political Hebraism and the Early Modern 'Respublica Hebraeorum,'" 59. On p. 62, Neuman sketches Cornelius Bertram's 1574 characterization of the Mosaic polity as a mixed regime – an account strikingly similar to that of Aquinas. Also quite relevant is the discussion on pp. 158–62 of Miriam Bodian's chapter in the same volume: "The Biblical 'Jewish Republic' and the Dutch New Israel in Seventeenth-Century Dutch Thought," in *Political Hebraism*, ed. Schochet, Oz-Salzberger, and Jones. Bodian discusses a 1683/1684 work by Daniel Levi de Barrios that parcels out the monarchical, aristocratic, and democratic aspects of Jewish political existence into separate historical moments: "There was, [De Barrios] insisted, no single model of Israelite government. Under Moses, Saul, David, and Solomon, Israelite government was monarchic. Under Joshua, the Judges, and the Maccabees, it was aristocratic. In exile – in Egypt, Babylonia, and the post-antique diaspora (including his own time) – it was democratic." Hence: "God did not ordain a certain form of Israelite government as the proper one for all time," but instead allowed the Jews to adopt different forms of governance in different phases of their history (p. 159).

64 *Basic Writings of Saint Thomas Aquinas*, 927.

65 Ibid., 928. The rare biblical texts in which the people either choose members of the Sanhedrin or choose kings seem a slender basis upon which to claim that democracy is an established component of the regime. If there were more evidence, presumably Aquinas would have cited it.

66 Kries, "Thomas Aquinas and the Politics of Moses," 90.

67 Ibid., 90–3.

68 *Basic Writings of Saint Thomas Aquinas*, 928.

69 If in Aquinas's view the ancient Hebrews were naturally prone to these severe vices (cf. ibid., p. 943, reply to objection 3), one would be interested to know why he thinks that God nonetheless elected them to be his chosen people.

70 Ibid., 928. As Aquinas rightly notes, God consented to the inauguration of a human monarchy on account of his "being indignant with" the people, rather than on the basis of its excellence as a regime. When Aquinas states in the reply to objection 2 that "a kingdom is the best form of government of the people, *so long as it is not corrupt*" (my italics), the qualifying phrase in effect cancels out the assertion of monarchy being the best regime. The Hebrew Bible itself tells us very emphatically to expect corruption in a human king.
71 Ibid.
72 Ibid., 924–5.
73 Ibid., 945. The King James Version has "righteous altogether" where the *Basic Writings* has "justified in themselves" (from the Douay-Rheims Bible).
74 Ibid., 931.
75 Ibid., 937.
76 Ibid., 938; cf. 942, reply to objection 1.
77 Ibid., 938.
78 Ibid., 941.
79 Ibid., 942.
80 Kries, "Thomas Aquinas and the Politics of Moses," 97. The claim about just war is implausible because even in the case of cities *not* covered by the policy of *herem* (i.e., cities where, according to the words of Deuteronomy 20:14, the Hebrews were instructed to "take unto thyself" the women and children rather than slaughtering them all), these were still unprovoked wars of aggression.
81 *Basic Writings of Saint Thomas Aquinas*, 942. Aquinas surely overstates the "moderation" of the Israelites' divinely sanctioned conduct of war. He asserts that God insisted on a just cause for war, but as Aquinas must know, what counted as just cause in this context was simply that the rival nations happened to be inhabiting territory that had been promised to the Hebrews by God. Moreover, as we have discussed elsewhere, in cases where the type of warfare that was commanded involved "sparing women," the purpose for which they were spared admits of far less generous interpretations.
82 Ibid., 943; my italics.
83 Ibid. Aquinas cites Deuteronomy 9:5, invoking "the wickedness of these nations."
84 Josephus, *Jewish Antiquities* 4.223–4, also invokes a classical doctrine of the best regime, putting the following speech in the mouth of Moses: "Aristocracy, with the life that is lived thereunder, is indeed the best: let no craving possess you for another polity, but be content with this, having the laws for your masters and governing all your

actions by them; for God sufficeth for your ruler." This is a strange speech since it clearly implies that the regime established by Moses is a kind of "aristocracy," yet it offers no explanation for why the Mosaic regime, with God serving as its "ruler," should be described as such. The speech goes on to warn the Hebrews that "should ye become enamoured of a king," they should take care that the king remains subordinate to the "superior wisdom" of God and God's laws. "Let him do nothing without the high priest and the counsel of his senators," in order that the king "be restrained from becoming more powerful than is expedient for [the people's] welfare." *Jewish Antiquities* bks. 4–6, trans. H. St. J. Thackeray and Ralph Marcus (Cambridge, MA: Harvard University Press, 1998), 109, 111. This text is cited in John Milton, *Political Writings*, ed. Martin Dzelzainis (Cambridge: Cambridge University Press, 1991), 81, with Milton, as one would expect, emphasizing the restraints on kingship implicit in Josephus's interpretation of the regime as "aristocratic." Is Josephus suggesting that Moses, the high priest, and the seventy senatorial magistrates collectively constitute an aristocratic regime by virtue of their fidelity to divine law? Aquinas refers to Josephus a couple of times in the context of the ceremonial precepts (see *Basic Writings of Saint Thomas Aquinas*, 878–9, 891), but not in the context of the judicial precepts.

85 In question 105, article 1's third objection, Aquinas acknowledges that the "destruction [of the Jewish people] was brought about by the division of the kingdom." Why did a well-ordered regime regulated by wise precepts succumb to "destruction" in this way? See also the reply to objection 3 (p. 929), where Aquinas notes the people's "many dissensions, especially against the just rule of David."

86 Kries, "Thomas Aquinas and the Politics of Moses," 98: "For the most part, Thomas argues that the *Torah* and the *Politics* are in agreement." Also, p. 101: "In Thomas's view, the best natural regime and the best revealed regime are actually the same regime."

87 Ibid., 99.

88 As I point out in chapter 1, "Kingdom of God" is how Hobbes characterizes the Mosaic regime. I'm grateful to Charles Lesch for originally spurring my interest in Buber's book, and also to Michael Rosenthal for later organizing a reading group aimed at working through some of the book's perplexities.

89 Spinoza, *Theological-Political Treatise*, 189–90. As we pointed out in the earlier discussion, this original democracy, according to Spinoza, was dissolved in pretty short order. The people, terrified of interacting

directly with God, relinquished the "right to consult God, to receive and interpret his laws" entirely to Moses; hence the original fully democratic covenant was "abrogated," to be replaced by a new covenant that it seems hard to distinguish from "absolute monarchy" (p. 191), on Spinoza's own account. It's fairly clear that Spinoza, in common with Harrington (and even Hobbes), insists on this short-lived democracy in order to underscore the point that the *normative foundations* of the polity are strictly democratic, even if the substance of the regime isn't.

90 As should surprise no one, Buber's *Kingship of God* never mentions Spinoza.

91 Buber, *Kingship of God*, 15.

92 Robert Alter, trans., *The Hebrew Bible: A Translation with Commentary*, vol. 2 (New York: W.W. Norton, 2019), 113. As Buber notes, some scholars have suggested that this text is in tension with Judges 9:2, where Gideon's son Abimelech makes an apparent bid for monarchical authority. However, Buber marshals various arguments as to why the latter text shouldn't be seen as negating the force of the principle proclaimed in Judges 8:23 (*Kingship of God*, 60–2).

93 Buber, *Kingship of God*, 59–60. See 205n42 for Buber's argument that the Mosaic regime is never a theocracy in the sense of "government by priests." He cites as evidence the fact that "Moses' successor, to whom his prerogatives pass, is an Ephraimite" and that the high priest "has no political authority." Moses's "office as leader is by nature un-priestly and does not pass over to the priesthood."

94 Ibid., 64.

95 Ibid. If Wellhausen is right that as a matter of historical judgment there never was a stable or organized form of government in Mosaic Israel, this would suggest that attributing to it this or that regime is simply a way of asserting various normative claims within the medium of political philosophy. This in turn would help to render intelligible why the regime question becomes a kind of football being perennially contested on the playfield of Western political philosophy. The question we're pursuing in this section is whether more or less the same applies to Buber with his assertion of God's kingship as a paradoxical regime/non-regime.

96 Buber, *Kingship of God*, 64–5, 67.

97 Ibid., 75.

98 Alter, *The Hebrew Bible*, 159.

99 Buber, *Kingship of God*, 83.

100 Ibid., 77.
101 Ibid., 76.
102 Ibid., 78, 83–4.
103 Ibid., 83: "Something has been attempted ... but it has failed ... This 'something' is that which I call *the primitive theocracy*"; Buber's italics.
104 Ibid., 88.
105 Ibid., 93.
106 Ibid., 25.
107 Ibid., 84. Cf. 119: YHWH "makes known His will first of all as constitution"; and p. 131: "the constitution which has emerged from revelation."
108 Ibid., 107. Is this a clarification? Or does it further muddle what Buber means by "kingship" or "theocracy"? On p. 128, Buber tells us, without further explanation, that YHWH's "*melekh*-ship" gave Israel a "more leader-like than ruler-like *melekh*." One wishes for more clarity, but what Buber's formulation seems to indicate is that the *melekh*-ship of YHWH pertained mainly to leadership of tribes that had not yet consolidated themselves into a real state. On p. 135 he writes that the divine kingship constituted "a religio-political, institutional reality." But how institutional was it?
109 Ibid., 119.
110 Ibid., 126.
111 Ibid., 127.
112 Martin Buber, *Moses* (Oxford: East and West Library, 1946), 106.
113 Ibid., 107.
114 Buber, *Kingship of God*, 124.
115 Recall Spinoza's formulation quoted at the start of this section: "They all shared equally in the government of the state."
116 Buber, *Kingship of God*, 129, 207–8n63. "Meek" is the King James translation; Robert Alter and Everett Fox translate it as "humble." Robert Alter, trans., *The Hebrew Bible: A Translation with Commentary*, vol. 1 (New York: W.W. Norton, 2019), 518; Everett Fox, trans., *The Five Books of Moses: Genesis, Exodus, Leviticus, Numbers, Deuteronomy*, Schocken Bible, vol. 1 (New York: Schocken Books, 1997), 719.
117 This is the case in *Kingship of God*, at least. It's true that twelve years later, Moses gets a separate book-length treatment – thus, it might be said, repairing his neglect in the 1932 book.
118 Buber, *Kingship of God*, 136. Remarkably, Buber never even mentions Moses's name in this context. As regards the fact that divine kingship and dynastic power are mutually exclusive, consider Buber's important observation that "the Samuelic crisis [that led to the inauguration of human kingship] begins with Samuel's bare intention to bequeath his authority to his sons" (ibid.).

119 Ibid., 141; my italics. Cf. 140 and 157, referring to "the limited mission" of Moses. Buber's reference to a limited Mosaic mission suggests the notion (though Buber doesn't spell it out explicitly) of Moses as the first of the "judges" (cf. p. 160).

120 From a Jewish perspective, Buber's emphasis on Joshua as the privileged completer of the mission seems risky, since Christians can apply typological interpretations according to which Joshua merely foreshadows his later namesake Jesus (= Yeshua): see Northrup Frye, *The Great Code* (Toronto: Academic Press Canada, 1982), 172. As regards the question of the extent to which Joshua did or didn't fulfil this "great mission," the book of Judges (Judges 1:1) corrects the mistaken impression given by the book of Joshua that Israel had basically conquered the whole of Canaan: see Fox, *The Early Prophets*, 136. Cf. Buber, *Kingship of God*, 141.

121 Buber, *Kingship of God*, 147.

122 Paul Mendes-Flohr, "The Kingdom of God: Martin Buber's Critique of Messianic Politics," *Behemoth: A Journal on Civilization* 1, no. 2 (2008): 33.

123 Charles H.T. Lesch, *Solidarity in a Secular Age: From Political Theology to Jewish Philosophy* (New York: Oxford University Press, 2022), 150. Cf. Buber, *Kingship of God*, 136: "According to its negative content [the covenant at Sinai] signifies that no man is to be called king of the sons of Israel." That is, it's impossible to affirm God as king without simultaneously repudiating comparable power for human beings.

124 Lesch, *Solidarity in a Secular Age*, 157; Lesch's italics. Cf. 154: According to Buber's argument, Israel found in theopolitics "a novel means of realizing non-domination: When all human beings are fully dependent on God's will, no human being is dependent on merely human will." Interestingly, Buber, in *Kingship of God*, 136–8, claims that the same "theocratic" impulse is present in early Islam, and Buber traces it back to what he sees as a perennial "libertarian" or "anarchic" feature of nomadic Bedouin culture (cf. p. 161). In all three cases (pre-Islamic Bedouin desert existence, Mosaic Judaism, and early Islam), there is, according to Buber, a "drive of man to be independent of man" and hence a refusal to bow to merely human rulership (p. 138). Buber refers to the "Bedouin-ness" of the Hebrews in explaining "why the confederation of half-nomadic tribes wandering out of Egypt did not elevate its human leader [namely Moses] as *melekh*" (ibid.). Cf. Buber, *Moses*, 88: "the unbridled craving for independence, which was common to semi-nomadic Israelites of ancient times and to the Bedouins."

125 Lesch, *Solidarity in a Secular Age*, 159; Lesch's italics. One significant problem for this narrative that no human being should have dominion over another human being because dominion belongs only to God is the fact that God-ruled Israel tolerated slavery. Following Buber, Lesch

(pp. 158–9) draws attention to the fact that the Jubilee mandated periodic liberation of slaves. But of course periodic liberation of slaves means that human beings continue to be in bondage to other human beings. We return to this troubling problem in chapter 4.

126 Lesch, *Solidarity in a Secular Age*, 246n6, suggests that Buber deliberately "submerged his political aims" in *Kingship of God* because he was trying to use the book to win favour within "Weimar German academia." This may well be correct.

127 It should be noted that in the *Moses* book as well, Buber opts for consistently apologetic interpretations, as I have occasion to document in various endnotes elsewhere in this book.

128 Arguably, the most unpersuasive line in the whole book is where Buber writes: "The theocratic order … envisions community as voluntariness" (*Kingship of God*, 148). How can one read the story of the golden calf and write such a sentence?

129 Relevant here is the debate that John Milton conducts with Salmatius in chap. 2 of *A Defence of the People of England*. By way of direct challenge to Salmatius's view that Moses "was a king with supreme power," Milton insists, in Buber-like fashion, that "the king of the people was Jehovah; Moses was, as it were, only an interpreter of Jehovah the king." Milton, *Political Writings*, 99–100. Clearly, it's only on the basis of denying the kingship of Moses that it's possible for Milton to appeal normatively to "the ancient Mosaic form of commonwealth" (p. 138). For a helpful sketch of the context informing Milton's polemic against Salmatius, see Dzelzainis's introduction, xix–xxv. See also Daniel Jeremy Silver, *Images of Moses* (New York: Basic Books, 1982), 239–40, on the issue ventilated within Talmudic literature about whether it was appropriate to conceive Moses as "a king"; and Jonathan Kirsch, *Moses: A Life* (New York: Random House, 1998), 300, quoted by Harrison Fluss in chap. 3; according to Kirsch it was precisely the perception of Moses as a monarch that generated the repeated mutinies in the wilderness.

130 Lesch, *Solidarity in a Secular Age*, 155: "Buber argues that divine rule in ancient Israel was understood to be exclusive and direct. *None was permitted to serve as God's intermediary*" (my italics). This strikes me as a very radical circumvention of the role of Moses as it is presented in the Bible's version of the story. In chapter 1 of *Images of Moses*, Silver provides an interesting survey of a long Jewish tradition, rooted in the Hebrew Bible itself, of a deliberate "diminishing" of the role of Moses. It might be said that *Kingship of God* is faithful to this tradition.

131 Fluss, in his chapter on Korah, aptly quotes Spinoza: "The people believed that those men had been destroyed not by God who was their judge but rather by the craft of Moses."

132 *Political Works of James Harrington*, 174.
133 Ibid., 175.
134 Ibid.
135 Ibid.
136 Fox, *The Five Books of Moses*, 703. King James Version: "All the assembly shall assemble themselves to thee [Moses] at the door of the tabernacle of the congregation."
137 *Political Works of James Harrington*, 175.
138 Ibid.
139 Ibid., 175–6.
140 Ibid., 176. For some reason, Harrington treats the episode of Eldad and Medad in Numbers 11:26–7 as bound up with the question of how elders or members of the senate were selected. The problem that Harrington seems to be wrestling with is that Moses summoned the seventy elders around the tent or tabernacle so that God could address them (Numbers 11:24–5), yet these two men "remained in the camp" (11:26), suggesting that they were in some sense part of the council of elders and in some sense not. "With the Talmudists I conceive that Eldad and Medad had the suffrage of the tribes, and so were written as competitors for magistracy; but, coming afterwards unto the lot, failed of it and therefore went not up unto the Tabernacle, or place of confirmation by God, or to the session house of the senate with the seventy upon whom the lot fell to the senators; for the session house of the Sanhedrim was first in the court of the Tabernacle, and afterwards in that of the Temple" (ibid.). The biblical text is far too compressed for it to be a plausible basis upon which to spin out such issues; but possibly the Talmudic exegeses consulted by Harrington help make sense of such a puzzling interpretation.
141 Ibid.
142 When one looks at the introduction of the institution of the seventy elders in Exodus 18:15–27, it is indeed strictly for the purpose of lightening Moses's burden with respect to judicial matters (Fox, *The Five Books of Moses*, 357–8). But when one compares the parallel discussion in Numbers 11:16–17, we are told that the seventy elders will share "the burden of the people" carried by Moses without explicitly limiting this to the judicial aspect of his office (Fox, *The Five Books of Moses*, 714–15).
143 *Political Works of James Harrington*, 176.
144 Ibid., 176–7. Harrington notes that this text appears to privilege "the Levitical priests" (Fox, *The Five Books of Moses*, 929). But he explains this by pointing out that "the priests and the Levites, … being in the younger years of this commonwealth those that were best studied in the laws, were the most frequently elected into the Sanhedrim."

3. Exodus Betrayed: Korah, Moses, and Class Struggle in the Wilderness

1 Israel Abrahams, *Pathways in Judaism: Selected Essays on Jewish Themes* (Cape Town: Hebrew Congregation, 1968), 44.

2 James. H. Meisel, *Counterrevolution: How Revolutions Die* (New York: Routledge, 2017), 4.

3 Jan Assmann, *Moses the Egyptian* (Cambridge: Harvard University Press, 1997), 2. When it comes to the golden calf episode, Assmann makes the important point that what "'displeases' Yahweh is not the curtailment of his offerings and festivals but the introduction of 'heathen' customs and the recidivism symbolized by the Golden Calf. Israel's phobia was the worship of false gods, Egypt's the neglect of the gods." Assmann, *The Mind of Egypt: History and Meaning in the Time of the Pharaohs* (Cambridge: Harvard University Press, 2002), 406.

4 See Richard Wolin's trenchant critique of Assmann (and Assmann's reply) in "Biblical Blame Shift: Is the Egyptologist Jan Assmann Fueling Anti-Semitism?," *Chronicle of Higher Education*, 15 April 2013, https://www.chronicle.com/article/biblical-blame-shift/. For Latour's use of Assmann to make his case against the Mosaic dispensation as proto-modern and totalitarian, see Bruno Latour, *Facing Gaia: Eight Lectures on the New Climatic Regime*, trans. Catherine Porter (Cambridge: Polity, 2017), 155–7. For a Nietzschean treatment/critique of the golden calf episode as illustrating the inherent intolerance of Abrahamic religiosity, see Peter Sloterdijk, *In the Shadow of Mount Sinai* (Cambridge: Polity, 2016).

5 Thomas Paine, *The Age of Reason* (New York: Barnes and Noble, 2006), 90.

6 For Eugene V. Debs's use of the imagery of Exodus to illustrate labour struggles, see Nick Salvatore, *Eugene V. Debs: Citizen and Socialist* (Urbana and Chicago: University of Chicago Press, 1982), 63. Debs did not want to be considered the Moses of American socialism, however: "I would not be a Moses to lead you into a promised land, for someone would lead you out again." Eugene V. Debs, "A Glimpse into the Future," *Appeal to Reason*, 10 March 1906. For a comprehensive look at how the Exodus played a role in abolitionist struggles in the United States and in liberation theology, there is Joel S. Baden, *The Book of Exodus: A Biography* (Princeton: Princeton University Press, 2019), 157–215. While not invalidating the struggles and experiences of leaders from Harriet Tubman ("the American Moses") to Martin Luther King Jr., Baden does not shy away from the question of how the Hebrew Bible could also be used to justify slavery by Southern apologists of the "peculiar institution."

There is of course a reactionary critique of Moses that emanates from modern anti-Semitic politics, which one can trace from nineteenth-century reactions against the French Revolution and the Paris Commune right up to National Socialism. In what is a Nazi version of a Platonic dialogue, Adolf Hitler tells his mentor, Dietrich Eckart, that Moses was a Jacobin and a Bolshevik; that the Exodus itself is a prototypical model for subversive revolutionary movements everywhere. What Moses did to the Egyptians, Judeo-Bolshevism will do to the world. Bolshevism, according to Hitler in this lurid conspiracy theory, was Jewish right from the start, with the Jews themselves acting as harbingers of revolutionary plague and the downfall of white civilization. Dietrich Eckart, *Bolshevism from Moses to Lenin: A Dialogue between Adolf Hitler and Me*, trans. William L. Pierce, in *National Socialist World* (Fall 1966): 13–33.

Reactionary appreciations of the Hebrew Bible in the history of late modern political philosophy exist as well. These understand the god of Moses not as an emblem of human liberation, but as a god of war and virile conquest against universal solidarity. This is the perspective of Friedrich Nietzsche, taking as his cue the biblical exegesis of Julius Wellhausen with respect to kings versus prophets. Admittedly, Nietzsche sees much to criticize in the Decalogue (such as the fifth commandment, against unjust killing). Still, he celebrates an image of the Jews as conquerors and kings, which is seen as far preferable to the rabble-rousing of the prophets. Echoing Ernest Renan, who argues that Christian universalism begins with the prophets, the ethno-state of King David for Nietzsche is superior to the stateless internationalism of Isaiah. However, whether it is the condemnation of the Exodus as Jacobin or a re-conception of the Jews before the Babylon Captivity as a chauvinistic war machine to be praised, this right-wing view hinges on particularistic and anti-modern premises. For an in-depth discussion of Nietzsche's reading of the Hebrew Bible, see Jan Rehmann, *Deconstructing Postmodernist Nietzscheanism: Deleuze and Foucault* (Leiden: Brill, 2022), 107–18; see p. 111 on Nietzsche's debt to Wellhausen. For a discussion of Nietzsche's critique of the Decalogue (and why he thinks the "free spirits" should not be restrained by old tablets), see Domenico Losurdo, *Nietzsche: The Aristocratic Rebel* (Leiden: Brill, 2019), 597.

7 This is Isaac Deutscher's paraphrase of Thomas Carlyle's introduction to Oliver Cromwell's speeches. But unlike Carlyle, who sought to present Cromwell as the Puritan Moses of the English Civil War, Deutscher was attempting to rehabilitate Trotsky from under a mountain of calumny and oblivion. *The Prophet Unarmed: Trotsky: 1921–1929* (New York: Verso, 2003), vii.

8 Eric Voegelin suggests that when the YHWH cult became centralized in Jerusalem, the Levites left their villages and demanded equal wages with the Jerusalem priests. But the priests ignored their complaints. Also, as we shall see from the narrative in Numbers, YHWH himself brutally punished

the recalcitrant Levites represented by Korah. *Order and History*, vol. 1, *Israel and Revelation* (Columbia: University of Missouri Press, 2001), 421.

9 See John Rees for the comparison of the Levellers to Korahites in *The Leveller Revolution: Radical Political Organisation in England, 1640–1650* (London: Verso, 2016), 450. Matters get confusing, since the leader of the Levellers, John Lilburne, compared Cromwell to Korah, using Korah as an example of treachery against legitimate authority. In the hands of John Milton under Cromwell's Protectorate, Korah became an empty signifier to describe anyone politically unfaithful to the rightful government of Cromwell (left or right). For instance, he condemned as Korahite both the politics of the Presbyterian party and the politics of royalist sympathizers. Milton refers to the Korah rebellion elsewhere in his *Christian Doctrine* and even planned and outlined a tragedy devoted to Korah's rebellion. It is also no coincidence that Milton was writing *Paradise Lost* as he wrote polemics against those whom he saw as the Korahites of his day. Indeed, in book 5 of the poem, when Lucifer is demanding equality with God and his son, the angel Abdiel directly alludes to Korah in his counter-arguments. According to Abdiel's injunction, Lucifer and his fellow angels should not rebel, lest God punish "these wicked tents" – i.e., the tents where Korah led his challenge to Moses in the wilderness. Ironically, during the Restoration, Anglican preachers recast the entire rebellion of Cromwell and all regicides as Korahite. And as someone who publicly defended regicide, this would also include Milton himself! David Loewenstein, *Representing Revolution in Milton and His Contemporaries: Religion, Politics, and Polemics in Radical Puritanism* (Cambridge: Cambridge University Press, 2001), 235.

10 It is possible to conceive the caste of priests empowered by Moses and consolidated in their power by the defeat of the Korah rebellion as a "bureaucratic" caste. This bureaucratic caste can be defined (in the Marxist sense) as a conservative layer of officials who administer a centralized organization and whose social position comes with privileges and interests antagonistic to the masses. But we should stress that these priests of ancient Israel are a political-religious caste and not a distinct socio-economic class, as their role does not extend to economic ownership.

11 It is certainly true that non-Stalinists on the Left have accused Trotsky of being authoritarian during the period of the Russian Civil War, citing the Red Army's suppression of the 1921 Kronstadt revolt. Perhaps this suggests how Trotsky is not deserving of "Korahite" status. However, from Trotsky's perspective, one can make a distinction between actions taken to defend a revolution and actions taken to reverse it. As for Korah himself, we do not notice any dissent from Moses's policies until Numbers 16, implying that he approved of them, including Moses's suppression of the golden calf worshippers at Mount Sinai. This would mean that Korah is

more of a Left Oppositionist to bureaucratic encroachments of the Mosaic regime than an anarchistic rebel. On the Bolsheviks' role in the Kronstadt rebellion, see Paul Avrich, *Kronstadt, 1921* (Princeton: Princeton University Press, 1970). For Trotsky's own justification, see "Hue and Cry over Kronstadt," in *Writings of Leon Trotsky: 1937–38* (New York: Pathfinder, 1973), 134–45.

12 Robert Alter, trans., *The Hebrew Bible: A Translation with Commentary*, vol. 1 (New York: W.W. Norton, 2019), 533.

13 Robert Alter, trans., *The Five Books of Moses: A Translation with Commentary* (New York: W.W. Norton, 2004), 762. Throughout this chapter, I generally cite the Alter translation in the first instance for references to the Torah.

14 See note 9 above.

15 Alter, *The Five Books of Moses*, 762–3.

16 Ibid., 762.

17 For a general look at Stalin's purges, see John Getty, *Origins of the Great Purges: The Soviet Communist Party Reconsidered, 1933–1938* (Cambridge: Cambridge University Press, 1987). On the specific logic of political amalgams of Stalin's purges, see Vadim Rogovin, *1937: Stalin's Year of Terror* (Royal Oak, MI: Mehring Books, 1998), 65; Leon Trotsky, "A Trial Balance of the Stalin Amalgam," *New Militant*, February 1935, https://www.marxists.org/archive/trotsky/1935/01/amalgam.htm; and Trotsky's son, Lev Sedov, for his own analysis of Stalinist amalgams in *The Red Book: On the Moscow Trials* (Royal Oak, MI: New Park, 1980). Sedov was likely murdered by Stalin's agents, meeting a fate like that of his father. Sam Miller, "The Trotskys Betrayed," *Left Voice*, 20 August 2020, https://www.leftvoice.org/the-trotskys-betrayed/.

18 Alter, *The Hebrew Bible*, 535.

19 Alter, *The Five Books of Moses*, 762.

20 Robert Pinsky, *Life of David* (New York: Random House, 2005), 154.

21 Jonathan Kirsch, *Moses: A Life* (New York: Random House, 1998), 84.

22 Jan Assmann, *The Invention of Religion: Faith and Covenant in the Book of Exodus* (Princeton: Princeton University Press, 2020), 260.

23 Alter, *The Hebrew Bible*, 533.

24 Alter, *The Five Books of Moses*, 763.

25 Kirsch calls this Moses's "Nixonian moment," and his commentary is in sympathy with the rebels: "Even the biblical author was moved to report that Moses defended himself against the charges laid against him by Korah and the other rebels, and his apologia inevitably reminds the modern reader of Nixon's 'I am not a crook' speech: 'I have not taken one ass from them …' Perhaps Moses protested too much when he protested at all, but even if he were innocent of any abuse of power, the fact remains

that Korah and the other rebels do not appear quite as blameworthy to the contemporary reader as they did to the biblical sources. Indeed, if we prefer to see Moses as a man who 'proclaimed liberty throughout the land,' then we might begin to see Korah, Dathan, and Abiram too, as freedom fighters." Kirsch, *Moses: A Life*, 303.

26 Alter, *The Five Books of Moses*, 763.

27 For more on Korah's baldness as related to his heresy, see David Biale, "Korah in the Midrash: The Hairless Heretic as Hero," in *Jewish History* 30, no. 1/2 (2016): 15–28. In the Qur'an 28:76–81, Korah (or Qarun in the text) is presented as arrogant and greedy, obsessed with accumulating wealth, and not with true knowledge. That is why Allah causes the earth to swallow up him and his entire household. *The Qur'an*, trans. M.A.S. Abdel Haleem (Oxford: Oxford University Press, 2005), 250.

28 Alter, *The Five Books of Moses*, 764.

29 Ibid., 765.

30 Ibid.

31 Alter, *The Hebrew Bible*, 535–6.

32 Alter, *The Five Books of Moses*, 766.

33 Alter, *The Hebrew Bible*, 536.

34 Alter, *The Five Books of Moses*, 767.

35 Ibid.

36 For the Korahite rebellion as anticipating (or inspiring?) Milton's depiction of Lucifer's war in heaven, see note 9 above.

37 Kirsch, *Moses: A Life*, 300.

38 Ibid., 301.

39 Alter, *The Five Books of Moses*, 771.

40 Alter, *The Hebrew Bible*, 540.

41 Ibid.

42 Alter, *The Five Books of Moses*, 772.

43 For Korah's revolt as proto-Protestant, or proto-congregationalist, see Donald H. Akenson, *Surpassing Wonder: The Invention of the Bible and the Talmuds* (Chicago: University of Chicago Press, 2001), 96.

44 Alter, *The Hebrew Bible*, 540.

45 As Alter puts it, the "logic of placing these laws immediately after the story of Korah's rebellion is manifest." Alter, *The Five Books of Moses*, 773.

46 Thomas Hobbes, *Leviathan*, ed. Richard Tuck, rev. student ed. (Cambridge: Cambridge University Press, 1996), 312.

47 Quoted from Toma Mastnak, "Godly Democracy," in *Hobbes's Behemoth: Religion and Democracy*, ed. Toma Mastnak (Exeter: Imprint Academic, 2009), 308.

48 William Kolbrener, *Open Minded Torah: Of Irony, Fundamentalism, and Love* (London: Bloomsbury, 2011), 76.

49 Hobbes, *Leviathan*, 324. In his own infamous study devoted to Hobbes's *Leviathan*, the fascist Carl Schmitt summarizes the state of nature leading to the establishment of absolute authority in political-theological terms: "The terror of the state of nature drives anguished individuals to come together; their fear rises to an extreme; a spark of reason (*ratio*) flashes, and suddenly there stands in front of them a new god." Carl Schmitt, *The Leviathan in the State Theory of Thomas Hobbes: Meaning and Failure of a Political Symbol* (London: Greenwood, 1996), 30.

50 Hobbes, *Leviathan*, 324–5.

51 Ibid., 325.

52 Ibid., 326.

53 Kolbrener, *Open Minded Torah*, 76.

54 Quoted from John Aubrey, in Steven Nadler, *A Book Forged in Hell: Spinoza's Scandalous Treatise and the Birth of the Secular Age* (Princeton: Princeton University Press, 2011), 30. Hobbes sees the threat of Korah against Moses's authority in both doctrinal and political terms. It is as if he combines the ancient concerns of Josephus and Philo into one (counter-revolutionary) account. For Philo of Alexandria, a Hellenistic Jew who sees Moses as a Platonic statesman, Korah's rebellion represents chaos since he challenges Moses's divine authority itself. The very concept of divine revelation is at stake. Only unreasonable pride can motivate someone to overthrow divine revelation. For Flavius Josephus, the first-century Roman-Jewish historian and military leader, Korah is portrayed as he is by the rabbinic tradition as perhaps one of the mightiest adversaries that Moses ever dealt with in the wilderness. But, unlike the rabbis, Josephus depicts Korah in the manner of a Hellenistic statesman, whose main crime is political sedition and treachery, in the manner of Greeks acting badly in Thucydides. Korah does not act stoically but is overwhelmed by irrational passions for power. For a comparison of Philo and Josephus on Korah, see Louis H. Feldman, "Josephus' Portrait of Korah," *Old Testament Essays* 6 (1993): 399–426.

55 Kolbrener, *Open Minded Torah*, 78. As for Kolbrener's criticism of Hobbes, namely that he cannot prevent a Spinozistic threat from emerging on Hobbes's own theoretical premises, Carl Schmitt approaches the Spinozistic threat against *Leviathan* from a much different and much more disturbing angle. The fascist Schmitt agreed with the rabbis of Amsterdam that Spinoza deserved to be excommunicated. But instead of asserting the transcendence of the Torah as a safeguard against Spinozism, in his book on Hobbes's *Leviathan*, Schmitt argues for Christian fundamentalism to protect the state/community. Hobbes's doctrine of inner piety or freedom of conscience allows for too much freedom of thought; thus, Schmitt wants the Hobbesian polity to have doctrinal uniformity in body and mind, with

all and sundry believing that "Jesus is the Christ." But unlike Kolbrener, such theological transcendence is meant to protect the polity from the Jews themselves, who are now cast by Schmitt as dangerous, rootless cosmopolitans. Schmitt sees Spinoza's rereading of Hobbes as allowing the Jews to enter Hobbes's Christian state – i.e., the sovereign state that Hobbes calls the Leviathan, subverting it from the inside. Schmitt, *The Leviathan in The State Theory of Thomas Hobbes*, 57–8.

56 Akenson, *Surpassing Wonder*, 96.

57 Avivah Gottlieb Zornberg, *Moses: A Human Life* (New Haven: Yale University Press 2016), 128.

58 Ibid., 129.

59 Ibid.; Zornberg's italics.

60 Ibid.

61 Ibid., 130.

62 Ibid., 138.

63 Ibid., 140. Even if Zornberg does not mention it, it is worth discussing in passing Walter Benjamin's brief treatment of the Korah episode in his 1921 essay "The Critique of Violence": see Walter Benjamin, *Selected Writings*, vol. 1, *1913–1926*, ed. Marcus Bullock and Michael W. Jennings (Cambridge, MA: Belknap Press, 1996), 236–53. In the essay, Benjamin distinguishes two types of violence: divine and mythic. Divine violence is antinomic, law-destroying, revolutionary, and emancipatory, while mythic violence is authoritarian, law-making, and ultimately conservative. Benjamin claims that Korah's destruction was in fact an act of divine violence. Indeed, and strangely, it was not even properly violent but a kind of violent non-violence. It was, as he puts it, "lethal without spilling blood" (pp. 249–50). Benjamin sees this as an act of divine left-wing violence in part because God was striking against the Korahites as privileged Levites. But what is bizarre and ironic about this argument is that Korah's revolt was specifically against the spiritual aristocracy of Moses and Aaron and that God's violence had nothing to do with his populism. Quite the opposite. Richard Bernstein notes against Benjamin's interpretation the following: "And we should not forget – although Benjamin doesn't mention it – that when the surviving people protest, when they murmur against Moses, the Lord – as the Hebrew Bible tells us – sends a plague that kills 14,700 of them." Of course, the ultimate irony when it comes to Korah is that it's precisely his revolt that seems to accord more with Benjamin's idea of justified "divine violence": The revolt was "an act of rebellion – a revolutionary act – against the authority of Moses and his [arguably mythic] law." Richard J. Bernstein, *Violence: Thinking without Banisters* (Cambridge: Polity, 2017), 62. As another commentator bluntly puts it, this isn't bloodless divine violence but a "bloody

massacre." Christopher Tomlins, *In the Matter of Nat Turner: A Speculative History* (Princeton: Princeton University Press, 2022), 279.

64 Karl Marx, "The Philosophical Manifesto of the Historical School of Law" (1842), in *Marx-Engels Collected Works, Volume 1: 1835–1843* (New York: International Publishers, 1975), 203–6.

65 For the connection between some types of Christian Pyrrhonism and political-religious conservatism, see Richard Popkin, *The History of Scepticism: From Savonarola to Bayle* (Oxford: Oxford University Press, 2003).

66 Zornberg, *Moses: A Human Life*, 145–6.

67 Spinoza, *Theological-Political Treatise*, ed. Jonathan Israel (Cambridge: Cambridge University Press, 2015), 208.

68 Lewis S. Feuer, *Spinoza and the Rise of Liberalism* (New York: Routledge, 2017), 285.

69 Spinoza, *Theological-Political Treatise*, 226.

70 This is a frequent tension in Spinoza's biblical hermeneutics – perhaps a result of writing under persecution. Spinoza sometimes reinterprets the meaning of certain passages that literally say that God acted out of anger or jealousy. But this goes against his own hermeneutics: not to make interpretative excuses à la Maimonides, but to present the text as is, warts and all. As Spinoza himself demonstrates against rationalizing interpreters, commentators cannot have their cake and eat it too.

71 Spinoza, *Theological-Political Treatise*, 226.

72 Ibid., 227.

73 Ibid.

74 Ibid.

75 Ibid., 228.

76 Ibid.

77 Ibid., 229.

78 Ibid., 228.

79 Kirsch, *Moses: A Life*, 301.

80 Ibid., 302.

81 S.S. Prawer, *Karl Marx and World Literature* (Oxford: Oxford University Press 1978), 420.

82 Karl Marx, *Capital: A Critique of Political Economy*, vol. 1 (New York: Penguin, 1982), 742.

83 *The Marx-Engels Reader*, ed. Robert C. Tucker, 2nd ed. (New York: Norton, 1978), 592.

84 Shlomo Avineri, *Karl Marx: Philosophy and Revolution* (New Haven: Yale University Press, 2019), 9.

85 From Marx's *Grundrisse*, where he singles Moses out as one of the greatest lawgivers of antiquity: "All the law-givers of antiquity, Moses above all, founded their success in commanding virtue, integrity and proper custom

on landed property, or at least on secured, hereditary possession of land, for the greatest possible number of citizens … The individual is placed in such conditions of earning his living as to make not the acquiring of wealth his object, but self-sustenance, his own reproduction as a member of the community; the reproduction of himself as proprietor of the parcel of ground, and, in that quality, as a member of the commune." *Grundrisse* (New York: Vintage Books, 1973), 476. Marx also invokes Moses's laws against Christian hypocrisy in *Capital*: "Moses said: 'Thou shalt not muzzle the ox when he treadeth out the corn' [Deuteronomy 25:4]. But the Christian philanthropists of Germany fastened a wooden board round the necks of their serfs, whom they used as a motive power for grinding, in order to prevent them from putting flour into their mouths with their hands." *Capital*, 496.

86 Heinrich Heine, *Prose Writings* (London: Walter Scott, 1887), 314–15. One can compare Heine's praise of Moses's Jubilee year with Spinoza's praise in the TTP. Despite Spinoza's criticisms of Moses above, he agrees with Heine and Marx that it was Moses's agrarian reforms that kept the state stronger than it would have been: "For nowhere else did citizens hold their possessions with a stronger right than this state's subjects. They held an equal portion of the lands and fields with their leader, and each one was the perpetual owner of his share. If anyone was compelled by poverty to sell his estate or field, he had to be restored to it again when the Jubilee came around, and there were other customs of this kind to ensure that no one could be dispossessed of his allotted property. Nowhere could poverty be more tolerable." *Theological-Political Treatise*, 224. It would not be surprising if Marx and Heine had these passages from Spinoza's TTP in mind when writing about Moses's law-giving concerning land possession.

87 Unfortunately, Lunacharsky's book remains untranslated from the original Russian, along with the majority of his writings. Lunacharsky was a prolific scholar and commissar of enlightenment in the USSR under Lenin. His writings on the Hebrew Bible and the prophets are an important part of left-wing approaches to religion. One can access his 1908 study, *Religion and Socialism*, at the Lunacharsky archive online: http://lunacharsky.newgod.su/lib/religiya-i-socializm-t-1/

88 Some may balk at connecting Korah's "spiritual egalitarianism" to Marx at all, as (1) Marx was a materialist, not a "spiritualist"; and (2) it is not clear that Marx was even an egalitarian, since equality might be treated (reductively) as a category of bourgeois society. Obviously, Marx was a secular atheist, but he did appreciate how theological and spiritual debates can be translated into real political and material struggles. As the young Marx pointed out to Arnold Ruge in 1843, religion is "the table of contents of the theoretical struggles of mankind." We find Korah's

challenge to Moses to be democratic and uncannily modern (and arguably "materialist") in its implications. As for whether Marx believed in equality, it seems clear that the call for the abolition of class society is an egalitarian one. The main slogan of Marxian socialism is "from each according to their abilities, to each according to their needs" and not to *some* according to their needs. As the young Marx put it, equality (as emphasized in the French Revolution and its aftermath) is a confirmation of our shared human essence, or what Marx called our "species-being." For Marx's letter to Ruge, see *Writings of the Young Marx on Philosophy and Society* (Indianapolis, IN: Hackett, 1967), 213. For Marx's praise of the French notion of equality as the "groundwork for communism," see Karl Marx and Friedrich Engels, *The Economic and Philosophic Manuscripts of 1844 and the Communist Manifesto* (Amherst, NY: Prometheus Books, 1988), 123.

89 Roland Boer, *Marxist Criticism of the Bible: A Critical Introduction to Marxist Literary Theory and the Bible* (New York: Bloomsbury, 2003), 140.

90 Ernst Bloch, *Atheism in Christianity* (London: Verso, 2009), 67–8.

91 Ibid., 68.

92 Ibid.

93 Ibid.

94 For a critical assessment of Ernst Bloch's relationship with Stalinism, see Doug Greene, *Stalinism and the Dialectics of Saturn: Anticommunism, Marxism, and the Fate of the Soviet Union*, foreword by Harrison Fluss (London: Lexington, 2023), 121–3.

95 This issue of separating mythic image from philosophical content is elaborated on in Harrison Fluss and Landon Frim, *Prometheus and Gaia: Technology, Ecology, and Anti-humanism* (London: Anthem, 2022).

4. The Moses Story in the Hebrew Bible: Puzzles and Paradoxes

1 Vladimir Sharov, *The Rehearsals*, trans. Oliver Ready (Sawtry, UK: Dedalus, 2018), 24.

2 Alexis de Tocqueville, *Democracy in America*, trans. Harvey C. Mansfield and Delba Winthrop (Chicago: University of Chicago Press, 2000), 37–8, commenting on Connecticut's Code of 1650.

3 Jan Assmann, in *The Invention of Religion* (Princeton: Princeton University Press, 2018), 68, highlights a tension between universalism and particularism within the Hebrew Bible itself: The book of Genesis, he suggests, "represents God from a universalistic perspective as the creator of heaven and earth, interacting with the human race as a whole … The Book of Exodus, by contrast, adopts a decidedly particularist perspective." Cf. 72, referring to the "opposition between the inclusive, universalistic, and irenic tendency of the tales of the forefathers [in Genesis] and the

exclusive, particularistic, and aggressive spirit of the Exodus story." Assmann also points out (pp. 65–6) that in Amos 9:7, YHWH is presented as *not* privileging the Israelites as a chosen people, but on the contrary acting as the guardian of various other peoples. YHWH has brought "the Philistines from Caphtor, and the Syrians from Kir" just as he has "brought up Israel out of the land of Egypt." Donald Harman Akenson similarly points out that the original version of the divine covenant in Genesis 9:8–17 was not limited to any particular tribe or nation: see *God's Peoples: Covenant and Land in South Africa, Israel, and Ulster* (Montreal: McGill-Queen's University Press, 1991), 14. See also Eric Voegelin's reference to "the conflict between spiritual universalism and patriotic parochialism that had been inherent from the beginning in the conception of a Chosen People": *Order and History*, vol. 1, *Israel and Revelation* (Baton Rouge: Louisiana State University Press, 1956), 357.

4 For an excellent one-paragraph summary of the kinds of paradoxes surveyed in this chapter, see Louis H. Feldman, *Philo's Portrayal of Moses in the Context of Ancient Judaism* (Notre Dame, IN: University of Notre Dame Press, 2007), xi.

5 Robert Alter, trans., *The Hebrew Bible: A Translation with Commentary*, vol. 1 (New York: W.W. Norton, 2019), 518. In the remainder of this chapter, I generally cite the Everett Fox translation (Everett Fox, trans., *The Five Books of Moses: Genesis, Exodus, Leviticus, Numbers, Deuteronomy*, Schocken Bible, vol. 1 [New York: Schocken Books, 1997]) in the first instance, but I often follow this with citations from the Alter translation and/or the King James Version (KJV) where they are interestingly different so as to avoid dependence on a single rendering.

6 Baruch Spinoza, *Theological-Political Treatise*, trans. Samuel Shirley, 2nd ed. (Indianapolis: Hackett, 2001), 28.

7 Daniel Jeremy Silver, *Images of Moses* (New York: Basic Books, 1982), 40. James Bernard Murphy in a recent book has pointed out that Moses belongs to a tradition, extending from Abraham to Jeremiah, of prophets who "talk God down from some of his threats." As Murphy puts it (without noting how strange this is): "The best prophets bring out the best in their God." *The Third Sword: On the Political Role of Prophets* (Cambridge: Cambridge University Press, 2023), 19. Cf. Thomas L. Pangle, *Political Philosophy and the God of Abraham* (Baltimore: Johns Hopkins University Press, 2003), 109: "God is repeatedly said to 'change His mind,' to 'regret,' or to 'repent' … to alter His intended deeds and His plans, in response to human actions…. The prophets Isaiah, Jeremiah, Joel, Amos and Jonah repeatedly teach that God is capable of 'repenting.'" Pangle rightly asks, "If we take literally these scriptural texts ascribing repentance or regret and change of mind to God, can we still speak intelligibly of divine omnipotence?"

8 Cf. Pangle, *Political Philosophy and the God of Abraham*, 103: Scripture responds to human errancy by means of "the rule of a specific code of positive divine law, delivered and taught through prophecy to a chosen people … But the peculiarities of this answer are so great as to make it far from easy to comprehend. Why a chosen people? Why this positive law, for just this one people?" One should consider Freud's interesting suggestion that the nation of Israel was *Moses's* chosen people, not *God's* chosen people: *The Standard Edition of the Complete Psychological Works of Sigmund Freud*, vol. 23 (London: Vintage, 2001), 45, 106. Freud says the same thing in a letter to Lou Andreas-Salomé reproduced in Richard J. Bernstein, *Freud and the Legacy of Moses* (Cambridge: Cambridge University Press, 1998), 117.

9 Martin Buber, *Moses* (Oxford: East and West Library, 1946), 76.

10 Michael Walzer, "The Strangeness of Jewish Leftism," in *Jews and Leftist Politics*, ed. Jack Jacobs (Cambridge: Cambridge University Press, 2017), 29–39; see 31. In this essay, Walzer surveys a whole series of tensions between his leftist commitments and Judaism. I'm grateful to Igor Shoikhedbrod for bringing this interesting text to my attention.

11 Fox, *The Five Books of Moses*, 448, 455.

12 Spinoza, *Theological-Political Treatise*, 35.

13 Thomas L. Pangle and Timothy W. Burns, *The Key Texts of Political Philosophy: An Introduction* (New York: Cambridge University Press, 2015), 129–30.

14 Max Weber, *Ancient Judaism*, trans. H.H. Gerth and D. Martindale (New York: Free Press, 1952), 364; my italics. Cf. *The New Science of Giambattista Vico*, trans. T.G. Bergin and M.H. Fisch (Ithaca, NY: Cornell University Press, 1984), 49, where Vico points out that according to the Hebrew Bible itself, the Egyptian overlords mocked their Hebrew slaves by "scornfully [asking] the Hebrews why the God they adored did not come to liberate them from their hands."

15 John Bright, *A History of Israel*, 2nd rev. ed. (London: SCM Press, 1972), 348. Freud offers quite similar statements in *Standard Edition*, 64, 112, 134. See also Freud's hard-to-dispute suggestion that "Allah showed himself far more grateful to his chosen people than Yahweh did to his" (p. 92).

16 Walzer, "The Strangeness of Jewish Leftism," 31. Novelist Matt Cohen evokes a similar sense of the bittersweet quality of God's supposed favour when he offers the following playful interpretation of Moses's failure to make it to the Promised Land: "He had been thinking about Moses in the desert. The story told was that because he broke his magic staff, God had punished him by denying him the Promised Land. How could Moses have been so stupid? But there had been so many promises. The truth was that Moses had broken his staff on purpose. After a certain point a man wants

to stay where he is. No one could say history had proven Moses wrong." *Elizabeth and After* (Toronto: Vintage Canada, 2000), 37.

17 See Akenson, *God's Peoples*, 175–6. As I note in chapter 2, note 120, there is a telling contradiction within the Hebrew Bible itself on the question of whether Joshua did or did not conquer the whole of Canaan.

18 Jean-Jacques Rousseau, *On the Social Contract*, ed. Roger D. Masters (New York: St. Martin's, 1978), 125: Pagan gods, not being "jealous Gods" like the God of the Israelites, "divided dominion over the world among themselves." However, "Moses himself and the Hebrew people accepted this idea sometimes when speaking of the God of Israel" (i.e., seemed to acknowledge, at least in specific parts of the text, that he was merely another national god, on a par with the pagan gods, rather than a universal, all-sovereign god). This is correct. I think Rousseau tends to see this as a worst-of-both-worlds scenario: On the "jealous God" side, one gets the religious imperialism that's typical of monotheistic religions. But "an exclusive national religion" (p. 131) suffers severe pathologies as well, and Mosaic religion qua national religion also participates in those. As we saw in the Freud section in chapter 1, Freud develops quite similar insights by distinguishing between two different gods that get fused at the origins of Mosaic religion: YHWH (a national god) and Aten (a properly monotheistic god).

19 Note that Genesis 6:1–4 refers to "divine beings" other than God, at least according to the translation in Fox, *The Five Books of Moses*, 33. Both KJV and Alter, *The Hebrew Bible*, 25, call them "sons of God."

20 Fox, *The Five Books of Moses*, in note 33 on p. 835, points out that murder was one of the two major causes of "biblical pollution," the other being adultery.

21 Robert A. Paul, *Moses and Civilization* (New Haven: Yale University Press, 1996), 210; my italics. Paul interprets the Mosaic revolt against Pharaoh according to the Freudian template of the myth of the primal horde, and his book as a whole is intended to explain (in psychoanalytic terms, obviously) in what sense the Mosaic revolt against the pharaoh of Egypt entailed murder of his "father," adultery, and so on. One should add that it's possible to gain insight into the various dimensions of Moses's transgressiveness without necessarily buying into the full psychoanalytic story that Paul ingeniously constructs. In a similar vein, see also Lincoln Steffens, *Moses in Red* (Pittsburgh: Dorrance, 1926), 85: "At the time of the exodus, good intentions, good will, good records were of no account; Moses himself had killed a man; the conspirators all joined in a lie to Pharaoh (about the feast in the wilderness); the whole tribe of Israel had stolen jewelry and everything they required from the Egyptians … The whole plot was immoral, from the human point of view."

22 Paul, *Moses and Civilization*, 246n9.

23 Alter, *The Hebrew Bible*, on p. 343 (note to Exodus 32:27) calls them "the sacerdotal tribe." However, strictly speaking, it appears that the Levites are, or become, attendants to the priests rather than priests in the full sense, as Fox spells out (*The Five Books of Moses*, 744). According to Fox, this subordinate status (or at least its "more strict enforcement") is a consequence of the fact that the revolt of Korah was a Levite revolt: "[Enforcing] the separate roles of priest and Levite [was] necessitated by the rebellion of Korah." As we discussed in our summary of the Moses story in the introduction, Moses's speech in response to Korah's challenge in fact emphasizes the fact that the Levites are mere "under-priests," so to speak, and aspire to the status of full priests (see Numbers 16:9–10). But if this resentment about inferior religious status is what was driving the revolt, then it seems strange to suggest that that status as attendants was a *consequence* of the revolt.

24 Martin Buber's interpretation of the Moses story is so apologetic that he even avoids acknowledging any responsibility on the part of Moses for this unspeakable atrocity. See Buber, *Moses*, 152–3, where Buber characterizes the episode as "a riot" among the Levites. "The revolt is suppressed at the order of Moses" (p. 153). Cf. 147: The Levites "go forth with the sword at [Moses's] behest 'from gate to gate,' and reduce all resistance"; as well as p. 149, where it is suggested that according to northern kingdom tradition, King Jeroboam, in opting for non-Levite priests, was taking "a stand … against the 'people-slaying' Levites," with the implication that "the Levites abused the orders which they had received," thus preserving "the reverence requisite towards Moses." At the opposite end of the hermeneutical spectrum is the description of the Levites by Graham Hammill (in the context of a discussion of Machiavelli) as a "militia [that] Moses could use to enforce his authority when his words failed"; see *The Mosaic Constitution* (Chicago: University of Chicago Press, 2012), 57.

25 Fox, *The Five Books of Moses*, 894. Alter, *The Hebrew Bible*, 652, also uses the language of intercession, but KJV doesn't. It merely says, "I prayed for Aaron."

26 It should be noted that the translation as "jealous/jealousy" is disputed. See Martin Buber, *Moses*, 144, which discusses this issue and opts for "zealous/zeal." As regards the Exodus 34:14 text, Fox, *The Five Books of Moses*, 456, translates it as: "You are not to bow down to any other god! For YWHW – Zealous-One is his name – a zealous God is he!" Fox sides with Buber in describing "jealous" as a mistranslation; Everett Fox, trans., *The Early Prophets: Joshua, Judges, Samuel, and Kings*, Schocken Bible, vol. 2 (New York: Schocken Books, 2014), 121 (editorial note to Joshua 24:19). Both Alter and KJV, by contrast, opt for "jealous." "For you shall not bow

to another god, for the LORD, His name is Jealous, a jealous God He is" (Alter, *The Hebrew Bible*, 350). KJV: "For thou shalt worship no other god: for the LORD, whose name is Jealous, is a jealous God." As regards Numbers 25:11, Fox, *The Five Books of Moses*, 785, and KJV opt for "in my jealousy," whereas Alter, *The Hebrew Bible*, 572, offers "through my zeal." However, one should also consider Deuteronomy 4:24, where Fox, *The Five Books of Moses*, 868, Alter, *The Hebrew Bible*, 633, and KJV all converge on translating the text as "a jealous God."

27 Fox, *The Five Books of Moses*, 448. Alter, *The Hebrew Bible*, 344, also refers to it as "the calf that Aaron made," as does KJV.

28 Fox, *The Five Books of Moses*, 445, 441. Both KJV and Alter (*The Hebrew Bible*, 342, 339) are more or less the same, though Alter actually uses "mold."

29 Thomas Hobbes, *Leviathan*, ed. Richard Tuck, rev. student ed. (Cambridge: Cambridge University Press, 1996), 487. Augustine claims, in *City of God*, book 14, chapter 11, that "when the people went astray, [Aaron] did not consent to the making of an idol because he was persuaded by them; rather, he yielded to compulsion" – comparing the relationship of Aaron to the erring people to Adam being lured into sin by Eve. However, the Hebrew Bible (as we have just demonstrated) is not consistent with respect to the question of whether Aaron's participation in this transgression was active or passive.

30 Joep Dubbink, "'Don't Stop Me Now!' – Exod 32:10 and YHWH's Intention to Destroy His Own People," in *Nomos and Violence*, ed. Victor Ber (Zurich: Lit Verlag, 2019), 47. Cf. Voltaire, *A Pocket Philosophical Dictionary*, trans. John Fletcher (Oxford: Oxford University Press, 2011), 208–9: "Instead of punishing your unworthy brother you make him our high priest."

31 See Silver, *Images of Moses*, 39: "God punishes [Miriam] with 'snow white scales,' presumably leprosy." Lincoln Steffens interprets the "white leprosy" inflicted upon Miriam "as a satirical rebuke for her color prejudice: The Lord made her whiter than she could possibly have desired Moses' Ethiopian wife to be"; see *Moses in Red*, 135.

32 Quoted from KJV. Alter, *The Hebrew Bible*, 520: "The Lord's wrath flared against them"; cf. Fox, *The Five Books of Moses*, 719. It's probably worth recalling that there might have been no Moses at all but for Miriam's efforts to help save him as an infant, as recounted in Exodus 2:7–8. For discussion of this incident, see Paul, *Moses and Civilization*, 78.

33 Steffens, *Moses in Red*, 135.

34 For an example of a commentator who tries to brush this aside, see Martin Buber's apologetic account of the Hebrew institution of slavery on p. 145 of *Moses*. For Buber, the core of the Israelite law governing slavery is its recognition of the Hebrew slave (*but not foreign slaves*) as "a person" rather than as chattel, as well as its recognition of "personal freedom of choice" –

since the Hebrew slave can opt not to accept the emancipation offered after six years of enslavement. (Leviticus 25:44–6 makes clear that the liberation of slaves during the sabbatical year does not apply to non-Israelites; they can be owned in perpetuity.) Because it is left to the will of Hebrew slaves to accept or renounce liberty when the latter is available, Buber claims that the relationship between owner and slave is "mutual" and not just "unilateral." This seems a rather perverse way of characterizing the institution of slavery, even if Mosaic law makes allowance for liberation of at least certain slaves every seventh year.

35 Michael Walzer, *In God's Shadow: Politics in the Hebrew Bible* (New Haven: Yale University Press, 2012), 21. As I discuss briefly in the introduction, there is some dispute about whether what the Israelites suffered in Pharaoh's Egypt counts as slavery in the full sense. Locke's commentary on the institution of slavery among the Hebrews is relevant (though not necessarily convincing): "I confess, we find among the *Jews*, as well as other Nations, that Men did sell themselves; but, 'tis plain, this was only to *Drudgery, not to Slavery*." He cites Exodus chapter 21, according to which slaves had to be released in the jubilee year, and masters were forbidden from killing or maiming their slaves. For Locke, this means that the kind of "slavery" involved was less than "Absolute, Arbitrary, Despotical Power," hence not really slavery. See John Locke, *Second Treatise of Government*, ed. C.B. Macpherson (Indianapolis: Hackett, 1980), 18; Locke's italics. Fox, *The Five Books of Moses*, 325, translates Exodus 13:14 as "YHWH brought us out of Egypt, out of a house of *serfs*" (my italics).

36 Cf. Walzer, *In God's Shadow*, 25–6; and Joel S. Baden, *The Book of Exodus: A Biography* (Princeton: Princeton University Press, 2019), 159–62. "Nowhere does God (or Moses, or anyone else) signal that all slavery is wrong." Baden, *The Book of Exodus*, 160. Montesquieu condemns the Mosaic law of slavery as a violation of natural law. *The Spirit of the Laws*, ed. Anne Cohler, Basia Miller, and Harold Stone (Cambridge: Cambridge University Press, 1989), 260 (bk. 15, chap. 17).

37 George Fitzhugh, *Sociology for the South: Or the Failure of Free Society* (Richmond, VA: A. Morris, 1854), 96. This is from the opening of a chapter entitled "Scriptural Authority for Slavery." Nor is the problem limited to the Jewish and Christian holy scriptures. Graeme Wood, in *The Way of the Strangers* (New York: Random House, 2017), 19–22, offers a discussion of the Koran's openness toward slavery and on p. 19 cites the analogy with the Hebrew Bible, which suffers from the same problem.

38 Consider Paul's remarkable portrait of the Israelite God as a "jealous, persecuting primal father" in accordance with the Freudian account in *Totem and Taboo*: *Moses and Civilization*, 53–4. Paul, on p. 18, relatedly cites Freud's description (in *Group Psychology and the Analysis of the Ego*) of "the

violent and jealous father" reigning over the primal horde, of whom Freud comments that he was "at the very beginning of the history of mankind ... the 'superman' whom Nietzsche only expected from the future." It seems pretty clear that Freud's image of the domineering – and in fact "filicidal" – primal father is seen by Freud as fully inscribed in YHWH as the Hebrew Bible presents him.

39 Fox, *The Five Books of Moses*, 381n17; cf. Fox's commentary on Deuteronomy 18:9–14 on p. 932. A similar claim is made by Freud: Mosaic religion "condemns magic and sorcery in the severest terms, while in [Egyptian religion] they proliferate with the greatest luxuriance." *Standard Edition*, 19. Also p. 36: "a religion in which all magic and spells were proscribed in the strictest terms"; and p. 50: a deity "averse to all ceremonial and magic."

40 Fox, *The Five Books of Moses*, 455, and Alter, *The Hebrew Bible*, 349. KJV: "I will do marvels." Cf. Deuteronomy 26:8: "YHWH took us out of Egypt ... with great awe-inspiring (acts) and with signs and portents" (Fox, *The Five Books of Moses*, 969; Alter, *The Hebrew Bible*, 705). KJV: "with signs, and with wonders." Also Deuteronomy 34:11: "all the signs and portents that YHWH sent [Moses] to do in the land of Egypt" (Fox, *The Five Books of Moses*, 1014; Alter, *The Hebrew Bible*, 744). KJV: "the signs and the wonders."

41 Silver, *Images of Moses*, 224; cf. 223: "As a magician *Moshe Rabbenu* is Merlin, a royal wizard." The whole of chapter 6 of Silver's book is relevant.

42 See the discussion in ibid., 70–2. Assmann, *The Invention of Religion*, 61, calls it "a magic contest between YHWH, Moses, and Aaron on one side, and Pharaoh with his sorcerer-priests on the other." Cf. Voegelin, *Israel and Revelation*, 385, 390. Voegelin (pp. 333, 426) interprets the third of the Ten Commandments – "Thou shalt not take the name of the Lord thy God in vain" – as prohibiting the invocation of God "for magic practices." If this suggestion is correct, then Moses was surely in violation of the third commandment in his contest with Pharaoh's magicians. Rousseau, in the *Letters Written from the Mountain*, also disparages the story of the ten plagues as a mere contest of "magic tricks": *The Collected Writings of Rousseau*, vol. 9, ed. Christopher Kelly and Eve Grace (Hanover, NH: University Press of New England, 2001), 179–81; cf. 70 ("Letter to Beaumont"). See also Jean-Jacques Rousseau, *Emile*, trans. Allan Bloom (New York: Basic Books, 1979), 299.

43 Pierre Bayle, *Various Thoughts on the Occasion of a Comet*, trans. Robert C. Bartlett (Albany, NY: State University of New York Press, 2000), 263. One gets a similar story in the hyper-Spinozistic tract *Traité des trois Imposteurs*: see Abraham Anderson, *The Treatise of the Three Impostors and the Problem of Enlightenment* (Lanham, MD: Rowman and Littlefield, 1997), 18–22.

44 Ashley Walsh, *Civil Religion and the Enlightenment in England, 1707–1800* (Woodbridge, Suffolk: Boydell Press, 2020), 88; cf. 7–8, 45–6. For further discussion of Bolingbroke's views as well as Voltaire's debt to Bolingbroke, see Bronisław Baczko, "Moïse, législateur …," in *Reappraisals of Rousseau*, ed. S. Harvey, M. Hobson, D. Kelley, and S.S.B. Taylor (Manchester: Manchester University Press, 1980), 113–16. I offer a sketch of Shaftesbury's views on this topic in Ronald Beiner, "Shaftesbury's *Characteristics* and the Problem of Priestcraft," in *Challenging Theocracy: Ancient Lessons for Global Politics*, ed. Toivo Koivukovski, David Edward Tabachnick, and Hermino Teixeira (Toronto: University of Toronto Press, 2018), 317–20.

45 Buber, *Moses*, 51, 53. Cf. Martin Buber, *Kingship of God*, trans. Richard Scheimann (New York: Harper & Row, 1967), 105–6.

46 Buber, *Moses*, 67, 77. Cf. 123, where Buber rejects the notion of Moses as "sorcerer," as "Faustian magician."

47 Irving M. Zeitlin, *Ancient Judaism* (Cambridge: Polity Press, 1984), ix–xii. However, if one consults Max Weber, *Ancient Judaism*, 219–25, one sees that Weber's view on this topic is somewhat more qualified than Zeitlin's. (Zeitlin's book is explicitly presented as an updating of Weber's *Ancient Judaism*.) Weber's views about "the Judaic hostility to magic" is also a recurring theme in John Love, "Max Weber's *Ancient Judaism*," in *The Cambridge Companion to Weber*, ed. Stephen Turner (Cambridge: Cambridge University Press, 2000), 200–20.

48 Zeitlin, *Ancient Judaism*, 30–2.

49 Ibid., 31.

50 Ibid., 88.

51 Ibid., 87; contrast Fox, *The Five Books of Moses*, 505: "victory of the biblical God over the gods of Egypt."

52 Mary Douglas, *Purity and Danger* (London: Routledge, 2002), 22.

53 As Douglas puts it on p. 27 of *Purity and Danger*, the mistake committed by this tradition (which includes Durkheim) was to "cut off magic from morals and religion." As she by contrast sees it, magic and religion belong indissolubly together with respect to what makes a culture of interest to anthropologists.

54 Fox, *The Five Books of Moses*, 245.

55 Fox, *The Five Books of Moses*, 453. Alter, *The Hebrew Bible*, 347, is more or less the same. KJV: "Thou shalt see my back parts."

56 Joshua was also part of this group, so presumably he saw God too. Exodus 24:11 seems to express surprise that their viewing of God did not exact severe divine vengeance: "He did not send forth his hand" (Fox, *The Five Books of Moses*, 392, and Alter, *The Hebrew Bible*, 315); "he laid not his hand" (KJV).

57 Fox, *The Five Books of Moses*, 490, and Alter, *The Hebrew Bible*, 367. KJV: "in the sight of all the house of Israel." Fox, *The Five Books of Moses*, 22, in a note commenting on Genesis 3:8 ("hid themselves from the face of YHWH"), writes, "The 'face' or presence of God is a dominating theme in many biblical stories and in the book of Psalms. People seek God's face or hide from it; God reveals it to them or hides it from them." Cf. Genesis 4:14 ("From your face must I conceal myself"); Genesis 12:7 ("YHWH was seen by Avram"); Genesis 18:1 ("And YHWH was seen by [Avraham]"); Genesis 18:22 ("Avraham still stood in the presence of YHWH"); Genesis 26:2 and 26:24 ("And YHWH was seen by [Yitzhak"]; Genesis 32:31 ("I [Yaakov] have seen God, face to face"); Genesis 33:10 ("I have ... seen your face, as one sees the face of God"); Genesis 35:1 ("God was seen by you"); Genesis 34:9 ("God was seen by Yaakov again"); Leviticus 9:4 ("for today, YHWH will make-himself-seen by you!"); and Leviticus 9:23 ("and the Glory of YHWH was seen by the entire people"). All of these citations are from Fox. Also Isaiah 6:5: "Mine eyes have seen the King, the LORD of hosts" (KJV). As regards the last of these texts, Buber, *Moses*, 40, notes that this offered a more corporeal access to God than what was granted to Moses at the burning bush.

58 Buber, *Moses*, 8.

59 See ibid., 117–18, where Buber tries to give an account of how to deal with the paradox of "an invisible God who, however, becomes visible at will"; "becoming manifest yet remaining invisible." Cf. 125–27 (p. 127: "the invisible, who permits Himself to be seen") and 131: "His invisible but nevertheless manifesting presence."

60 Eli Zaretsky, *Political Freud: A History* (New York: Columbia Press, 2015), 96.

61 Fox, *The Five Books of Moses*, 452, and Alter, *The Hebrew Bible*, 347. KJV: "I beseech thee, shew me thy glory."

62 Fox, *The Five Books of Moses*, 451. Alter, *The Hebrew Bible*, 346, has "as a man speaks to his fellow." KJV has "as a man speaketh unto his friend."

63 Spinoza, *Theological-Political Treatise*, 30.

64 Ibid., 10–14.

65 Ibid., 14. Thomas L. Pangle similarly relates the issue of the visibility/invisibility of God to God's ambiguous corporeality/incorporeality: *Political Philosophy and the God of Abraham*, 54.

66 Spinoza, *Theological-Political Treatise*, 12.

67 Ibid., 14; my italics.

68 Cf. our discussion of the Spinoza-Freud contrast in chapter 1, note 105.

69 See Zaretsky, *Political Freud*, 114.

70 Cf. Walzer, "The Strangeness of Jewish Leftism," 35: "Moses did not have to look for a politics that would vindicate his authority; God acted directly to destroy all those who rebelled against him"; as well as Hobbes's

suggestion in chapter 12 of *Leviathan* that Moses had no choice but to bolster his authority by performing miracles. When there was a pause in the performance of miracles, the faith of the people failed and so the Israelites rebelled. *Leviathan*, 85.

71 Phrasing the argument in this way may make it sound as if I am privileging a consequentialist political philosophy, as was pointed out by one of the publisher's reviewers. However, it's not my purpose here to take sides in a philosophical debate between Kantians and utilitarians, since both are equally committed to adjudicating the ends of political life within the bounds of secular reason.

72 "Transcript: President Obama on How U.S. Will Address Islamic State," *NPR*, 10 September 2014, https://www.npr.org/2014/09/10/347515100/transcript-president-obama-on-how-u-s-will-address-islamic-state.

73 Salman Rushdie, *Languages of Truth: Essays 2003–2020* (New York: Random House, 2021), 140.

74 *The Complete Essays of Montaigne*, trans. Donald M. Frame (Stanford, CA: Stanford University Press, 1965), 477 (bk. 2, chap. 16). I owe this reference to Zachariah Black.

75 I've tried to make a case for such a secularist political vision in Ronald Beiner, "Secularism as a Common Good," in *Citizenship and Multiculturalism in Western Liberal Democracies*, ed. David Edward Tabachnick and Leah Bradshaw (Lanham, MD: Lexington Books, 2017), 37–55.

76 See Aaron Wildavsky's commentary: *Moses as Political Leader* (Jerusalem: Shalem Press, 2005), 46–50.

77 Of course, circumcision would only have the effect of separating the Hebrews from all other peoples (as Rousseau applauds and Spinoza condemns) if it were in fact unique to the Hebrews. However, it is widely reported that circumcision was never a uniquely Hebrew practice. Jacques Derrida, for instance, in *Archive Fever* (Chicago: University of Chicago Press, 1996), 42n6, refers to it as an Egyptian "indigenous practice," but this is merely the restatement of an argument by Freud, according to whom the claim is traceable back to Herodotus: *Standard Edition*, 26–7, 30n2, 44–5. Herodotus, though, is merely one source for what is actually a long historical tradition that sees the Hebrew practice of circumcision as deriving from the Egyptians, as I discuss in "Shaftesbury's *Characteristics* and the Problem of Priestcraft," 319, 329n71. In any case, as Freud correctly points out (p. 45), as a way of hiving off the chosen people from all other peoples, circumcision is "a particularly clumsy invention. As a mark that is to distinguish one person from others and prefer him to them, one would choose something that is not to be found in other people; one would *not* choose something that can be exhibited in the same way by millions of other people";

Freud's italics. See also Bonnie Honig, *Democracy and the Foreigner* (Princeton, NJ: Princeton University Press, 2001), 138n35.

78 Wildavsky, *Moses as Political Leader*, 128.

79 This has to be qualified; as discussed elsewhere in this book, there *are* biblical texts where YHWH urges genocide against nations practising idolatry, seemingly *because* they are practising idolatry. There doesn't seem to be consistency in the divine policy on this matter.

80 Fox, *The Five Books of Moses*, 867; Alter, *The Hebrew Bible*, 632: "allotted them."

81 Fox, *The Five Books of Moses*, 991. Alter, *The Hebrew Bible*, 719, also uses "apportion."

82 Fox, *The Five Books of Moses*, 1002: "At his dividing the human-race, he stationed boundaries for people by the number of the gods." Alter, *The Hebrew Bible*, 729: "He set out the boundaries of people, by the number of the sundry gods." KJV makes no reference to non-Hebrew gods.

83 Fox, *The Five Books of Moses*, 1005. Alter, *The Hebrew Bible*, 733: "No god is by My side." KJV: "There is no god with me."

84 Fox, *The Five Books of Moses*, 827. Alter, *The Hebrew Bible*, 597: "destroy," "demolish." KJV: "Destroy all their pictures, and destroy all their molten images, and quite pluck down all their high places." Cf. the text in Exodus 34:13 cited in the "Are Non-Hebrew Religions Tolerated?" section below.

85 See Wildavsky's commentary: *Moses as Political Leader*, 129–33.

86 Michael Walzer, *Exodus and Revolution* (New York: Basic Books, 1985). Cf. James Joyce, *Ulysses*, ed. Hans Walter Gabler (New York: Vintage Books, 1986), 116–17, where the Mosaic narrative is presented as the tale of an oppressed people asserting itself against imperial arrogance (implying a model for the pre-independence Irish in liberating themselves from the English). My thanks to Gabriel Beiner for reminding me of this interesting text.

87 Assmann, *The Invention of Religion*, 228–9; cf. p. 88. See also Edward W. Said, "Michael Walzer's "Exodus and Revolution': A Canaanite Reading," *Grand Street* 5, no. 2 (Winter 1986): 91–3. Historically, the rhetoric of "chosenness" has of course wreaked much political damage in different political contexts. For an important account of how this rhetoric was drawn upon by the Afrikaners in South Africa, by the Ulster-Scots in Northern Ireland, and by 20th-century Zionists, see Akenson, *God's Peoples*.

88 Joshua's conquest of Canaan figures interestingly in a debate between Hannah Arendt and Carl Schmitt on the relationship between law and conquest as reconstructed by Anna Jurkevics in "Hannah Arendt Reads Carl Schmitt's *The Nomos of the Earth*," *European Journal of Political Theory* 16, no. 3 (July 2017): 345–66. Jurkevics (p. 352) suggests that Joshua is "paradigmatic" of Schmitt's idea that taking possession of territory is what founds a *nomos*. For the Schmitt text appealing to Joshua, see Carl Schmitt, *The Nomos of the Earth* (New York: Telos, 2006), 81.

89 Fox, *The Early Prophets*, 78, 115. Caleb, one may recall, is one of the two scouts, the other being Joshua, who are exempted by YHWH from his blanket denial of entry to the Promised Land for the wilderness generation (even including Moses and Aaron).

90 Paul, *Moses and Civilization*, 60–1, makes the interesting point that the presentation of "Ham, the father of Canaan" as a "sexual outlaw" in Genesis 9:21–2 helps to legitimize Israelite usurpation of the lands of the Canaanites. Paul also importantly notes that the Israelites "had long since usurped" these lands at the time of the writing of this biblical text.

91 Akenson, *God's Peoples*, 42.

92 Fox, *The Five Books of Moses*, 891. KJV: "The LORD thy God doth drive them out from before thee."

93 Fox, *The Five Books of Moses*, 933; cf. Alter, *The Hebrew Bible*, 680. KJV: "because of these abominations the LORD thy God doth drive them out from before thee." Hence the KJV translation for what Fox and Alter translate as "dispossession" is the same as for Deuteronomy 9:3–5, quoted in the previous note.

94 Fox, *The Five Books of Moses*, 877.

95 Ibid., 881; cf. Joshua: 24:13. It's telling, with respect to the apologetic character of Buber's *Moses*, that there's no acknowledgment anywhere in the chapter devoted to "The Land" (pp. 172–81) that there might be something problematic about the God of the Hebrews expropriating Canaanite land on behalf of his chosen people. One sees further evidence of this same apologetic purpose when Buber describes Israel's wars in the era of the Judges and of Saul as "a war of liberation" (p. 165).

96 One can also find the image of Moses as lawgiver in Montesquieu's *Spirit of the Laws*, which consistently refers to "les lois de Moïse" (characterized in bk. 15, chap. 17 as "bien rude"), which pretty clearly implies that the laws of the Hebrews were designed by Moses as civil legislator. Interestingly, Eric Voegelin detects a significant shift within the Hebrew Bible itself: "The words and ordinances which in Exodus emanate from Yahweh, flow in Deuteronomy from the authority of Moses." On Voegelin's interpretation, Deuteronomy executes this shift from God to Moses because it is seizing upon a "fictitious Moses" in the conscious "creation of a myth of political order." That is, it is a civil religion constructed by "priests under prophetic influence." *Israel and Revelation*, 364, 363, 359; cf. 383.

97 Walzer, *Exodus and Revolution*, 68. Walzer's view should perhaps be qualified in light of the suggestion in Silver, *Images of Moses*, 308, that Philo was not alone within the Jewish tradition in anticipating the later image of Moses as a civil-religionist lawgiver: "To a Jew conditioned by Hellenistic cultural norms Moses was a lawgiver who founded the civil religion of Jerusalem, not unlike Solon or Lycurgus, who had founded the respected civil religions of Athens and Sparta."

98 Hobbes, *Leviathan*, 487.

99 Cf. Thomas Hobbes, *On the Citizen*, ed. Richard Tuck and Michael Silverthorne (Cambridge: Cambridge University Press, 1998), 192: "what laws God made for them."

100 Hobbes, *Leviathan*, 82.

101 Rousseau, *On the Social Contract*, 70.

102 Fox, *The Five Books of Moses*, 452; my italics. KJV: "So shall we be separated, I and thy people, from all the people that are upon the face of the earth."

103 Fox, *The Five Books of Moses*, 884. Alter, *The Hebrew Bible*, 644: "You shall not intermarry with them." KJV: "Neither shalt thou make marriages with them."

104 See Fox, *The Five Books of Moses*, 718, and Alter, *The Hebrew Bible*, 518. Both Fox and Alter, in their editorial notes, point to an ambiguity here, since some scholars view Cush as possibly encompassing Midian. Hence, despite KJV's reference to an Ethiopian wife, there is at least a possibility that the wife being complained about here is in fact Zipporah. Either way, Aaron and Miriam clearly see Moses's choice of marital partner as sufficiently transgressive that it serves as a basis for challenging or subverting his authority. For an interesting discussion, see Silver, *Images of Moses*, 65–6, 79–80. Silver (p. 80) is quite sceptical that the Cushite woman and Zipporah are the same wife. Thomas Mann, in his Moses novel, has some fun spinning out the comic possibilities of Moses's entanglement with this putative second wife: see *The Tables of the Law*, trans. Marion Faber and Stephen Lehmann (London: Haus, 2012), 76–83.

105 John Toland, *Nazarenus*, ed. Justin Champion (Oxford: Voltaire Foundation, 1999), 237. Zeitlin, *Ancient Judaism*, 53–4, highlights the fact that intermarriage was common among the Hebrew patriarchs; he refers to Isaac, Jacob, Judah, Simeon, and Joseph. Zeitlin concludes, "The Scriptures tell us clearly and unabashedly that the people of Israel was formed of mixed ethnic stock: Hebrew, Aramean, Canaanite and Egyptian." He also claims (p. 78) that the Bible presents Moses, with his Egyptian education and his intermarriage with a Midianite, "as a figure transcending the bounds of any one culture. In this respect he resembles the patriarchs." See also p. 185, where Zeitlin comments on the many non-Israelite wives of David and Solomon. Rehoboam, heir to Solomon's throne, was the offspring of one such intermarriage. Finally, see Buber, *Moses*, 31: In contrast to Genesis 24:3–4's prohibition on Isaac's acquiring a Canaanite wife, "Judah marries a Canaanite woman, Joseph an Egyptian and Moses a Midianite without Scripture finding any cause for censure in their doing so."

106 Walzer, *In God's Shadow*, 44. On the theme of intermarriage, see also pp. 2–4, 39, 43. Akenson, *God's Peoples*, 24, relates "the horror with which the [Hebrew] scriptures view intermarriage" to a specifically biological notion of "blood purity."

107 Jean-Jacques Rousseau, *The Government of Poland*, trans. Willmoore Kendall (Indianapolis: Hackett, 1985), 12.

108 Ibid., 14.

109 Ibid., 6.

110 Fox, *The Five Books of Moses*, 765.

111 Ibid.

112 The fact that Moses and Aaron are Egyptian, not Hebrew, names is noted by Fox, *The Five Books of Moses*, in note 7 on p. 784; cf. p. 264n10. See *Standard Edition*, 7–10, where Freud makes this business of the non-Hebrew name central to his theory of Moses as Egyptian; and Yosef Hayim Yerushalmi, *Freud's Moses: Judaism Terminable and Interminable* (New Haven: Yale University Press, 1991), 5, 85–6, 114n14, where Yerushalmi traces Freud's thesis about Moses's name back to Josephus. If Moses was adopted by Pharaoh's daughter, it shouldn't be surprising that he bears an Egyptian name. In that sense, the fact that Aaron as well has an Egyptian name seems somewhat more surprising, though it is hardly uncommon for minority cultures to adopt names current in the majority culture.

113 Fox, *The Five Books of Moses*, 784n7; John Toland, *Tetradymus* (1720; repr., Whitefish, Montana: Kessinger, 2010, 50–7). An identical theory is offered in the *Traité des trois Imposteurs*: see Anderson, *The Treatise of the Three Impostors and the Problem of Enlightenment*, 21. As discussed in note 6 of our introduction, there seems to be more than a little ambiguity about whether Hobab was the son of Jethro or instead another name for Jethro (= Reuel). Toland certainly takes Hobab to be the *son* of Jethro. Hobab is also referred to by the author or authors of *Traité des trois Imposteurs* as Moses's brother-in-law. As is pointed out in Jan Assmann, *Moses the Egyptian* (Cambridge, MA: Harvard University Press, 1997), 238n8, it can't be ruled out that Toland himself had some involvement in producing the *Treatise*.

114 Again (see previous note), on some readings of the relevant texts, Jethro and Hobab are taken to be the same person. If the Hobab = Jethro interpretation is correct, then these "two relatives" are really one relative.

115 See Fox, *The Five Books of Moses*, 456n13. KJV refers merely to "altars," "images," and "groves." Alter, *The Hebrew Bible*, 350, refers to "altars," "pillars," and "cultic poles." Cf. Vico, who speaks of Moses's "burning of the sacred groves" ("clearings leveled in the midst of the forest") where pagan tribes tended to worship their gods: *The New Science of Giambattista*

Vico, 11 (para. 16), 160–1 (paras. 479, 481). See Harrison Fluss and Landon Frim, *Prometheus and Gaia* (London: Anthem, 2022), 55–6, for discussion of a specifically feminist interpretation of the Israelite destruction of the sacred groves. See also Petrus Cunaeus, *The Hebrew Republic*, trans. Peter Wyetzner (Jerusalem: Shalem Press, 2006), 133–4.

116 Fox, *The Five Books of Moses*, 452. Alter, *The Hebrew Bible*, 347: "I shall grant grace to whom I grant grace and have compassion for whom I have compassion."

117 Fox, *The Five Books of Moses*, 754, commenting on Numbers 20:8–12 and 20:24; cf. Numbers 27:13–14. As Richard A. Gabriel plausibly puts it: "In Exodus, Yahweh repeatedly slays the Israelites over what seem to be trivial ritual infractions." *God's Generals: The Military Lives of Moses, Buddha, and Muhammad* (New York: Skyhorse Publishing, 2017), 182.

118 According to Buber, *Moses*, 196, there is no clear elucidation in the Pentateuch as to what exactly was the transgression that caused Moses to be banned from the Promised Land.

119 In the Fox translation (*The Five Books of Moses*, 307), God describes himself as "capricious" (Exodus 10:2). However, the other translations are quite different. Alter, *The Hebrew Bible*, 252: "How I toyed with Egypt." KJV: "What things I have wrought."

120 Someone might say: Well, the Hebrew Bible is literature, and literature is not philosophy. One doesn't need to buy into a deconstructionist blurring of the boundary between philosophy and literature in order to disagree. Plato's *Republic* is literature. Montesquieu's *Persian Letters* is literature. Rousseau's *Emile* is literature. So is Nietzsche's *Thus Spoke Zarathustra*. Yet all of them embody political philosophies that can be judged according to the canons of rational truth-seeking that define and animate the philosophical tradition. In principle, there is no reason why the Hebrew Bible can't admit of a similar treatment, which is why it has engaged both thinkers of the traditional Western canon and contemporary theorists and philosophers.

121 All quotations to follow come from Orwin's text "Comment on Walzer's *In God's Shadow*," delivered in the context of the Tikvah Summer Program in Jewish Thought at Princeton University on 30 July 2012. I'm grateful to Orwin for sharing this text with me.

122 See Walzer's account of *In God's Shadow* in his conversation with Astrid von Busekist: Michael Walzer and Astrid von Busekist, *Justice Is Steady Work: A Conversation on Political Theory* (Cambridge, UK: Polity Press, 2020), chap. 9. At some points in the conversation, Walzer verges on an Orwin-like view ("My focus is … on biblical anti-politics, [the idea] that the gentiles, the goyim, need politics, but we [Jews] don't – because God takes care of us"). However, at other points in the conversation

(see esp. p. 164), he embraces a conception of politics far broader than Orwin's.

123 Cf. Yoram Hazony, who asks, "What is it, exactly, that prevents the [Hebrew] Bible from being treated as 'political philosophy'? After all, it seems to be preoccupied with precisely those matters that are of concern to political theorists: War and peace, justice and injustice, rulers and ruled, obedience and disobedience, power and right, individual and state, empire and anarchy" (foreword to Wildavsky, *Moses as Political Leader*, x). Hazony claims that prior to Wildavsky publishing his book, the Hebrew Bible was unjustifiably shut out of the canon of Western political philosophy (pp. ix–x). This may well have been true prior to the original publication of Wildavsky's book (viz., 1984); but as should be evident throughout this book, many political theorists and philosophers in recent years have been exerting themselves to set this right.

124 Walzer, in the discussion with von Busekist, points out that "there are about a hundred or more treatises published in the late sixteenth and in the seventeenth century with titles like 'the Hebrew Commonwealth.'" Walzer and von Busekist, *Justice Is Steady Work*, 155. If the Hebrew Bible really were "anti-political," it would be hard to imagine how that would be possible.

125 Buber, *Moses*, 186; cf. 205. Buber's view is fully endorsed by Voegelin, who considers the essential meaning of the Mosaic narrative to be the founding of a "new dispensation" that is rightly characterized as a "theopolity": see *Israel and Revelation*, chap. 12.

126 My co-author disagrees. Here is part of an email to me in which Harrison Fluss expresses his rather different position on this fundamentally important question: "There has to be a distinction between image and argument. The Bible isn't a systematic treatise, but a work of literature, so there are many different elements (including philosophical ones) that don't form a coherent whole, including stories where the message or moral or even doctrine isn't obvious. Of course, there might be tensions in an ostensible philosophical treatise, but we work them out philosophically. With the story of Moses, it's more ambiguous, precisely because it's to a large degree a story. This is why religion is a mytho-poetic, and not a philosophical, means of grasping truth – what Spinoza calls obedience to God and not love of God (*Theological-Political Treatise*, ed. Jonathan Israel [Cambridge: Cambridge University Press, 2015], 272). We need to be careful to distinguish which stories we're talking about, which intentions, etc. We can't deduce a comprehensive philosophy that doesn't exist." I agree with Fluss's claim in the concluding section of chapter 3 that mere exegesis cannot be a substitute for independent philosophical argument. But I worry

that if we enforce too strict a division between "stories" on the one side and Euclidean rational "demonstration" on the other, too much of the established political-philosophy canon will find itself on the wrong side of the dividing line alongside the Hebrew Bible read as a collection of sub-philosophical myths and stories. (Cf. note 120 above.) To be sure, the authors of the Hebrew scriptures were not in the business of constructing a tightly reasoned treatise; nor should one underestimate the daunting challenges associated with imputing a consistent integral world view to a text that was almost certainly stitched together from diverse source documents. But the essential point is this: The contest of rival visions of human life that composes our tradition of political philosophy is articulated in a very wide range of media and genres. Better to err on the side of an expansive conception of what deserves inclusion.

127 Fox, *The Five Books of Moses*, 327 and Alter, *The Hebrew Bible*, 268. KJV has "went up harnessed."

128 Fox, *The Five Books of Moses*, 335 and Alter, *The Hebrew Bible*, 274. KJV also has "a man of war."

129 Fox, *The Five Books of Moses*, 457 and Alter, *The Hebrew Bible*, 351. KJV: "I will cast out the nations before thee, and enlarge thy borders."

130 Fox, *The Five Books of Moses*, 863. Alter, *The Hebrew Bible*, 629: "It is the LORD your God Who does battle for you." KJV: "The LORD your God he shall fight for you." Cf. Exodus 14:14 (Fox, *The Five Books of Moses*, 332): "YHWH will make war for you."

131 Moshe Halbertal and Stephen Holmes, *The Beginning of Politics* (Princeton: Princeton University Press, 2017), 27.

132 The translation here is from KJV. Fox, *The Five Books of Moses*, 941: "You are not to leave-alive any breath"; "devote-them-to-destruction." Alter, *The Hebrew Bible*, 686: "You shall let no breathing creature live"; "you shall surely put them under the ban." Voegelin claims that there is an exterminationist aspect to Deuteronomy that is not present elsewhere in the Five Books of Moses: see *Israel and Revelation*, 375–6. That claim seems questionable to me, though it may be true that Deuteronomy goes furthest in this direction.

133 Гюндуз Мамедов/Gyunduz Mamedov (@MamedovGyunduz), "Two former commanders of Wagner Group confessed to killing children in Bakhmut & Soledar. They said about Prigozhin's order 'to kill everyone.' They told that shot more than 20 children, including a 5-year-old girl. Also, they 'cleared' a basement of a 9-storey building in Bakhmut with 300-400 civilians. Important information for investigating authorities." Twitter, 17 April 2023, 11:16 a.m, https://twitter.com/MamedovGyunduz /status/1647982387957997571.

Gyunduz Mamedov was the deputy prosecutor general of Ukraine between October 2019 and July 2021.

134 *The Works of Lord Bolingbroke*, vol. 3 (London, 1844), 27; quoted in Walsh, *Civil Religion and the Enlightenment in England, 1707–1800*, 89. The Hebrew Bible's tribalist principle is nicely encapsulated in Exodus 33:16 when Moses says, "We are distinct, I and your people, from every people that is on the face of the soil." Fox, *The Five Books of Moses*, 452. Cf. Leviticus 20:24 and 20:26 and Deuteronomy 14:2.

135 Akenson, *God's Peoples*, 42. See Akenson's important discussion of the notion of "purity of the seed," implicit in the conception of a chosen people, on pp. 22–5; cf. pp. 209–10 and 252. In this context it's germane to point out – as a supplement to Walzer's story that the book of Exodus naturally lends itself to leftist appropriations – that far-right appropriations of the Hebrew Bible exist as well. For instance, a prominent tendency within the twentieth-century white-supremacist movement – what is now referred to as white nationalism – is something called Christian Identity. Adherents of this bizarre ideology believe in a nutty – and dangerous – version of the biblical saga according to which God is "white," both Moses and the nation that he liberated from slavery were "Aryan," and the Mosaic tribes, migrating via Europe, eventually arrived in North America. Far from the Hebrew Bible being a narrative about Jews and Judaism, the Jews are cast as the *enemies* of the true Moses and his authentic people: they are "children of Satan." The Israelites are in fact a community founded on *race* (as understood by nineteenth- and early twentieth-century racialists). It's hard to imagine how anyone could come to these insane conclusions if they had actually read the Bible; but the crucial point for our purposes is that holy texts provide a potential resource for just about any ideology that one cares to cook up, provided that one is willing to take some liberties with the text (which all appropriations of whatever complexion obviously do). Hence, however logic-defying this might seem, the Hebrew Bible can even be a bible for Nazis! See Raphael S. Ezekiel, *The Racist Mind* (New York: Penguin Books, 1995), xxvi, 40; Nicholas Goodrick-Clarke, *Black Sun* (New York: New York University Press, 2002), chap. 12; and Michael Barkun, *Religion and the Racist Right*, rev. ed. (Chapel Hill: University of North Carolina Press, 1997). One significant aspect of the story as presented by Barkun is that, according to the view of the originators of Christian Identity, "God's primal command to Adam's descendants was the prohibition on racial intermarriage" and that the Jews were necessarily excluded "from God's design" on account of their inability to honour this essential commandment. *Religion and the Racist Right*, 142–3. Relatedly, Akenson, *God's Peoples*, 94–95, discusses how Afrikaner culture drew racist

conclusions from the Hebrew Bible, namely, the story of Noah and Ham in Genesis 9:18–27.

136 For a full account, see Ronald Beiner, *Civil Religion* (New York: Cambridge University Press, 2011), chap. 11.

137 *Basic Writings of Nietzsche*, trans. Walter Kaufmann (New York: Modern Library, 1968), 580 (*Genealogy of Morals*, 3rd essay, sec. 22); Nietzsche's italics. By contrast, here is Freud's synoptic judgment on ancient Israel, offered in a 1932 letter to Arnold Zweig (quoted in Yerushalmi, *Freud's Moses*, 15): "This tragically mad land ... is connected with no other progress, no discovery or invention ... Palestine has never produced anything but religions, sacred frenzies, presumptuous attempts to overcome the outward world of appearances by means of the inner world of wishful thinking." It's surely interesting that despite Nietzsche's powerful animus against the whole Judeo-Christian inheritance, he was nonetheless able to appreciate the grandeur of Israel, whereas Freud clearly wasn't.

138 I try to explore these questions systematically in chapter 30 of *Civil Religion*.

139 For an acute discussion, see Domenico Losurdo, *Nietzsche, the Aristocratic Rebel*, trans. Gregor Benton (Leiden: Brill, 2019), 765–768.

140 Although Nietzsche hardly ever refers to Moses, it's very telling that he goes out of his way to make clear that the one aspect of the Mosaic legacy that he thoroughly repudiates is the prohibition of murder: see *The Gay Science*, trans. Walter Kaufmann (New York: Vintage, 1974), 100 (sec. 26). In *The Antichrist*, Nietzsche proposes his own counter-morality. *The Portable Nietzsche*, ed. Walter Kaufmann (New York: Viking Press, 1968), 570 (sec. 2).

141 As has been rightly pointed out by one of the publisher's reviewers, there is an important philosophical tradition (including but not limited to al-Farabi, Maimonides, and Thomas Aquinas) that seeks to reconcile reason and revelation, or incorporate them in a higher synthesis. If one of these philosophical systems had made good on its intellectual ambition, it would be possible to say that human beings are not obliged to choose between reason and revelation. It is beyond our competence to evaluate the philosophical outcome of these grand projects to transcend the reason/revelation distinction, but honesty requires us to confess our strong scepticism that any Islamic or Jewish or Christian philosopher has in fact succeeded in overcoming the evident tensions between what we can draw from unaided human reason and the claims to normative authority that have been historically attributed to a transcendent divinity. Since Aquinas is clearly part of this tradition of trying to harmonize reason and revelation, my commentary on Aquinas in chapter 2 is relevant here.

142 Spinoza, *Theological-Political Treatise*, trans. Shirley, 225. The full subtitle of Spinoza's book is "Various Disquisitions, By means of which it is shown not only that Freedom of Philosophising can be allowed in Preserving Piety and the Peace of the Republic: but also that it is not possible for such Freedom to be upheld except when accompanied by the Peace of the Republic and Piety Themselves" (p. xlix).

143 Immanuel Kant, *Critique of Pure Reason*, trans. Norman Kemp Smith (London: Macmillan, 1980), 9, note a.

144 Here's a good illustration: Ian McEwan's novel *The Children Act* (Toronto: Vintage Canada, 2015) features a courtroom exchange between a Jehovah's Witness father of a son who will die without a blood transfusion and the lawyer representing the hospital anxious to save the son's life. Here's the relevant exchange (p. 81):

> [LAWYER:] But at the time of these Iron Age texts, transfusions didn't exist. How could it be forbidden?
>
> [FATHER:] It certainly existed in the mind of God. You need to understand that these books are his word. He inspired his chosen prophets to write down his will. It doesn't matter what age it was, Stone, Bronze or whatever.

145 One should note that Freud, in a manner that may look paradoxical, actually sides with "the common man … and his religion [which Freud considers 'infantile'!] – *the only religion which ought to bear that name*" (my italics): "It is … humiliating to discover how large a number of people living to-day, who cannot but see that that [religion conceived in the image of a providential guardian] is not tenable, nevertheless try to defend it piece by piece in a series of pitiful rearguard actions. One would like to mix among the ranks of the believers in order to meet these philosophers, who think they can rescue the God of religion by replacing him by an impersonal, shadowy and abstract principle, and to address them with the warning words: 'Thou shalt not take the name of the Lord thy God in vain!'" *Civilization and Its Discontents*, ed. James Strachey (London: Hogarth Press, 1972), 11. Freud is equally disdainful of attempts to water down traditional religion in a letter to Marie Bonaparte dated 19 March 1929: "One is in danger of overestimating the frequency of an irreligious attitude among intellectuals … That comes from the most varied drinks being offered under the name of 'religion,' with a minimal percentage of alcohol – really non-alcoholic; but they still get drunk on it. The old drinkers were after all a respectable body, but to get tipsy on pomerit [apple juice] is really ridiculous." Ernest Jones, *The Life and Work of Sigmund Freud*, vol. 3 (New York: Basic Books, 1957), 447. As regards the question of what truly motivates people to embrace religion, Freud

spells this out on p. 12 of *Civilization and Its Discontents*, where he refers to it as one of the "palliative measures" allowing us to cope with the fact that "life, as we find it, is too hard for us; it brings too many pains, disappointments and impossible tasks."

146 Fox, *The Five Books of Moses*, 435. The KJV translation is identical.

147 Wood, *The Way of the Strangers*, 52. Moreover, Osama bin Laden, in his "Letter to the American People" of November 2002, wrote: "It is the Muslims who are the inheritors of Moses (peace be upon him) … If the followers of Moses have been promised a right to Palestine in the Torah, then the Muslims are the [nation most worthy] of this." "Osama bin Laden's Letter to America: Transcript in Full," *Newsweek*, 17 November 2023, https://www.newsweek.com/osama-bin-laden-letter-america-transcript-full-1844662.

148 Akenson, *God's Peoples*, 10.

149 Ibid., 20. With respect to Akenson's notion of "theologizing away the grittier aspects of the Word" (p. 10), cf. the suggestion on p. 30, quoted from Harold Bloom, that "there was no Jewish theology before Philo" and that "Yahweh is an uncanny personality, and not at all a concept."

150 David Hume, *Writings on Religion*, ed. Anthony Flew (La Salle, IL: Open Court, 1992), 155–6.

151 I'm grateful to Zachariah Black, Andrew Sabl, and Stephen Newman for extremely thoughtful and helpful critical responses to an early version of this chapter. As goes without saying, I owe a huge debt to my co-author, Harrison Fluss, whose help and encouragement have been essential in turning this into a book. I might also mention that the original spark for the thoughts that led to this book came from a dinner for Benjamin Hertzberg at which Teresa Bejan asked me if I had ever taught the Bible, and if not, what part of it I would want to teach. It was a good question.

Index